IT Auditing *and* Sarbanes-Oxley Compliance

Key Strategies *for* Business Improvement

IT AUDITING *AND* SARBANES-OXLEY COMPLIANCE

KEY STRATEGIES *FOR* BUSINESS IMPROVEMENT

DIMITRIS N. CHORAFAS

CRC Press
Taylor & Francis Group
Boca Raton London New York

CRC Press is an imprint of the
Taylor & Francis Group, an **informa** business
AN AUERBACH BOOK

CRC Press
Taylor & Francis Group
6000 Broken Sound Parkway NW, Suite 300
Boca Raton, FL 33487-2742

First issued in paperback 2019

ISBN-13: 978-1-4200-8617-1 (hbk)
ISBN-13: 978-0-367-38650-4 (pbk)

Library of Congress Cataloging-in-Publication Data

Chorafas, Dimitris N.
IT auditing and Sarbanes-Oxley compliance : key strategies for business improvement / Dimitris N. Chorafas.
p. cm.
Includes bibliographical references and index.
ISBN 978-1-4200-8617-1 (alk. paper)
1. Information technology--Auditing. 2. Auditing, Internal. I. Title.

HD30.2.C477 2008
657'.458--dc22 2008014241

Visit the Taylor & Francis Web site at
http://www.taylorandfrancis.com

and the CRC Press Web site at
http://www.crcpress.com

Contents

Preface

Written as a contribution to the accounting and auditing professions, this book brings under one cover two key strategies for business improvement: information technology (IT) auditing and Sarbanes-Oxley (SOX) compliance. Superficially, these seem to be strange bedfellows, yet they belong together for several reasons, not the least being that they both require

- Ethical accounting practices,
- Focused auditing activities,
- A functioning system of internal control, and
- A very careful watch by the board's audit committee and chief executive officer.

From the Bubble Act of 1720 to the Sarbanes-Oxley Act of 2002, the history of financial legislation is the *child of crisis* and of the inevitable complaints of those who were harmed by malfeasance. When new laws are voted into effect, or when rules and regulations change, the impact is felt by both

- The accounting profession, because accounting is the gatekeeper of financial information, and
- Information technology, particularly that part of it addressing account keeping and financial reporting, hence the need for IT auditing.

The text has been designed to give the reader a practical knowledge of modern IT auditing, all the way to compliance issues. The practical examples and case studies included in this book have been written with the hope that they may assist in raising the professional standards. Therefore, not surprisingly, the readership is principally auditors, accountants, and information system specialists at large. Because not all readers are necessarily versatile in internal control and audit prerequisites, Part I focuses on those issues that are needed to provide a level playing field.

Chapter 1 introduces the reader to the concept of internal control and explains how and why internal control and information technology correlate. As the text demonstrates, a similar statement can be made in regard to internal control and auditing.

Case studies on the contribution of internal control to sound governance, particularly in connection to operational risk, have been included in Chapter 2. Design reviews are examined under the aspect of an internal control instrument, and internal control is treated not only as a feedback channel but also as the process that, to be effective, must be endowed with analytical capabilities.

The theme of Chapter 3 is auditing functions. Auditing is the systematic verification of books of account, vouchers, and other financial and legal records for the purpose of determining accuracy and integrity of accounting and record keeping, including IT records. As such, auditing involves the in-depth examination of financial and other reports by challenging the "obvious" and through proper understanding of the business under audit.

Originally, the purpose of an audit was to trace fraudulent transactions and accounting errors. Late in the 20th century, new functions began to make their appearance. Auditing theory and practice have developed at a rapid rate to include the audit of internal controls, operational risks, and information technology. This requires auditors well trained not only in accounting but also in economics, finance, law, and technology—acting in two capacities as both controllers and advisers. The Sarbanes-Oxley Act is taken as an example of the change that has occurred in terms of audit objectives and of compliance.

Audits, Chapter 4 points out, can be internally conducted by regular employees of the organization or externally by hired professional auditors. As this text suggests, whether auditing is internal or external, the auditors should be investigative, comply with the laws of the land, and do their work with diligence, accuracy, and integrity.

Chapter 5 deals with the responsibilities of the board of directors in connection with internal control and audit. It documents the reasons why internal and external auditors should not report to line management but, rather, to the audit committee of the board. This is the best way to ensure the auditors' independence of opinion and the transparency of results.

Part II presents the reader with real-life case studies in which the author had a role to play. As the principles and conduct of business have changed over the recent years, and as financial operations (including their immediate and further-out ramifications) have become more complex, the purposes of audits are now covering a far wider scope than they formerly did.

The subject of how information technology should be audited, from IT policies to procedures, is treated in Chapter 6. The case of technology risk is deliberately brought into perspective so that the IT auditor is made aware that, while the effect of technology is generally positive, there are also cases where IT may be a drawback or even a source of errors and fraud. Left to its own devices, technology risk may morph into legal risk.

The case study in Chapters 7 and 8 is based on the IT audit of a well-known credit institution, undertaken at the demand of the board. Chapter 7 presents the bad news. The external IT auditor was asked by the bank's chairman and CEO to present an independent opinion. To do so, he conducted personal interviews with all senior executives and key IT team members, and gave them the chance to develop and defend their own views while

- Probing for weak spots in the systems specialists' reasoning, and in their work;
- Guiding them back to basic issues if they strayed off the path; and
- Helping them to keep things simple by thinking clearly, realistically, and creatively.

In contrast, the text of Chapter 8 reflects an adviser's job: a positive contribution by the external information technology auditor to the IT solution the institution needed to remain competitive. This part of the mission was characterized by intramural discussions in which the company's executives played a major role by coming up with suggestions. The Socratic method was at the kernel of IT auditing in this phase, while in the first phase (Chapter 7), the focal point was the bank's IT people, books, and deliverables.

The constructive approach followed in Chapter 8 continues in Chapter 9, which analyzes the underlying reasons for failures in IT projects and how they can be avoided. The case studies in this chapter are drawn from different industries. The intent is not to make the reader an instant expert in IT audit. Rather, the thoughtful discussion is intended to help the reader gain a general feel for what goes into an IT audit, including company politics.

Part III takes a different approach altogether. Its method is pedagogical, which has much to be said for it, but which differs from the case studies at the general management level presented in Part II. The chosen approach has been Cicero's method, which has the advantage of getting more deeply into an issue and focusing on questions, but also puts limits on their coverage.

Two themes have been chosen for Part III, each including technical issues for which an IT auditor can exercise his or her skills. Chapters 10 and 11 concentrate on some of the most critical technical questions concerning any information technology, where auditing functions must penetrate to the core of the subject matter. First the chosen subject is presented as "matter of fact"; then questions are raised—similar to the queries an IT auditor should be asking—to guide the reader's hand. In each chapter, the questions being asked on the IT auditor's behalf pertain to issues under discussion; this is not an all-weather-type IT inspection.

Chapter 10 discusses auditing problems closely related to system reliability and response time, i.e., issues that have complex technical and financial ramifications. It needs no explaining that—neither through paper records nor through remembrance—managers and professionals cannot hope to have all of the various data of their business at their fingertips at all times. Modern business relies upon information technology for support in a great number of daily operations, and this support is conditioned by availability, reliability, and response time. Therefore, all three must be subject to established corporate standards, and they have to be regularly audited.

As Chapter 11 demonstrates, a similar statement is valid about the ways and means employed by the firm for enhancing security. An audit that centers on IT security must be polyvalent and, as such, it is characterized by a number of critical issues that include abiding by top management's security policies, sizing up situations where security is in doubt, appraising administrative controls, identifying weaknesses that hackers can exploit, assessing security risks despite all of the measures being taken, and planning and corrective action.

Part IV follows the conceptual framework of Part III in terms of conducting an examination, but its focal point is managerial auditing, with a focus on compliance. The Sarbanes-Oxley Act, which is presented to the reader in Chapter 3, constitutes the background scenario. Chapter 12 explains that the better approach to compliance rests on clear and unambiguous top-management policies and evidently involves a fair amount of IT.

The same chapter also brings to the reader's attention methods of approach that help to promote effective compliance. One is the corporate memory facility (CMF). All decisions, along with their rationales and their outcomes, must be registered and mined to serve in a wide variety of applications, ranging from compliance to decisions regarding extension of credit, contemplated investments, prevailing trends, profitability of operations, and more. Most evident, the CMF must be audited.

Moreover, as Chapter 12 documents, any implementation of information technology that does not employ a high quotient of knowledge engineering is one that costs too much and delivers too little. Therefore, the IT audit must examine the company's use of agents and expert systems. The results will be a reliable reference source on the state of the art of the firm's information technology.

While closely linked to the central theme of Chapter 12, Chapter 13 presents the reader with a "what if" scenario. This scenario is primarily related to the Sarbanes-Oxley Act and secondarily to technology, taking as a reference the actions of Enron, WorldCom, and Enron's banks. What if SOX legislation had passed the U.S. Congress in the late 1990s or even 2000? How might this have influenced the financial statements of Enron and WorldCom? What about the credits that banks extended to them, and the new financial instruments they designed for them? What kind of role might technology have played in averting these bankruptcies?

Behind these queries is the issue of compliance and, with it, management intent and management policies. The strategy of the aforementioned companies was one of deception, and it is safe to bet is that no tactical moves could correct such strategic flaws. In the end, both companies proved to be empty sacks, and as Benjamin Franklin wrote in his autobiography, "It is hard for an empty sack to stand upright."

Because all issues treated in this book's 13 chapters have a touch of normal human frailties as well as strengths, it has been a deliberate choice to use constructive criticism—but criticism nevertheless—in connection with the case studies. Like any other audit, an IT audit must establish in a factual and documented way which new problems confront the organization in regard to its information technology and its functions. Changes in both the operational risk factors and the impact of the unexpected must, in fact, be expected.

About the Author

Since 1961, **Dr. Dimitris N. Chorafas** has advised financial institutions and industrial corporations in strategic planning, risk management, computers and communications systems, and internal controls. A graduate of the University of California, Los Angeles, the University of Paris, and the Technical University of Athens, Dr. Chorafas is also a Fulbright scholar.

Financial institutions that have sought his assistance include the Union Bank of Switzerland, Bank Vontobel, CEDEL, the Bank of Scotland, Credit Agricole, Österreichische Länderbank (Bank Austria), First Austrian Bank, Commerzbank, Dresdner Bank, Demir Bank, Mid-Med Bank, Banca Nazionale dell'Agricoltura, Istituto Bancario Italiano, Credito Commerciale, and Banca Provinciale Lombarda.

Among multinational corporations, Dr. Chorafas has worked as a consultant to top management for General Electric-Bull, Univac, Honeywell, Digital Equipment Corporation, Olivetti, Nestlé, Omega, Italcementi, Italmobiliare, AEG-Telefunken, Olympia, Osram, Antar, Pechiney, the American Management Association, and a host of other client firms in Europe and the United States.

Dr. Chorafas has served on the faculty of the Catholic University of America and as a visiting professor at Washington State University, George Washington University, University of Vermont, University of Florida, Georgia Institute of Technology, University of Alberta, Technical University of Karlsruhe, Ecole d'Etudes Industrielles de l'Université de Genève, École Polytechnic Fédérale de Lausanne, Polish Academy of Sciences, and Russian Academy of Sciences.

More than 8,000 banking, industrial, and government executives have participated in his seminars in the United States, England, Germany, Italy, other European countries, Asia, and Latin America.

Dr. Chorafas is the author of 145 books, some of which have been translated into 16 languages.

Acknowledgments

My debts go to a long list of knowledgeable people who contributed to the research that led to this text. Without their contributions, the book the reader has in hand would not have been possible. I am indebted not only for their input, but also for their constructive criticism during the preparation of the manuscript.

Let me take this opportunity to thank John Wyzalek for suggesting this project, and Ari Silver for the editing work and production effort. To Eva-Maria Binder goes the credit for compiling the research results, typing the text, and making the camera-ready artwork.

Dr. Dimitris N. Chorafas
Valmer and Vitznau

MANAGEMENT CONTROL

I

Chapter 1

Internal Control and Information Technology

1.1 Internal Control Defined

Internal control (IC) is a formal system of safeguards established by top management to provide a feedback on the way a financial institution, industrial organization, or any other entity observes the board's and senior management's policies, plans, directives, and rules as well as the law of the land and regulatory requirements. This is in contrast to the *grapevine*, which is a feedback channel of hearsay. IC should be seen as a process:

- Promoting transparency,
- Enhancing communications, and
- Affecting all levels of personnel.

The competitive advantage of internal control is that it enables board members to supervise, and senior executives to manage, by tracking exposure to deviations from guidelines, programs, established courses of action, and regulations. Such deviations may increase in credit risk, market risk, operations risk, settlement risk, legal risk, or other exposures relating to transactions, assets, and liabilities as well as to fraud and other events due to breaches of security.

Beyond risks, internal control goals include the preservation of assets, account reconciliation, and compliance. Without any doubt, laws and regulations impact on IC, whose able management requires policies, organization, technology, open communications channels, reliable information, access to all transactions, quality control, experimentation, and corrective action. The major aims of IC aims are to

- Promote personnel accountability and
- Keep open the arteries of corporate communications.

The development, implementation, and proper functioning of an internal control system require the existence of clearly stated internal bylaws and directives; a rigorous sense of supervisory activity; compliance with government regulations; and an organization that is flexible, dynamic, and appreciative of the need for management control (Chapter 5). Advanced technology is required to support IC efforts.

Not everybody, or every company, has the same definition of what is and is not internal control. This is documented by the opinion of 76 talented people in the financial industry, including central banks, commercial bankers, investment bankers, brokers, and representatives of trade associations that participated in the research. "The internal control definition," said the executive vice president of a New York brokerage, "should reflect the necessary segregation of duties, and it should stress the quality of management—two issues well beyond pitch-up reports."

In the opinion of David L. Robinson, of the Federal Reserve Board, internal control should in principle be content-neutral; but a system designed to serve IC should be commensurate with the complexity of the banking business that it supports. This is a sound principle to follow in regard to organization and structure, particularly when it is enriched with concrete and measurable objectives.

A senior executive at the European Monetary Institute (EMI), predecessor of the European Central Bank (ECB), looked to an IC system as the process (including all controls, financial or otherwise) effected by a credit institution's board of directors, senior management, and other key personnel to provide reasonable assurance that corporate objectives are achieved, including

- Safeguarding of assets
- Accomplishment of established goals
- Effective and efficient use of resources
- Adequate control of various risks incurred
- Reliability and integrity of financial reporting and of internal management information
- Compliance with laws and regulations, as well as with policies, plans, internal rules, and procedures

The definition of internal controls by the Institute of Internal Auditors (IIA) states that the term stands for actions taken by management to plan, organize, and direct the performance of sufficient operations so as to provide reasonable assurance that corporate aims will be achieved. IIA's bullet points are very similar to those listed above by EMI.

The Committee on Working Procedures of the American Institute of Certified Public Accountants (AICPA) defines internal control as comprising the plan of organization—and of all coordinate methods and measures adopted within the business—with the objectives of safeguarding its assets, checking the accuracy and reliability of its accounting data and of its budget, promoting operational efficiency, and encouraging adherence to subscribed managerial policies.

Managers and executives from different branches of industry, who participated in this research, underlined the need for better tools than currently available to make internal control proactive, including IT-based tools and methods. "Most current tools are post-event," said Clifford Griep, of Standard & Poor's in New York, "but internal control must be proactive. It must deal with pre-transaction approval."

Some of the IC definitions recorded during the research meetings were broader than others because they incorporated budgetary control and feedback on standard costs, quality of work being done, operating results, statistical analyses, and more. The dissemination of such outputs was also a consideration. Additionally, some institutions divided internal control into two distinct but complementary parts. AICPA, for example, distinguishes between

- Accounting controls and
- Administrative controls.

Moreover, a number of financial institutions and regulators take IC as being part of risk management, while others make exactly the opposite statement. In reality, as Figure 1.1 demonstrates, up to a point, internal control, audit, accounting, and risk management overlap. But at the same time, each one of these functions has its own domain of specific characteristics.

Whatever the adopted IC definition and organizational solution may be, the surge in interest for internal controls is a direct result of senior management's decision to be in charge of the company's fortune. Top-tier control systems enable early detection of problems that, left alone or remaining undetected, lead to crises. A first-class IC also makes feasible more timely and effective damage control.

In conclusion, internal control is a dynamic system with feedback (and sometimes feed-forward) characteristics, covering all types of exposure, addressing fraud, assuring transparency, and promoting reliable financial reporting. The chairman, board members, chief executive officer (CEO), and senior managers are responsible and accountable for the proper functionality of internal control. Because even the best solutions and systems do not last forever, internal control must be regularly audited by internal and external auditors to ensure its rank and condition. Auditors should respond to the board's query about its status in the organization in a factual and documented manner. The audit committee (Chapter 5) must ascertain that

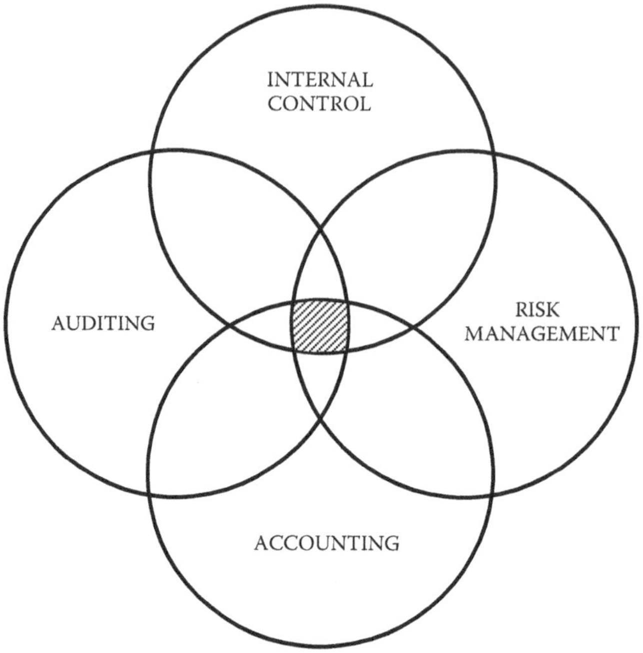

Figure 1.1 Internal control, internal auditing, risk management and accounting have a common core.

there is no cognitive dissonance at any level in connection to IC goals or duties and the way that these duties are carried out.

1.2 Internal Control and Service Science

The development of *service science* as a polyvalent but integrative field of management in the 21st century has greatly increased the need for effective internal control. The better way to appreciate the notion of service science is to start with a most basic query: What is meant by *service*? An orderly way of answering will look at fundamental issues underpinning the sense of conception, design, organization, and provision of a service, including its

- Nature
- Product characteristics
- Market offering
- Execution
- Profitability
- Feedback control

A couple of practical examples help in guiding the reader's mind. In 1882, journalists Charles Dow, 31, Edward Jones, 27, and Charles Bergstresser, 24, started Dow Jones & Co.—a service company. Its object was to pick up news and gossip and peddle them to brokers, bankers, investors, and speculators. Seven years later, in 1889, Dow Jones launched the *Wall Street Journal* (WSJ), another service product that came to life as a four-page stock-and-bond paper priced at 2 cents.

Throughout history, new services have been designed to cover a market need beyond what is addressed by existing services. One of the best recent examples is the emergence of Google on the Internet. Down to the bottom line, however, what counts most is *culture.* The offering of first-class services boils down to the people the firm employs, the responsibilities it assigns to them, the training it provides them with, and the way it rewards them for putting the firm's service interests above their own. Today, the component parts of service science are more complex than they used to be in previous centuries. They include

- Strategic planning
- Product and market studies
- Business partners
- Technical skills
- Analysis and experimentation
- Supply chain and logistics
- Quality assurance
- Internal control
- Information technology (IT)

Information technology became a branch of the service industry in the second half of the 20th century. Originally confined to number crunching and accounting, its domain has tremendously expanded. Among tier-1 firms, IT brings the concept of service orientation from the boardroom to the rank and file. Top-level IT tools promoting service science include

- Models
- Experiments
- Knowledge artifacts

(Because of its great importance in information technology, reference to *knowledge artifacts* is made in several parts of this book. This term, as well as the term *agents*, is defined in Chapter 12, to which the reader is referred in case he or she is not familiar with the aforementioned two concepts.)

Information technology assists internal control in delivering its messages, without delays, free of distortions, and at the right time. To enhance internal control, the better-managed companies use a wide range of methods, tools, and techniques, increasingly supported by real-time systems, sophisticated software, data mining, simulation, analytics, and interactive visualization of engineering, financial, and other reports.

In terms of service science, IT makes a significant contribution to *logistics*, which has been an established discipline since Alexander's time, more than 2300 years ago. The blending of IT with logistics, including its implementation on the Internet, has delivered the benefits of supply-chain management involving (in a way) both the real and virtual worlds. Indeed, many experts look at this present-day version of logistics as the forerunner of service science.

Real-enough-time *management reviews* provide another example. The way an article in *Business Week* had it, Boeing could not have accomplished all of its Dreamliner's design and supply requirements on its own. Traditionally, the aerospace company micromanaged design and production of a jet's components, an approach that caused the budget of its previous plane, the 777, to double in cost, from $6 billion to $12 billion.

With the Dreamliner, many of the details of the plane's design have been handled by suppliers in Japan, Italy, and the United States. Tokyo-based Mitsubishi Motors created the wing, while Italy's Alenia Aeronautica produced the rear fuselage and horizontal stabilizer. Outsourcing, however, is subject to centrifugal forces, hence the need for

- Real-enough-time project control by management and
- Online real-time supply-chain-linked business partners.

In the case of Boeing's example, one of the keys to pulling off integrative supply-chain management was the company's careful attention to managing *cultural change*.* This made close collaboration with business partners and customers feasible while also improving the quality of deliverables, shrinking development time, and helping to keep costs down.

Part of the cultural change to which the preceding paragraphs refer center on the orientation of the user organization in implementing advanced IT solutions. Many participants in this research commented that it becomes increasingly difficult to derive returns from information technology investments if the chief information officer (CIO) is not at the same time

- A business innovator,
- A service-level designer, and
- An agent of disruption and renewal.

This is a demanding task, but it is also a personal opportunity. In the new order, which is slowly but surely defined by service science, the CIO becomes more than anything else a chief process innovation officer, whose responsibility is to think hard about all company processes, analyze the extent to which they further the

* *BusinessWeek*, May 14, 2007.

firm's competitive position, and project new IT solutions that bring the company ahead of the curve (more on this in Section 6).

1.3 The Proverbial Long, Hard Look

Building a sound system for internal control is synonymous with taking a long, hard look at how the business should be planned, conducted, and controlled. This has been the majority opinion of the cognizant people who contributed to the study leading to this book. Is a tough setting of internal control working against the growth in business? Lev Borodovski, of Crédit Suisse First Boston, mentioned a principle he learned at Fidelity, his former employer: "If it is done properly, internal control does not suppress business. It helps it."

Timothy Stier, of the Office of Thrift Supervision (OTS), sees internal control under the twin aspects of risk management and compliance, because there is regulatory risk. "We view internal control as the process that makes up for risk management by providing the nuts and bolts," said Curtis Wong, of the Federal Deposit Insurance Corp (FDIC). The FDIC places greater emphasis than ever before on internal and external audits, which

- Are part of internal control and
- Contribute to better risk management.

In regard to the OTS reference, like any other credit institution, the savings and loans have two exposures that may get out of control and bring an entity to bankruptcy. One is credit risk. Figure 1.2 provides a snapshot of the building blocks that should enter into the able management of credit exposure. Notice that the functions briefly described by all of them can be significantly improved through IT. The other major exposure is interest rates: a market risk.

After the well-known problems of the later 1980s, OTS has instituted an excellent procedure for interest-rate risk control. The 1100 thrifts it supervises must report daily their liquidity position ±100, ±200, ±300, and ±400 basis points over and below the current rate; the ±200 bp is the main reference. (A basis point is 1/100, or 1 percent). In this case, too, IT plays a pivotal role. Being in charge of credit risk and market risk is not an option. It is a matter of regulatory compliance. In both cases, internal control and IT are instrumental in enabling the institution to comply with this directive by regulators (Chapter 13).

However, as Section 1 brought to the reader's attention, because all systems can malfunction, and because they decay with time, both internal control and IT must be regularly audited. Well-governed companies see to it that this is written in their bylaws, and they also appreciate that IC's proper functioning is part of the board's and of senior management's desire to confront their responsibilities.

It takes teamwork to understand where the risks occur, and nobody can say that the worst stories that have happened to others in the past "couldn't happen to

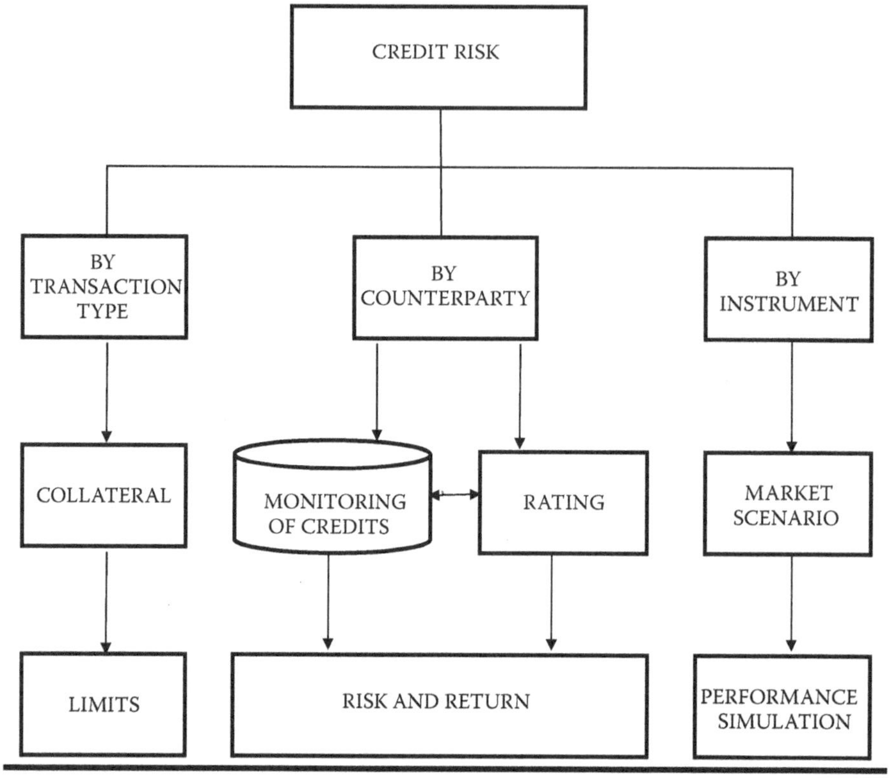

Figure 1.2 Building blocks of credit risk management.

us" in the future. Bear Stearns* probably thought so until adversity hit two of its hedge funds on June 20, 2007. Market risk is omnipresent, and any entity operating transborder is exposed to credit risk by counterparties it scantly knows.

Credit risk from unwillingness or inability to perform by counterparties as well as market risks from changes in foreign currency exchange rates, interest rates, leverage, and other reasons impact the entity's

- Cash flows,
- Financial position, and
- Results of operations.

Companies often manage their exposure to such market risks through derivative financial instruments. But even if derivatives are employed as risk management tools, and not for trading purposes, there are different types of exposures (frequently

---

* In early March 2008, after Bear Stearns ran out of both money and credit, JP Morgan Chase took it over, with the Federal Reserve acting as midwife and guarantour. The price was a paltry $2 per share, upped to $10. By late May 2008 the acquisition was completed and Bear Stearns ceased to exist.

covert) associated with assumed positions, which internal control should make transparent and bring to senior management's attention.

The principles that internal control and IT must be audited are honored by every well-governed company, although this is a recent development. By and large, until two or three decades ago, internal and external audits used to be verifications of the accounting system and of what was written in the company's books. Only enlightened persons had taken the position that internal control, too, must come under the microscope.

This is true of all entities, including the state. In a 1928 Supreme Court decision, Justice Louis Brandeis wrote in the case of *Olmstead v. United States*, "If the Government becomes a lawbreaker, it breeds contempt for law; it invites every man to become a law unto himself; it invites anarchy." This concept is fully applicable to every company regarding

- Its accounts,
- Its compliance with laws and regulations, and
- The way in which its internal control system operates.

"The role of bank managers is not only to assure the proper function of their institutions, but also to see to it that auditors obtain a consistent and coherent image of status and results," suggested Alain Coune, of the International Monetary Fund (IMF). Coune added that this has become part of both internal control and audit. Quantification has been enriched with qualification by the Sarbanes-Oxley Act (see Chapters 3, 12, and 13).

This dual approach is vital because an organization's control environment is the corporate atmosphere in which accounting operates, internal control exists, financial statements are prepared, and critical functions are audited. In the opinion of a senior audit executive, a well-studied internal control puts a saddle on a horse that never had one. A strong control environment reflects management's consciousness of and commitment to an effective system of internal control that

- Does not guarantee the absence of fraudulent financial reporting,
- But reduces the chance that management will override internal and regulatory accounting controls. (As we will see in Chapter 13, this is only partly true.)

A weak control environment undermines the effectiveness of a company's internal accounting system, and may reflect a predisposition toward misinterpretations or errors in financial statements. In contrast, an effective internal control structure enlarges the bandwidth of internal communications and improves the understanding of the organization's policies and objectives.

For instance, banks usually take a one-way street to risk management because they find it difficult to integrate different skills into one system. They either hire rocket scientists who are good in mathematics but know nothing of trading, or they hire

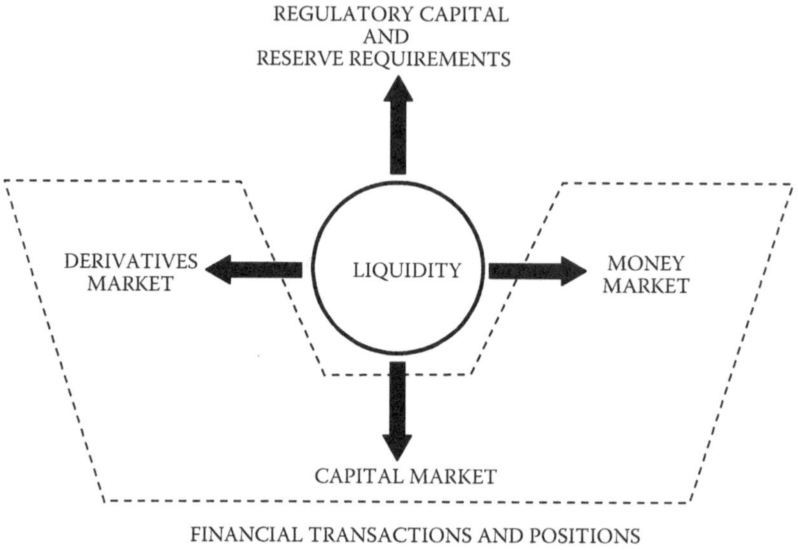

Figure 1.3 Four different dimensions of liquidity to be controlled intraday with results reaching top management through internal control.

ex-traders who grasp what makes sense in risk control, but who have no background in mathematical analysis. Contrary to this one-way street, organizations should be keen to merge trading and analytical skills, thereafter auditing the deliverables.

If the proverbial long, hard look is not very often in fashion in management circles, there exist some excellent positive examples. One of them is the conclusion reached by a 2005 blue ribbon banking committee under Gerald Corrigan, former chairman of New York Fed. In its conclusion, the committee differentiated between

- *Disturbances* as isolated problems and
- *Shocks* with systemic aftereffects.

Controls must be in place to register both and to differentiate between them. Frequently, the direct effect of shock is an increase in volatility, which, among other aftereffects, impacts negatively on investors' risk appetite. Another example is the disappearance, or near disappearance, of liquidity. As Figure 1.3 suggests, this impacts on financial transactions and positions.

- In the short run, there is no way to tell the difference between brief illiquidity problems and insolvency.*
- Therefore, liquidity must be controlled intraday through market data and feed-forward simulation.

* As Gerald Corrigan said in October 1987 to Alan Greenspan. See Bob Woodward, "Maestro: Greenspan's Fed and the American Boom," Simon and Schuster, New York, 2000.

The Corrigan Committee study also associated shocks with unexpected *tail risks* (of the assumed distribution of exposures) as well as to risk concentrations and risk contagion. These are issues addressed by a new generation of internal controls (see Section 4) that make good use of experimentation and whose information is boosted through stress tests.

(The Corrigan study identified relatively recent red zone shocks that greatly impact on financial stability: emerging market debt, of the mid-1980s; stock market crash of October 1987; debt instruments crisis of 1994; Asian Tigers crash of early to late 1997; Russian bankruptcy of August 1998; and LTCM's descent into the abyss in September 1998. The stock market crash of March/April 2000 provides another systemic risk example.)

1.4 Classical and New Internal Controls

Classical internal control issues included authorization for transactions, safeguards over assets and records, segregation of duties, documentation standards as well as verification duties, which tended to integrate internal control with auditing. Internal accounting control for industrial companies, merchandising firms, banks, and brokers included books and records of the firm's assets and liabilities, as well as segregated entries of customer property. The dual targets of such control have been

- Capital protection and
- Management compliance with existing rules and regulations.

The service economy has amplified these duties. As we saw in Section 2 on service science, in recent years the range of activities has been extended to cover new responsibilities that require both quantitative and qualitative judgments, for instance, on the degree of independence of different banking functions, including their relationships with

- Corporate governance rules and
- A growing range of compliance activities (Chapter 12).

Risks, too, must be controlled both quantitatively and qualitatively. Examples of quantitative measures are policies that pay adequate attention to risk limits and that ensure a rigorous process for measuring, evaluating, and instantly reporting exposures. In contrast, among other aims, qualitative controls put a premium on a strong control environment and make certain that the organization as a whole abides by ethical values.

One of the basic reasons why internal controls today play a more important function than ever is that the products and services offered by many service companies, credit institutions, and securities firms are becoming

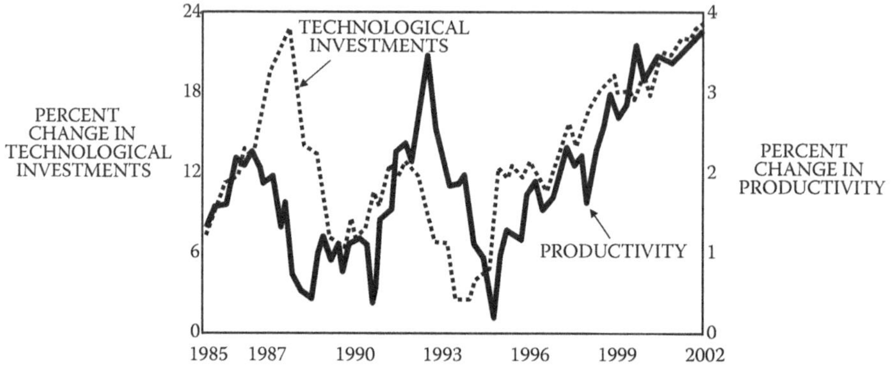

Figure 1.4 A pattern of non-farm labor productivity vs. technological investments in the United States. (2-Year annualized percent change. Statistics by bureau of economic analysis, Bureau of Labor Statistics).

- More complex and
- More exotic in their nature.

Precisely because of the growing complexity characterizing financial instruments and transactions, internal controls must produce not only words and numbers, but also patterns permitting one to judge, among other factors, individual and cumulative exposure. Patterns make it possible for every manager to be more confident when evaluating outstanding risk. As an example, Figure 1.4 presents a seven-year pattern of non-farm labor productivity versus technological investments in the United States.

Internal control and corporate governance correlate, because IC is a matter of *referential integrity*, addressing such questions as: How do we make sure our operations are clean of malfeasance and of conflicts of interest? How do we keep them clean? and other more personal queries. William McDonough, the former chairman of New York Fed, once said that corporate governance depends on more than a company's compliance with rules.

To a substantial extent, internal control is a matter of *management intent*. Management's *vigilance* and *virtue* make the difference between the chemists and alchemists of financial reporting and, by extension, the dependability of financial systems. Says Michael White in the biography of Sir Isaac Newton:

> The intellectual as opposed to the motivational foundations of chemistry and alchemy overlapped.... Chemists and alchemists dealt with the same compounds, even used the same apparatus and shared inherited knowledge; what lay between them was *approach* and *intent*.* (emphasis added)

* Michael White, *Isaac Newton, The Last Sorcerer* (London: Fourth Estate, 1997).

Management approach and intent are important issues that go hand in hand with the way a person, company, or state runs its business—in short, with *personal accountability*. That is why an integral part of the management approach is the institution of internal control and its attendant feedback.

In 2003, at the time of Allied Irish Banks (AIB) misfortunes in America, voices on Wall Street said that there was some evidence that senior management at AIB and Allfirst knew what was going on with Allfirst's rotten operations, but took no corrective action. The blowup came when Goldman Sachs stopped trading with Allfirst because they did not like what they saw in terms of control procedures.

Quite often, the board's and CEO's reluctance to act on evidence provided by internal control, and put the accounts straight, comes from the fact that a lot of people at the top do not understand what the professionals working for them are doing. Therefore, they can neither guide them nor control them.

In many banks, for instance, top management is very reliant on the expertise of a few people: traders, financial analysts, and some other professionals. But if management lacks knowledge on these issues and activities, it cannot comprehend how these people think and work or how they may overreach their limits. This makes it nearly impossible to be in charge of operations where (at times) exposure may skyrocket.

Such a state of affairs worries regulators. During the meeting at the Office of Thrift Supervision (OTS), an executive that I was talking to underlined that institutions should have a risk-control system in place that they consider to be an integral part of the responsibilities of the bank's senior management. To this he added that management control must promote

- Efficient operations within established risk limits,
- Reliable financial and regulatory reporting practices, and
- Compliance with relevant laws, regulations, and institutional policies.

Because supervisory authorities tacitly or explicitly approve dealing in new financial instruments, it is part of their duty to ensure that internal controls that are in place in institutions under their watch have the level of coverage, sophistication, and quality assurance necessary to

- Report exposure in factual terms and
- Enable management to be truly in charge.

Among tier-1 banks, this task is supported by technology, including knowledge-enriched software (Chapter 12), online database mining, and any-to-any intelligent multimedia networks. While the existence of state-of-the-art technology is no assurance that an adequate internal control environment exists, the lack of it is an indication of insufficient management attention paid to preservation of assets, competitive standing, and reputational risk.

1.5 Deficiencies and Conflicts in Internal Control

Many boards and CEOs think that their organization has a superb system of internal control (IC), only to find out the hard way that it is full of weak spots, saturated links, filtering nodes, and generally has many deficiencies that have not been addressed promptly, if at all. Even well-designed IC systems fall apart because, in dynamic markets, even the best solutions become obsolete, and if they are not regularly audited they cease to perform.

Some of internal control's deficiencies are structural; others are the result of half-baked policies and ill-studied procedures. Managers who are worth their salt know that once weak spots are identified, they should be corrected on a timely basis. Internal auditors (Chapter 4) should ensure that this is done by conducting follow-up reviews, and if the audit's statement is not unqualified, they should alert the audit committee of the board (Chapter 5).

Creative accounting is an example of a malfunction that sometimes finds its origin at top management. Creative accounting can thrive in the absence of rigorous internal control. Given that all accounting rules can be twisted to make the balance sheet and income statement look pretty, many profit reports reflect clever (but not ethical) use of accounting, rather than the accounting result of real operations that obey established standards (GAAP [generally accepted accounting principles] in the United States; IFRS [International Financial Reporting Standards] in the European Union).

From the downfall of Barings to the copper scam of Sumitomo Corporation, many organizations that suffered major losses did so because they neglected to continually assess the risks connected to their accounting practices, and to conduct in-depth analysis to spot unwarranted double- and triple-book practices. Quite frequently, the board fails to appreciate that classical-type control systems are unable to handle.

- Leveraged products and
- Complex market environments.

Market environments become complex for a number of reasons, such as the growing sophistication of investors and of financial products, absence of appropriate legislation and regulation (the case of hedge funds), differences in legislation of jurisdictions made prominent by globalization, and a growing amount of legal risk due to the propensity of litigation. After the 1997 financial meltdown in East Asia, analysts found that the balance sheets of even relatively healthy local banks were suspect.

- Gaps and defects in local legislation made it almost impossible to attach residual values to nonperforming loans.
- These banks could not recover money owed by recalcitrant companies because of the absence of effective bankruptcy legislation in their jurisdiction.

There was as well an inordinate amount of political patronage, which had led to granting loans to noncreditworthy firms and to a good deal of inappropriate business activities that should have been reported upward through formal internal control channels, but they were not reported because of

- Conflicts of interest and
- The many cases where even the concept of internal control was unknown.

In other cases, information contained in management reports was plainly inaccurate, creating the impression of a business situation that "was in control" while big losses accumulated. In connection with the 1997 meltdown of East Asia's "tigers," this situation was further compounded by

- Ineffective and inadequate audit programs and
- Substandard monitoring activities undertaken by senior management.

Many audits were superficially done, thereby impeding efforts to identify balance sheet weaknesses, while in other instances where auditors reported problems, no corrective action was taken by senior management. A frequently encountered control deficiency was that the effects of movements in foreign currency exchange rates were consistently skipped over, even if this was posing risks to profitability and to cash flow. Furthermore, scant attention was paid to the aftermath of potentially adverse changes in interest rates, even in transborder operations. Yet, interest rate changes resulted in losses in market value of the banks' assets due to differences between current market interest rates and rates at the inception of the loan. The net result was that a majority of East Asian banks suffered because they had failed to manage their exposure to interest rate changes.

Scant attention was also paid to counterparty creditworthiness, with the result that losses from loans were at the top of the list of weaknesses in the East Asian banks. Credit was extended with little consideration of the borrower's credit rating. In fact, in the majority of failed bank loans were handouts, and they depended on family connections, political pork barrel, or business acquaintances—not on quality of credit.

In western countries, conflicts of interest result when the same executive who is assessing the adequacy of loan documentation then monitors the borrower after loan origination, or provides information to customers about their positions while screening their loan applications or extending credit lines. Research has unearthed a steady pattern generated by such conflicts. Under these conditions, internal control becomes a fiction, if it exists at all. Confusion also seems to have prevailed in financial reporting between derivatives and other more classical instruments with relatively low exposure. In management control terms, "one size fits all" is risk control's version of creative accounting.

Also in western countries, postmortem examination of the factors contributing to a bank's bankruptcy has revealed a failure in segregation of duties, which is always a serious organizational deficiency, and one that is not limited to situations where the same person is in charge of front desk and back office. Other examples include giving the same executive responsibility for (a) approving the disbursement of funds as well as the authority of doing the actual disbursement or (b) handling in an integrative way customer accounts and proprietary accounts. Invariably,

- The bank's operating units that later reported significant losses, first reported profits because of intensive market activities, and
- These reported profits were, most frequently, far in excess of expectations for the reported level of risk; hence, they were eventually leading to highly anomalous results.

In well-governed credit institutions, internal control alerts responsible executives about all of these patterns, and senior management is seriously concerned about such alerts. This leads to corrective measures. In contrast, in poorly managed enterprises, because of the illusion that deviations from risk-and-return expectations tend to be positive, questions are not asked and investigations are not started until serious problems hit the radar screen.

In conclusion, senior management should appreciate that preventive action is an integral part of an organization's daily operations, and internal control is its agent. Prudential action is exemplified by limits and real-time reports on deviations, permitting senior management to effectively address risks the bank takes before they get out of control. Part of prudential control is that the board and senior management request live presentations and interactive performance reports that enable them to critically review exposure. This goes well beyond the status of more classical reports, which typically show risk-and-return information in a largely opaque form, and do not facilitate the detection of problems that can be addressed early on, well before they become catastrophic.

1.6 Internal Control Is IT's Current Frontier

Section 2 made reference to the observation that the huge changes taking place in IT organization and management are driving people to pick up new skills, while the CIO's performance is increasingly judged by how far and how well he or she can be a business innovator and service-level designer. The need for reinventing IT arises from deep underlying trends that are affecting

- The concepts as well as the nuts and bolts of corporate technology and
- Methods that companies employ to get the most out of their IT investment and their business at large.

Highly competitive IT systems cannot be replicas or patchworks of legacy systems, or even new developments based on them. They must be designed from the bottom up with an aim to respond to changes in business processes and market drivers. In this connection, it is the business of internal control to provide top management with factual information on

- The mind frame and performance of the CIO, project managers, and other IT professionals, and
- How well and how fast IT deliverables serve the company's strategic plan, respond to its information needs, and make everyone's job more effective.

Feedback on these types of results fit well with the most modern business management principles, which posit that sustainable competitive advantages require not only brilliant ideas, but also rapid action. If there were no other reason for rapid action (and there are several), it is definitely required to evaluate and rethink the CIO's role:

- He or she is no longer a backroom specialist, whose job was to make systems run.
- He or she is now a process innovator and designer, and therefore must be willing and able to learn the language of business management.

It is not necessarily obvious that business innovators are the best hope of the computer companies themselves, because they need to grow in an industry that is apparently stagnant. Take client-servers as an example. Profitability that can be derived from humdrum corporate servers supporting run-of-the-mill business applications is shrinking because server prices are falling faster than the growth in volume being shipped. Business innovators, however, appreciate that at the same time there is a parallel market that is expanding quickly. This is populated by unusually demanding customers who need powerful servers to

- Route their wares efficiently,
- Model complex products and processes, and
- Do simulations for design experimentation and forecasting.

Another category of users ahead of the curve includes the fast-growing Web 2.0 start-ups that handle huge amounts of multimedia information. A Silicon Valley term, Web 2.0 is not just software. It describes a collection of services, including processing, databasing, networking, and metalevels. This is an interesting paradigm because it allows the end user much greater freedom of interaction with the Internet as well as transitioning

- From a collection of Web sites
- To a fully fledged computing utility.

According to experts, the able use of what Web 2.0 has to offer facilitates online dynamic service agreements meeting the ever-changing needs of end users. An on-demand service approach replaces desktop computing and alters the perception of data processing. These are already real-life events, and therefore they are milestones that corporate IT must reach in terms of sophistication and effectiveness.

Developers of software for computer games are among the first entities capitalizing on Web 2.0's potential because they appeal to a market that demands a very fast response time and the best graphics. Therefore, they have become a guide and testing ground for the latest hardware/software developments and trends.

Sony's most important concession to Web 2.0 and *user-generated content* came with a demonstration of its LittleBigPlanet game. This game permits players to choose objects and manipulate physics to create customized spaces and then communicate that space or world to other players with whom they interact. Sony expects that LittleBigPlanet players will upload and share their versions with each other.

The reader may wonder how these developments affect the world of corporate computer operations. The answer is self-evident. Though still oriented to the private user, the foregoing references constitute an avant-garde of IT's potential in service science. Companies need to master Web 2.0 and other developments in the coming years to remain competitive.

1.7 The Audit of Advanced IT Operations

The examples presented in Section 6 are one of the first available references to the evolving application of service science (Section 2), and they lead toward the implementation of *software as a service*. Many experts look at Web 2.0 facilities—from games to user-generated content—as agents of the coming business process-oriented technology.

As the solutions this technology provides evolve into competitive applications, they will have a great impact on needed IT skills as well as on the mission of IT departments. Compared with today's data-processing-oriented systems, including ERP (enterprise resource planning) and supply-chain management, future systems will, in all likelihood, be

- Designed to be flexible and adaptable and
- Projected to combine at short notice pieces of different functions into new systems, which themselves may be ephemeral.

As Figure 1.5 points out, high technology is the first, and therefore most basic, layer of the infrastructure on which will rest the oncoming business edifice. To contribute to it, the CIO must, by definition, be a business innovator, and he or she must continue being an innovator. At the moment this person tries to turn service science into a legacy application, he or she will be professionally dead. At

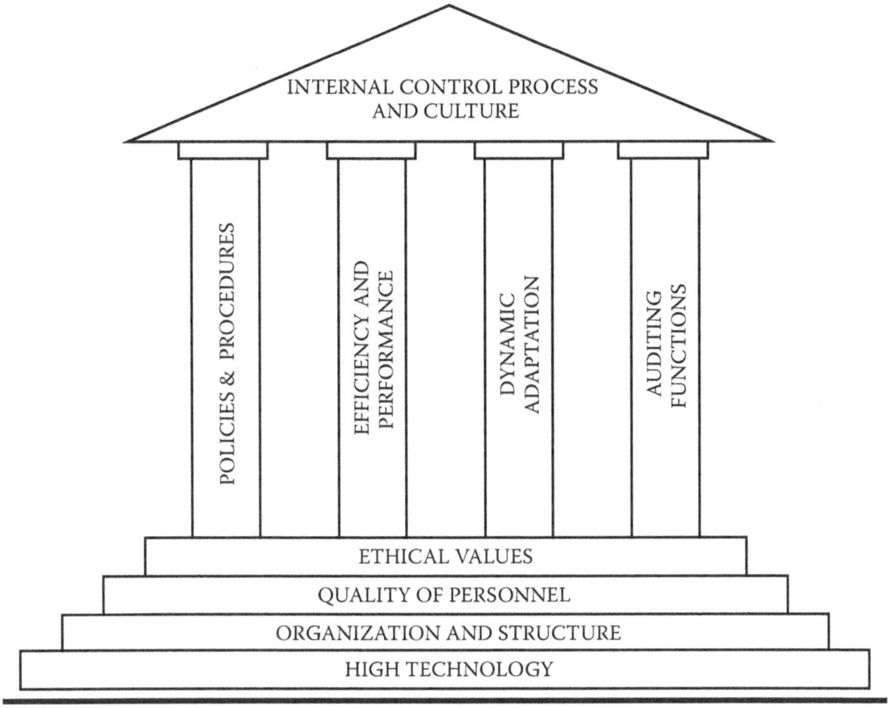

Figure 1.5 Infrastructure and pillars supporting a valid solution to internal control.

the same time, however, senior management must watch over and continue monitoring this innovation process in corporate IT. That is why, at the top of the edifice in Figure 1.5, one finds the internal control process and culture subject to regular audits.

The service-level designer's undisputed client is the end user. To serve the user best, the designer must squeeze more out of the company's current IT system and free resources that can be invested in projects way ahead of current ones. To maximize the use of resources, the CIO and service-level designers will have to ensure that all of a company's information elements, processes, and subprocesses are

- Properly captured and
- Maintained in a form making them readily available on request.

Within the perspective established by these two bulleted items, IT audit must concentrate on identifying failures to do what the previous paragraphs have briefly prescribed. A typical example would be a failure to provide quick, flexible, and effective service-level applications because of go-slow IT policies or too much of legacy-thinking residues.

Another negative to IT deliverables along service-science lines is the parochial applications that user organizations developed in the 1980s and 1990s to escape the yoke of centrally located mainframes. Commercial and investment banks tend to have separate IT systems aligned with different lines of business such as equities, fixed income, foreign exchange, and so on. However, provided that service-science principles are fully observed, competitiveness in the global market requires that

- These IT silos become fully integrated and
- Real-time interactive IT services be supported at a wide range of activities, but without duplications.

These are fundamental in allowing institutions and companies in other industrial sectors to continue developing their specific capabilities around their assets and markets. These are also important in responding in a timely and efficient way to commercial pressure and in reducing time to market for new products and services while closely tracking exposure associated with them.

IT auditors should appreciate that, in well-governed enterprises, they are confronted with two IT cultures, each requiring a different audit procedure: legacy, and that of the agents of disruption and renovation, whose job is to look beyond immediate business needs to find new opportunities served through advanced technology.

Apart from other advantages, a business-intensive IT solution makes it feasible to capitalize on innovative revenue-earning asset classes. Clear thinkers in management strategy have proposed a broad distinction inside companies between employees doing more-or-less routine work and those charged with

- Inventing,
- Deploying, and
- Optimizing a product or service.

The optimizers focus purely on efficiency, squeezing resources out of mature processes. This way, the cycle of inventing, which is quite often disruptive, and that of deploying and using can coexist. Microsoft and IBM provide an example. The upheaval that is under way in the software industry at large makes both companies increasingly dependent on:

- Technology shifts
- New competitive breakthroughs
- Use of drivers that are very different from those that have traditionally shaped the software business and its products

If, for example, IBM focuses its strategy on becoming a full *software as a service* provider, this would turn on its head the row of criticism that it has kept out of the applications business by concentrating too much on income from consulting.

It would also create a crisis in its highly profitable partnership with application software producers.

In the opinion of a growing number of experts, online *software as a service* will prove to be a most critical development to all software producers and marketers, changing the way companies procure many of their applications. This business has been pioneered by firms like Salesforce.com and Google, and it is still in its early development stage.

The auditors of IT departments and of IT service companies will be well advised to study the Web 2.0 possibilities and policies followed by the firms they work with in purchasing software products that meet the ever-changing needs of end users. The gathering of user-centric requirements and system-development techniques appropriate to an on-demand service approach is an activity totally different than that used in the IT we have known in past decades.

While CIOs become more exposed to the perceptions that end users and other stakeholders have of their departments, both the firm's ongoing IT operations and the service-on-demand experiences should be subjected to auditing and internal-control feedback. They should also be subjected to critical analysis of their upsides and downsides. It is rare to find a new service channel or business line that presents only an upside.

Chapter 2

Case Studies on Internal Control's Contribution

2.1 Internal Control and Operational Risk

The Basel Committee on Banking Supervision defines *operational risk* (op risk) as the risk of loss from inadequate internal processes or failed internal control. These processes may regard people, tools, methods, or systems. Operational risk also stems from external events outside the control of *our* organization, but in this chapter we will be concerned only with those generated within the organization—and their avoidance. To a very substantial degree, op risks are

- Causal,
- Event-oriented, and
- Result in loss or damage.

While there is always a tendency to classify operational risk in neat categories such as fraud (internal and external), workplace safety, damage to physical assets, exposure resulting from business practices, and the like, Figure 2.1 suggests that the domains where op risk can be found are much broader. This figure brings to the reader's attention the three main groups of operational risk that are present in practically every organization.

Every function, whether front-desk activity, back-office operation, trading, or the logistics unit, must identify, monitor, and manage the operational risks that

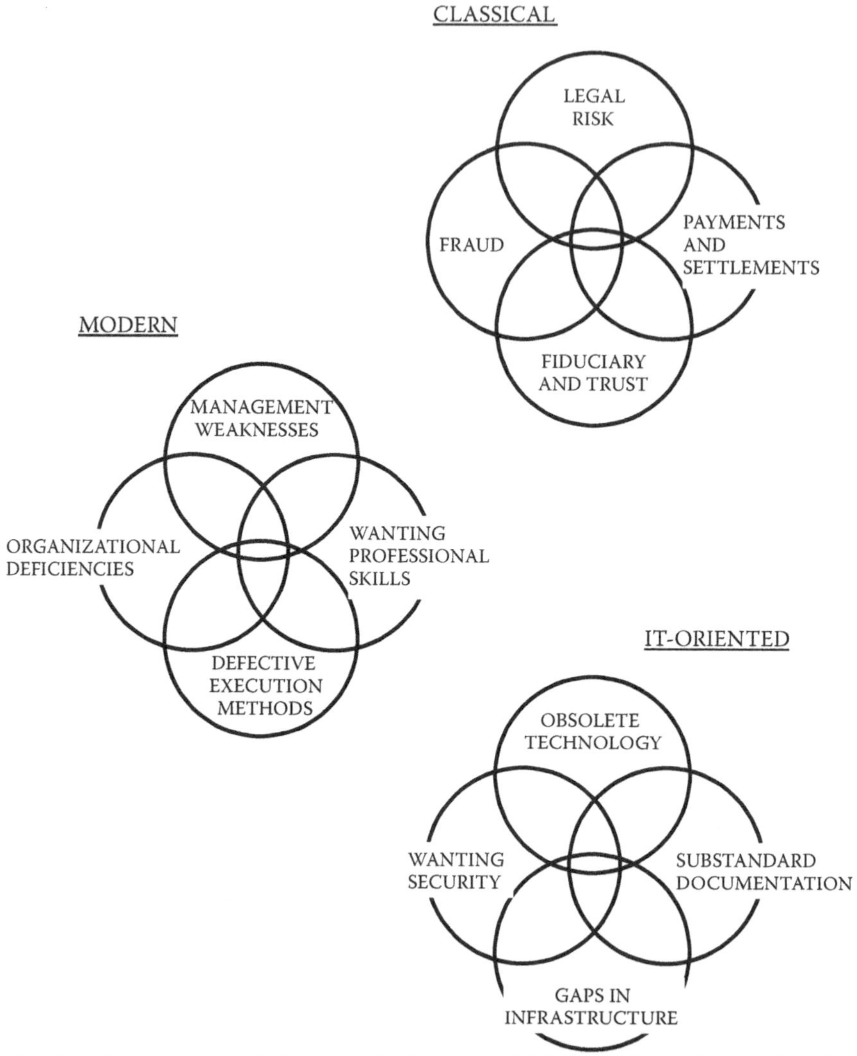

Figure 2.1 Three different groups of operational risk.

arise from its own business. Because these risks are pervasive, with a failure in one area potentially impacting several others, a sound framework must be based on mutual oversight across all functions, under centralized operational-risk control.

An operational-risk-control framework includes the definition of roles and responsibilities, so that those responsible can collectively ensure that they follow control standards and reach objectives necessary to protect the company's tangible and intangible assets and interests. Op-risk-control activities are based on specific types of operational risks that might arise, ranging

- From everyday reconciliation problems
- To potentially severe errors in payments and settlements.

As major operational-risk events occur, management must assess their causes and implications for the firm, whether or not they lead to direct financial loss. This includes events that could affect third parties that are relevant to the company's business if sufficient information were to be made public, which so often happens.

Classically, financial institutions and other entities have used a range of control techniques to keep op risk in check, but these were largely oriented toward the prevention of fraud. Examples include cross-checking, reconciliation of accounts, double signature, staff turnover, and limited access. Companies have also instituted follow-up procedures for breaches, whether done individually by one party, or by many. The audit department has usually handled such cases.

This has changed inasmuch as today's operational risk is more complex, and it can be much more costly than in the past. Therefore, well-managed entities use all available op-risk information to test their internal control framework. Even if an event does not lead to direct or indirect financial loss, it may indicate that the firm's internal control standards are defective or are not being complied with. Beyond an established threshold, operational risks must be reported as they happen to senior management, evaluated in terms of their

- Potential frequency of occurrence and
- Likely severity of the resulting impact (more on this in Section 3).

Until this greater awareness about operational-risk control became part of the general conscience (at least in the banking industry thanks to Basel II), the effectiveness of control procedures for op risk varied widely. This is not surprising, because the results depend on a number of factors to be controlled, ranging from the particular area to which the technique is applied to the quality of audit personnel, the tools being used, the type of organization, and the size of the business.

Other things being equal, the internal control effort has been more successful when the internal environment is better managed (because the control mission is not handicapped), and when a high degree of consideration is given to the internal control function by the CEO and the board. This reflects the principle that an entity's administration should be in charge, in a way consistent with

- The nature of the business and
- The pursuit of its objectives.

The organizational ills leading toward unwarranted operational risks include ineffective segregation of duties, confused lines of responsibility, and loopholes permitting concealment of violations of rules and regulations. While having a strong ethical culture does not guarantee that a financial institution will not take extraordinary op risks, its absence raises the probability by so much that such unwarranted risks will be assumed (we will return to this issue). A particular characteristic of op risk is that, without proper organization and training,

- People do not know *what* is targeted;
- People do not understand *how* to control op risk; and
- People do not like to be controlled in what they are doing.

Identification, quantification, and monitoring of operational risks provides useful data both for immediate corrective action and for the purpose of preventing its repetition. For example, appropriate preventive measures established as part of corporate policy help in reducing reputational risk. Making people aware of the materiality of losses helps in concentrating their attention on avoidance of op risk.

Theoretically, a company's operational risk will not necessarily bear any relationship to its market risk and credit risk. Practically, this is not true because, as Figure 2.2 shows, these three types of risk tend to overlap. Therefore, an organization keen in swamping operational risk would be well advised to do a comprehensive review of:

- The major op risks that it faces
- Existing correlation of these risks
- The policies necessary to be in charge of these exposures

The way to bet is that the methodology to be adopted for operational-risk control and for IC's contribution to this effort would require detailed research to establish benchmark ratios and the means to convert any op-risk exposure into a capital charge. The quantification of operational risk should be based on algorithms that are simple and straightforward, relating capital to the size of exposure on the basis of some logic. This is what the Basel Committee advises.*

Internal control should be very sensitive to the opportunities presented by, and limitations characterizing, metrics applied to the monitoring and measurement of operational risk. Correctly, Basel II directives make the board of directors and senior management responsible for operational risk and for integrity standards, as well as for establishing a culture that emphasizes the importance of internal controls.

There is plenty to be said on the cultural issue (see also Chapter 1). The prevailing concepts, attitudes, words, and actions of the board of directors and senior management affect the integrity and ethics of the bank as a whole, and most particularly the effectiveness of its controls. This is important, because an essential element of a strong internal control system is the recognition by every employee of the need to effectively carry out his or her responsibilities.

---

* D. N. Chorafas, *Operational Risk Control with Basle II: Basic Principles and Capital Requirements* (London: Butterworth-Heinemann, 2004).

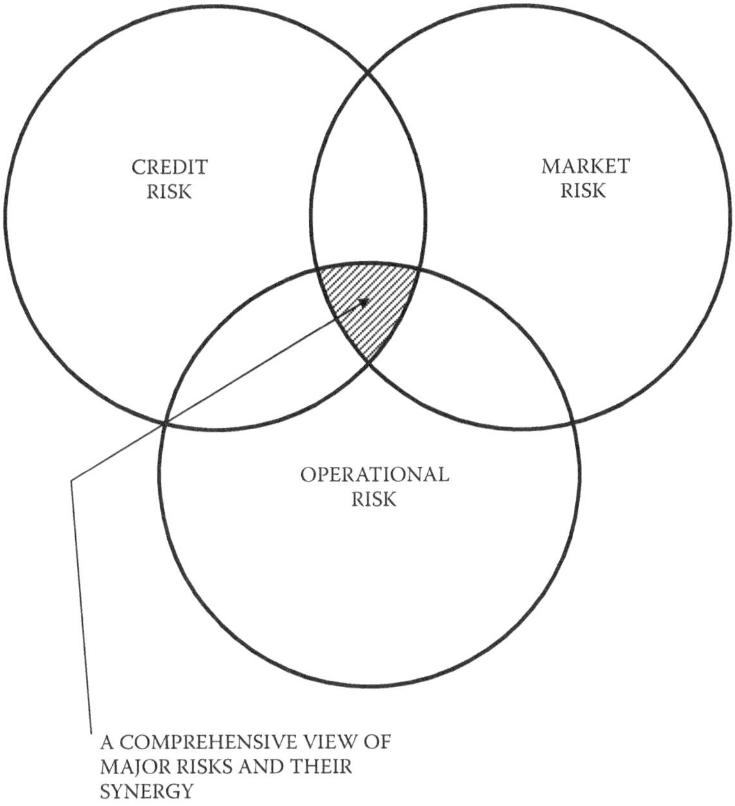

Figure 2.2 There are common elements in different types of risk. With new instruments these should be addressed from the drafting board.

2.2 Monitoring Functions of Internal Control

The success of internal control is indivisible from prudential policies (a) defined in accordance with the risk-taking strategy of the company, (b) supported by an advanced information technology that permits real-time response to op-risk events, and (c) is endowed with knowledge artifacts (Section 3). The IT plan should be comprehensive and cover all activities. It should also be commensurate with the nature and size of the firm, the business environment(s) in which it operates, the likelihood of operational risk, internal control requirements, and goals set by top management.

Leadership in IT is necessary, but leadership alone is not sufficient. The most basic prerequisite is *management intent*. Wise CEOs use their company's operational-risk framework as the basis for internal control assessments in areas such as legal, compliance, tax, fraud, financial accounts, and human resources. This framework also assists in meeting internal-control-related regulatory requirements, including Basel II and Sarbanes-Oxley Section 404 (see Chapter 3). In areas such as

- Governance at large,
- Regulatory reporting, and
- Assessment of policy implementation,

the impact of an operational-risk event may be larger than what its immediate monetary cost might suggest. For instance, a publicly disclosed regulatory fine may result in withdrawal of clients and other forms of loss of business. It is precisely because of regulatory and legal issues that the level of op risk is related to more than immediate financial losses, which at first sight are only indicative.

Members of the board, the CEO, and senior management should never forget that the wave of financial innovation and growth in the number and nature of financial instruments have made the issue of internal control both more demanding and more complex. Features and functions that, in the past, focused on reduction of fraud and other types of misappropriation are still important, but they are not sufficient in the new environment.

Legal risk, for example, has become more pervasive, encompassing new types of exposure for which appropriate reserves must be built. The establishment of financial reserves for legal risk should be governed by an assessment concept that can facilitate the identification, analysis, and management of all cases with legal risk potential. The most effective internal control is the one where

- Company communications are characterized by open channels,
- Policies and procedures provide incentives for compliance, and
- All employees are trained to high standards of behavior.

Deficient ethical standards and internal control failures have resulted in significant losses for banks and other industries. Such losses might have been substantially lessened if the board and chief executive officer had properly appreciated the risks and corrected issues that weakened the company's defenses. If left unattended, these issues promote and reward unscrupulous behavior.

A warning signal can be derived from what happens as well as from what should have happened but did not. Therefore, one of the basic goals of internal control is that of monitoring and recording *events* and *nonevents* associated with critical functions within the organization and their relations to business partners, particularly in connection with commitments that have been made.

The assignment of responsibilities provides another example. Risk-control functions should never be entrusted to traders or to persons accountable to traders. A policy of independence of opinion is indispensable to the establishment and maintenance of a system of checks and balances that permits executives to be immediately aware of any type of exposure that takes place in credit risk, market risk, or operational risk.

Quite often, internal controls are deficient because they are not formally set, and also because most institutions do not monitor every critical function in a dependable manner. Many executives tend to make judgments, implicitly or explicitly, that ignore some types of exposure or lack detail. For example, in terms of its ability to monitor market risk,

- The internal control system must be designed in accordance with the scale, complexity, and risk content of market activities conducted or projected, and
- The institution's strategy, trading practices, and market(s) in which it operates should be taken into full account in designing the control system.

For compliance purposes, internal controls must thoroughly reflect prevailing regulatory requirements by country of operations, type of institution, nature of instruments in which the entity trades and takes position, as well as other criteria specific to a given situation. The controls must ensure that regulations are honored at all times, by every transaction, wherever it is executed. (Compliance is discussed further in Chapter 12.)

For instance, in Germany, the prolongation of forward foreign exchange or option transactions at the rate of strike price of the original trade is permitted only if the following conditions are assured: The bank's senior management has expressly authorized such trades; prolongation is effected at the written request of a customer, other than another credit institution; the trade is verifiably based on a transaction in goods or services; and the customer undertakes to present appropriate documents at the bank's request in support of well-established criteria.

In conclusion, a reliable approach to the design, implementation, and daily functioning of internal control is an integral part of an overall risk monitoring and management structure covering *all* of an entity's areas of business. A prerequisite to effective operation of IC is that its mechanics facilitate identification and analysis of risks from trading and nontrading activities, with operational risk being a case point. A system of internal controls that is worth its salt will be flexible, enabling the company to respond at short notice to changes in the market and in its own operational conditions. IC's individual components, methods, tools, parameters, and computational procedures have to be studied, tested, and documented. They must also be audited and otherwise reviewed at least annually.

2.3 The Critical Role of Experimentation

Internal control will be so much more effective if plenty of attention is paid to experimentation, its rules, and its procedures, which often include the need for experimental design and for stress tests. Experimentation is an established discipline in engineering and in applied psychology, but it is a little-known world in business and finance. Yet, it is very important to both.

- When the number of unknowns increases, market conditions change at a fast pace, and uncertainty is king.
- Under these conditions, experimentation is not just the better policy; it is the only way to plan for success.

Here is an example from real life. As 1923 came to a close, five short years after WW I's end, the value of the French franc fell by 50 percent, and France found itself in full financial crisis. Frank Altschul, then leading partner of Lazard Frères New York, was invited by the French minister of finance to hear his views on solving the crisis.

Altschul called for the French government to make what he called an *experiment* aimed to stabilize the plunging currency.* His experiment was novel, as all experiments are. Using a $100-million loan (big money at that time) from J. P. Morgan, the French government bid the franc from 124 to the dollar to 61 to the dollar over the course of a few weeks. Speculators who had sold the franc short in expectation that its value would continue falling were hit by huge losses, and the franc stabilized.

All experiments involve risk, but when they are done under controlled conditions, the insiders who are in charge know how far they can go; the outsiders do not. The same applies in planning and testing our ability and preparation for dealing with operational-risk issues. In business, experiments can be so much more successful if we

- Design them properly and
- Establish clear responsibilities for carrying them out.

An example is experimenting on risks taken with what, at first sight, seems to be needed cost-effectiveness measures. Cost cutting is very often necessary, but it is no one-way street, and its final effectiveness should never be taken for granted.

In March 2005, 15 people were killed in an explosion at the BP refinery in Texas City, Texas, and another 500 people were injured. This was an operational accident—the worst industrial accident in 15 years in the United States. Postmortem, a discovery process revealed that not only BP itself, but also government regulators had failed to provide comprehensive scrutiny of the facility to uncover its alarming state of disrepair, largely due to swamping costs, which were a factor in the decision to operate without the benefit of an experiment on the consequences.

* William D. Cohan, *The Last Tycoons* (New York: Doubleday, 2007).

Based on its findings, the Chemical Safety and Hazard Investigation Board (CSB) blamed the accident on safety deficiencies at all levels of the BP corporation. Other critics added that the accident was promoted by a short-sighted business culture that idealized cost cutting. Costs matter, but so does safety. The CSB said that its two-year inquiry documented inadequate response to

- Multiple audits revealing safety lapses,
- Failure to thoroughly investigate and respond to previous accidents, and
- A policy of ignoring federal regulations by focusing on production rather than on safety.

Carolyn Merritt, CSB chair, commented that the March 2005 accident at BP was unavoidable—the inevitable result of a series of actions by the company that affected maintenance and safety by ignoring the implications of previous incidents that were red warning flags.* For its part, BP stated that it accepted responsibility for the explosion but disagreed with some of the CSB report. Still, BP management promised to

- Give full and careful consideration to the CSB's recommendations and
- Take steps to improve safety and confront the causes of this and similar operating risks.

One of the strong messages provided by this case is that many accidents are man-made. A 2007 study by Swiss Re, the Swiss reinsurance company, has revealed that such accidents tend to increase: There were 56 percent more major man-made disasters in 2006 than natural catastrophes. The trend in the number of natural and man-made catastrophes, from 1970 to 2006, is shown in Figure 2.3. In 2006, more than 31,000 people lost their lives in devastating high-impact events. The prerequisites to experimental analysis of results and projection of safety measures are

- Frequency by type of man-made accident
- Size of loss, determined in practical business terms
- Distinction between high-frequency (HF) events and low-frequency (LF) events
- Analysis of reasons behind high-impact (HI) and low-impact (LI) events

The best bet is that every company should have experimental goals. One example would be analysis of the drift that might exist from HF/LI to LF/HI events. Another would be the analytics of likely aftereffects of new events that were as-yet-unknown operational risks.

---

* *Financial Times*, March 21, 2007.

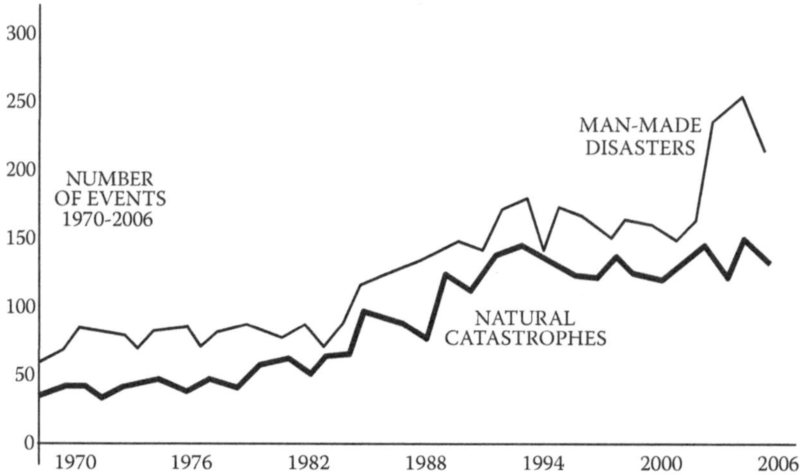

Figure 2.3 The number and impact of man-made disasters keeps on growing (statistics by Swiss Re' sigma no. 2/2007).

Several organizations collect operational-risk data, including losses analyzed by class, but most organizations do so in a not-so-dependable manner that does not allow subsequent experimentation. This is not independent of the fact that many companies lag behind in online, real-time data capture and data management.

Many companies have learned the value of obtaining a broader and deeper experimental view of exposure control, and this knowledge has been used to characterize market risk and credit risk. In contrast, the development of techniques for identifying, measuring, tracking, and monitoring of operational risks (and therefore man-made risks) is relatively limited, and such development varies widely from one entity to the next. The reasons for shortfalls in this area are fairly common, including

- Lack of strategic assessment
- Incomplete classification of operational risks
- Lack of definition for different types of operational risk
- Lack of information about the frequency of operational risks
- The fact that exposure is not always transparent and is not always material*
- Failure to explore the aftermath of operational risk to each process or service to which it is connected

Among commercial banks, the building of a first-class op-risk-events database has become mandatory, as the Basel Committee expects banks to include

* A material change (as well as a material error) is one which changes the results in a significant way. An accounting error of $1 million is not "material" in IBM's balance sheet, but it is highly material to a company with an annual turnover of $5 million.

operational risk in their *loss assessment* records. A prerequisite is clear policies regarding measurement of exposure by business line and op-risk type. Viable solutions for an operational-risk database capable of supporting experimentation include a number of steps:

- Addressing data quality issues at every point of each trade's or other operation's life cycle
- Associating loss events to each type of op risk, its frequency, and its impact
- Ensuring comprehensive coverage of op-risk events through better organization
- Increasing the frequency and accuracy of data collection to meet high-frequency financial data (HFFD) criteria

Among the better system solutions is intensive training of all personnel associated with the collection, storage, and management of op-risk data; assurance of a first-class data-validation process; data monitoring for early detection of operational risks; applying configural filters to transaction flow; establishing dynamic workflow adjustments; skill in experimental design; and developing state-of-the-art visualization and visibilization techniques.

2.4 Use of Threat Curves in IT

One of the few things on which the governments of the European Union seem to agree is that global warming will be bad not only for the planet, but as well for their citizens and the economy as a whole. However, they have found it much harder to come together on what to do about this challenge in an effective and lasting way.

On the surface, the EU countries have set themselves a target for stabilizing and then substantially reducing their output of carbon dioxide (CO_2). The downside is that plans are made of words and good intentions, much less so of specific commitments on

- *How* to deliver wanted results
- *Who* will be responsible for *which* contribution

Leaders of most of the world's other countries are also at a loss on how to implement their wordy commitments. So they keep on talking, usually by meeting at resort areas. International CO_2 tourism practically started with the June 1992 Rio Earth Summit, and it has been followed by the Kyoto Protocol and other just as ineffectual events. Notice that

- The greenhouse effect is an operational risk, and
- The conflict of interest in finding a sound solution comes from the fact that what underpins this op risk is well-being, travel, comfort, and employment.

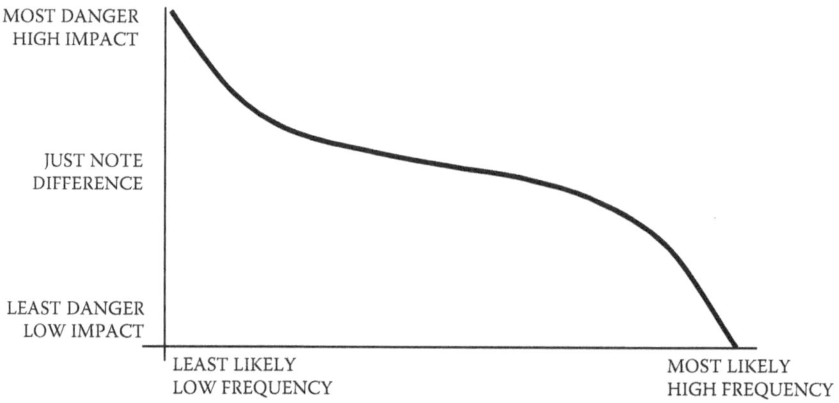

Figure 2.4 By ordering the probability associated to different risks, a threat curve assists in appreciating their likelihood.

Moreover, plenty of sacred cows contribute to CO_2 emissions. One of them (the theme of this section) is higher and higher power consumption by computers, databases, and communications links and nodes. Nobody really wants to be deprived of the fruits of technology. While the rapidly increasing use of computers has historically been welcomed as a sign of progress, this view is now confronting the reality of greenhouse emissions and the *threat curve* that goes with it. Figure 2.4 shows an example where the threat ranges

- From a minor event that is the most likely outcome but poses the least threat (HF/LI)
- To a major event that is the most unlikely outcome but represents the greatest danger (LF/HI).

Threat curves began to appear in NATO's intelligence offices in the mid-1980s. Their aim was to demonstrate the likelihood of certain dangers through an ordering, thereby permitting intelligence officers to channel a good share of resources to *probable risks*, not only the *worst case*, which may be unlikely. There are merits in applying the threat curve to the rapidly growing IT power consumption and the likelihood that it may derail the stated CO_2 control objectives.

Threat-curve graphics are a good analytical tool, allowing for events to be ordered in a way that expresses their likelihood on a scale of increasing probability, with (usually) the most dangerous threat being the least likely. Operational, financial, political, military, or any other crises have some common characteristics, ranging from their anticipation to their culmination and the need to establish the pattern presented by their threats. Examples where threat-curve implementation may be revealing are:

- Unexpected loan losses
- Mounting derivatives exposure
- Excessive use of resources
- Risks with IT projects
- Internal control deficiencies

Excessive energy consumption problems are in the domain of the last three bullets. Until about 2007, nobody really considered the high power consumption and environmental impact characterizing computer centers, PCs running 24 hours per day, portables, wired and wireless networks, and data warehouses. The awakening started with a study released in February 2007 by Lawrence National Laboratory, which found that

- Power consumption of data centers alone doubled between 2000 and 2005, and
- It now accounts for over 1.2 percent of *all* U.S. electrical consumption, a rapidly growing share.

In fact, adding all other information technology gear, including the Internet, brings technology's impact to 4 percent of U.S. power consumption. Although these figures are lower on a worldwide count, they are increasing fast, despite efforts to reduce emissions. Vodafone has reported a 10 percent drop in CO_2 emissions over 2005/2006, but because business is booming, over the same time frame, total electricity consumption increased by 23 percent.

One of the basic reasons power consumption has zoomed is the way in which computers have been historically designed: to maximize performance. Measures taken by some computer companies, like the PC-maker Dell, prompting their customers to plant trees to offset the carbon emissions generated by their computers, are nice but ineffectual. Neither is it enough to counterbalance the huge annual increase in computer usage by

- Installing more-efficient power suppliers and
- Switching to more-modern cooling systems.

The inescapable conclusion is that greater performance, high-density servers, more customers, more portables, and an increasing level of usage all represent threats because they produce more CO_2, and this greatly affects the environment despite what chiefs of state may say. According to published statistics, from 2000 to 2005 the total electricity use for *servers* in the world

- Increased from less than 60 billion kW·h per year to nearly 130, and
- This has been a direct effect of the number of servers, which went up 250 percent.

Worse yet, power consumption by high-end servers zoomed by almost 400 percent, while power needed for cooling and auxiliary equipment doubled. To bend the power consumption curve, AMD, Dell, HP, IBM, Intel, Microsoft, and Sun launched the *Green Grid* consortium, with fixes like multicore chips (by AMD and Intel), use of DC rather than AC, and on-demand cooling systems.

Sensors, actuators, and expert systems can help, but they will not do miracles. In spite of all these efforts, U.S. companies now spend 10 percent of their IT budget on electricity consumption, and this is expected to rise and equal expenditures for hardware. The same trend exists in the European Union, Japan, and other parts of the world.

To get a complete picture of the contribution of technology to global pollution, one must also consider the impact of waste equipment, such as huge loads of servers, PCs, and mobile phones discarded per year. For companies, too, electricity consumption grows inexorably with their size and business intensity, and the watch over CO_2 emissions, which has never been an issue in internal control, now requires internal control focus because the threat curve to the environment by IT is rapidly rising.

2.5 Design Review as an Internal Control Method

Project planning and execution is another fertile domain for exercise of internal control. A senior executive of the Royal Bank of Canada stated during a meeting that every IT project his organization has undertaken has a risk factor associated with it. This risk must be evaluated in a timely manner and corrected. Design reviews constitute an internal control method with feedback, and their patterns of findings can be expressed through a threat curve.

In several well-managed companies, minor design reviews of ongoing projects are made every week, evaluating both the project itself and its problems. Major design reviews are less frequent and target budgets and timetables as well as the projected effectiveness of the manager and the project members. To survive, project managers must *perform*. In my experience, performance is so much better if the project manager

- Puts his or her goals in writing,
- Sets priorities, and
- Commits himself or herself to a schedule, a budget, and the quality of deliverables.

Contrary to forecasts and projections, a design review, as an internal control instrument, deals with events that have happened. Except for extrapolations based on audited project results, they are not concerned with anticipations in general or

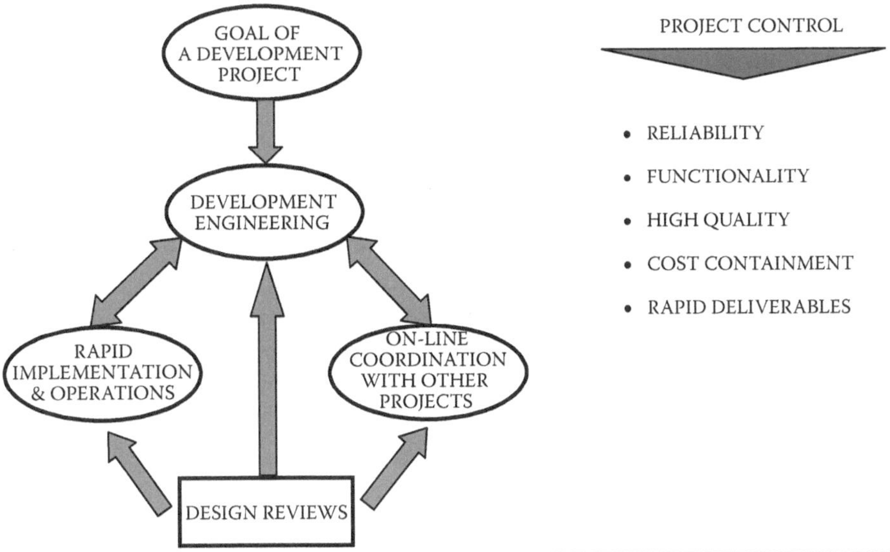

Figure 2.5 Able solutions to R&D must be functional, benefit from technology and be subject to design reviews.

with vague terms. Instead, they aim to reveal the worth of the project leader and his or her team.

This reference is valid of all research and development (R&D) projects, not only projects in IT. As Figure 2.5 suggests, viable solutions to development projects must be functional, benefit from high technology, observe standards (where they exist), and be subject to design reviews that watch over the critical variables established at the time of project definition. Figure 2.5 outlines five criteria for project control, but there may be more.

As an internal control method, design reviews contribute to management flexibility. Sam Walton, of Wal-Mart fame, had a policy that, in management, *flexibility* is the best policy. This can be characterized as the ability to turn on a dime. It is difficult to find a dictum that better fits the most basic characteristic of a good R&D project whose dynamics will typically rest on three pillars:

- Timetables that become faster and faster, leading to rapid compression of design schedules through simulation
- Effective coordination and avoidance of latent frictions, as engineers from different disciplines and driven by different priorities have to collaborate closely
- Conflicts that may arise because of the dual requirement of low cost but high quality, which must be solved through design reviews and not through the lengthy and ineffectual exchanges of documentation

As an internal control device, design reviews help the project manager not only by measuring progress against milestones, but also by asking the right questions and by having project members bring the answers in front of one another, not in private. Informed through internal control on how projects proceed, senior management can act, but should not change project leaders midstream unless the project has failed.

A project fails midstream if either its objective, its budget, its timetable, or some other crucial variable has failed. Moreover, many projects fail because their scope is ill-defined from the start; their human capital is not up to standards or is poorly led; the project manager ignores best practices and lessons learned; the chosen technology is substandard; or the project's sponsor(s) lost interest in it due to long delays or other reasons.

The results of the design review's examination of current and projected project progress reach senior management through internal control. This information typically includes strong and weak points identified by the design review, as well as assumptions used in estimating project completion, budget observance, and quality of deliverables.

- The design review is a *credibility test* for the project, over and above its other benefits.
- The design review does not subvert the project but, rather, assists in finding the reasons for deviations or delays, capitalizing on experience already gained with other similar projects.

A company can gain a great deal by dynamically exploiting knowledge from past projects, knowledge that is often hidden in a time closet and is available to only a very few persons, which is irrational. Yet, this does *not* require a great deal of virtuosity in knowledge management, because it can be effectively supported by the corporate memory facility (CMF, see Chapter 12).

Siemens, a company that operates in 190 countries and employs 470,000 people, provides an example. Its subsidiary in Malaysia wanted to bid for a high-speed data network linking Kuala Lumpur to its new airport, but lacked the necessary know-how. The competitive edge was provided by the company's *sharenet*, an internal Siemens system on which knowledge is posted for use throughout the firm's operations.

Using the sharenet facility, the Siemens subsidiary in Malaysia found that the parent firm was already working on a similar project in Denmark. The local people were able to adapt what had already been done and won an order for a pilot project. The reader should note, however, that the corporate memory facility is not just another database—it is a mindset.

It takes cultural change to classify, record, and exploit the knowledge accumulating over the years. But once this is done, it allows people at headquarters and faraway subsidiaries to develop and sell things in partnership, rather than fighting and stepping over each other's feet.

2.6 Internal Control and System Specifications

Because of increasing personalization of products and processes, and the need to sustain a steady reduction in time-to-market products coming out of development, projects must be *user driven* rather than *technology driven*. Regular internal control of engineering projects is a "must" to ensure that design premises honor that goal. Another basic mission assigned to design reviews in modern engineering is that of eliminating the classical technical disruptions in the transition between

- Research,
- Development,
- Manufacturing,
- Sales, and
- After-sales service.

Transition between different product phases should be properly planned from the start, as a seamless process. Such transition must be simple and effective, including the passage of product specifications and other files from research all the way to commercialization and field maintenance. A sound approach would eliminate the loss in efficiency that results when a project moves from one company department to the next, as shown in Figure 2.6. (This is based on my experience in the computer industry, but I found it applicable, as well, in other industry sectors.) This loss in efficiency happens because:

- Quite often, there is no single view of design specs among professionals supposed to cooperate.
- The risk of error-prone, phase-to-phase manual translation of specs in the design is always present.

Without high-technology support, it is difficult to explore component interactions inside a new product to their full extent. Additionally, there exist duplications of test benches among different intellectual centers working on the same project, and quite often there is a lack of integrative view of system design. This leads to misunderstandings and misapplications. Added to these factors is the fact that, because of differences in the backgrounds of team members, design specs quite often get misinterpreted.

From one company to the next, the challenges I have just enumerated may have different origins, but they all contribute to the same problem: a lack of a shared

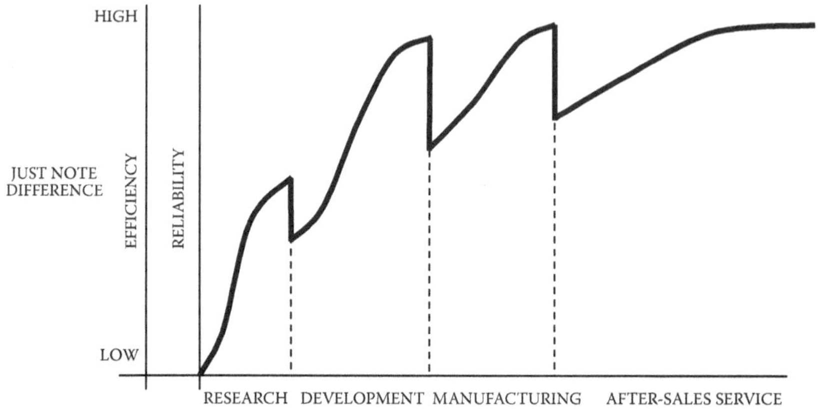

Figure 2.6 Non-seamless interfaces significantly reduce the efficiency and reliability of engineering work during product transition.

view of the product, which results in delays, high costs, and inadequate quality. What is necessary, therefore, is a common view, at the system-level, that makes it feasible for different members of the design team to make positive contributions in meeting coordinated technical requirements.

Based on these premises, internal control must ensure that no project is organized as a series of discrete steps or stages—or in "departmental silos," an expression the Basel Committee uses in regard to risk-management deficiencies. IT projects should *not*

- Start with esoteric algorithms and part-by-part specifications, and
- Then move through separate hardware and software designs to the testing phase.

Nothing should be done without a system view. IT auditors must ascertain whether this has happened and, if so, it must bring the malpractice to the attention of senior management. Auditors must also be aware that part-by-part approaches introduce errors that may not be detected until a prototype is built and tested.

- The auditors of a technical project are the independent experts participating in the major design review.
- An integral part of these auditors' mission is to discover and comment on discontinuities, suggesting such improvements as eliminating expensive and time-consuming integration errors.

Experience from engineering design demonstrates that up to 70 percent of development time can be spent in postmortem revising and revamping of projects rather than generating new intellectual property. This particularly happens when there is no method that can progressively integrate more-realistic representations of measurements and evaluation procedures. A well-managed IT project sees to it that concepts seamlessly flow aggregates into a reference design and its prototype, which then serve as:

- Executable specification
- Test bench for further refinement
- Reference model for measurement reasons

In every company hoping to play a leadership role in product design and product development as well as in manufacturing and sales, internal control should act as a watchdog in the aforementioned seamless transition. The elimination of inefficiencies in engineering phases is a most significant *value-added* element in global competition.

2.7 The Added Value of Prototyping

The statement made in the last paragraph of Section 6 is equally valid with *prototyping*. A prototype is not a theoretical system; rather, it is a working model reflecting product characteristics in the environment for which it has been conceived. A major advantage of prototyping is that it is a flexible, communication-intensive process that

- Facilitates an understanding of the product itself and
- Clarifies the larger process within which it is embedded.

Every company must have a policy of prototyping not only in R&D, regarding its main product lines, but in software development as well. Software prototypes are developed quickly, and their speedy employment compensates for the fact that end users do not always clearly define what needs to be done. At the same time, software developers do not necessarily understand what is in the end user's mind.

Over and above the technical issues associated with prototyping software products, this practice has proved to be instrumental in assisting in better internal control because the model is the message. Prototypes also make feasible timely and effective feedback in regard to the design and development processes, such as

- Helping to pinpoint cases where problems occurred and
- Permitting an effective visualization of specs and measurements.

Indeed, a major issue impacting the successful completion of a project is the analysis of timely and accurate measurements. This is a basic element of any science or engineering discipline. Measurements help in planning and controlling processes and products. For instance, the mapping of measurements through statistical quality control (SQC) charts permits

- Statistical teaching,
- Visualizing the observance of tolerances by a given process, and
- Accounting for the variability of production.

Up to a certain level, a system of measurement reflects only some chosen factors while abstracting other factors. This is deliberate, because what interests us is the physical characteristics of the chosen factors. What is essential is that the measurement process retain key relationships and quantitative references to those properties that are necessary to define the object. The resulting benefits range

- From the simplification of a complex system
- To the description of dimensions, surfaces, and other design criteria of key variables.

Prototypes accelerate and facilitate the process of measurement. To appreciate the prototype's contribution to internal control, consider a process by which numbers are assigned to attributes of entities in the real world in a way that describes weights, lengths, prices, or other target variables. This must be done according to clearly defined rules and is essentially a process of mapping empirical relationships of different attributes embedded in the design. This concept has a wide applicability because it characterizes the expansion of measurements from physics and engineering to other domains such as financial analysis, cost control, and software development. The bad news is that the more advanced is the application, including applications in the physical sciences, the more do current methods reveal deficiencies, which are often a consequence of employing

- Obsolete notions and
- Inadequate tools or methods.

Measurements may become invalid through untested procedures that are used to determine new parameters or for other reasons, leading to incorrect interpretations. Dependable measurements typically have a solid conceptual base and a procedure for meaningful empirical validation. Errors made during the construction of measurement methods include:

- Use of small samples with little significance to the project at hand
- Poor reliability in terms of data collection, clearances, and storage
- Misinterpretations associated with dependent variables, independent variables, and correlations

Measurement concepts, measurement processes, and results obtained from measurements should be audited, with the audited output fed into the entity's internal control system. This is stated with the understanding that the availability of reliable measurements has an impact on day-to-day management action. When dependable measurements are available, prediction systems can

- Provide a dependable definition of development relationships among key factors, and
- Facilitate the design of more-sophisticated solutions, all the way from engineering designs to financial instruments.

In conclusion, achieving first-class results in design—from engineering and software to finance—requires an internal control system that can provide feedback on measurements as well as a commensurate design culture that pays attention to detail and accuracy. Prototyping can best be viewed as an added-value facility supporting effective interaction between system designers and end users, thereby making better results feasible, whether the object be quality, performance, timetables, costs, or other factors affecting deliverables.

Chapter 3

Auditing Functions

3.1 Purpose of Auditing

The term *auditing* comes from a Latin word whose meaning is hearing. Listening or hearing is an important part of the auditing practice, but not the whole of it. Auditors must also do data research and analysis, as well as an evaluation based on personal interviews, in order to unearth managerial and accounting malpractices, commenting on them in their report. This is akin to the *discovery* process in legal practice, whereby both parties to a lawsuit exchange relevant documents with each other and search within these documents to establish legal shortcomings, for instance, to determine whether accounts and controls over accounts established by management had effectively been operating as required by law. Auditing is the mechanism that helps to verify whether controls are being followed; as a verification procedure, it includes:

- Internal audits, which in a bank should be independent of the trading desks and the revenue side of the business
- External audits by independent certified public accountants (CPAs) who, among other things, examine whether recommendations by auditing bodies and supervisors are properly implemented (for more on internal and external audits, see Chapter 4)

All business activities involve taking risks, and it is part of good management to understand those exposures and control them in the context of furthering the company's objectives. The CEO and his or her immediate assistants need to know that they are properly managing not only the risk of failure, but also their firm's business opportunities. To further this aim, auditors must provide a high degree of objectivity in their discovery and reporting.

In the best cases, internal and external performance evaluations incorporate a concept of examination and review that questions "the obvious." Verification has always been an essential element of any control system. Without a comprehensive verification, the risk of a breakdown in controls increases. Therefore, it is only natural that firms and supervisors need to determine that controls, once established by management, are operating as designed and keep pace with:

- New accounting standards
- Product innovation
- Market globalization
- Process revamping
- Industry technology

This verification process is expected to provide an independent review and appraisal of management, not just of financial accounts. Part of its function is to ascertain compliance with procedures, policies, regulations, and legislation. Another part of its function is to recommend improvements in performance, all the way to identifying waste and inefficiency, as well as controlling whether assets are safeguarded from fraud and other operational risks (see Chapter 2).

Figure 3.1 presents a bird's-eye view of internal and external audit connections in a business entity. Notice that both internal and external audit should report directly to the audit committee of the board of directors (see Chapter 5) for all matters under their responsibility. According to the Basel Committee on Banking Supervision, the scope of internal audit is broad, and it includes several major areas:

- Internal control systems
- Adherence to legal and regulatory requirements
- Risk management policies and practices
- Financial information systems
- Testing of transactions' observance of limits
- Testing of compliance with regulatory requirements
- Special investigations*

Nearly all companies consider the auditing of accounting records within the scope of internal audit, but few of them appreciate that, as the organization becomes larger and more dynamic, transactions become faster; change becomes the norm;

---

* Basel Committee, "Internal Audit in Banks and the Supervisors Relationship to Auditors," BIS, Basel, August 2002

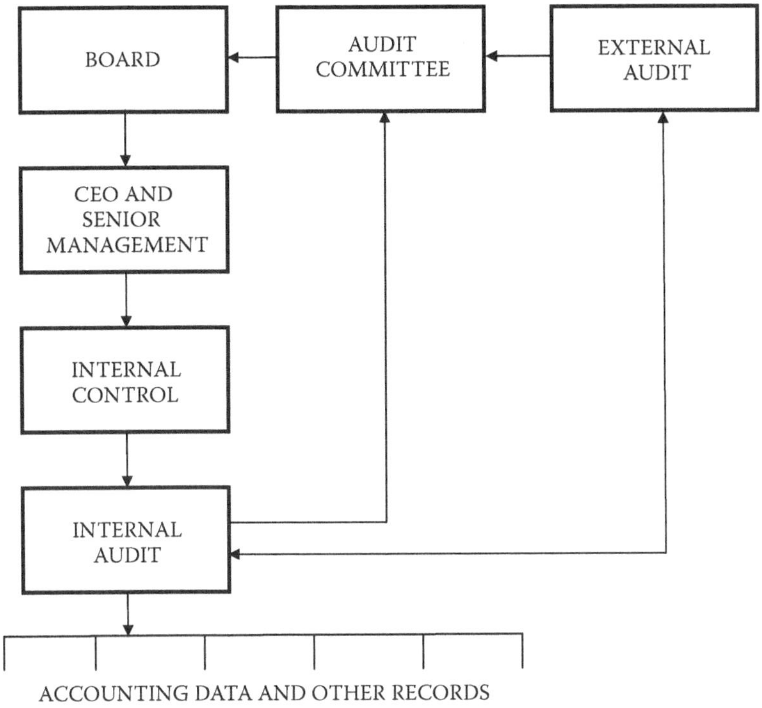

Figure 3.1 A birdseye view of audit connections in a business entity.

"observance of limits" requirements become more sophisticated; and the complexity of systems and procedures to be audited increases.

This is equally true of both internal audit and external audit. Internal auditing is no substitute for audit by a certified public accountant, and the opposite is also true. Each type of auditor renders a distinctive type of service that cannot fully be performed by the other. While the two domains of auditing have much in common—and to a certain degree they are complementary—their objectives are different.

A strong internal auditing department with a proper level of independence is a valuable agency not only to management, but also to the regulators and the certified public accountants, although the latter would control the work done by the former. The scope of the CPA's examination and the amount of detailed work that may be considered necessary will depend to a significant extent upon the external auditor's evaluation of the internal audit function.

- *If* the CPA accountant has complete confidence in the company's internal audit activity, and is satisfied that it has fully discharged its responsibilities,
- *Then* the CPA accountant may curtail the extent of his or her investigative work, using the results obtained through internal audits as well as the accountant's knowledge and experience.

It is clear that both internal and external audits should be done using well-established standards. The argument that the audit is no more than a contractual agreement between a company and its auditor, with standards subject to negotiation, is a sophistry. Indeed, because audit standards are set for the public good, they must be uniform among all companies (and, in a globalized economy, among all countries, although such global uniformity remains a chimera rather than a fact).

As the sophistication of business activities increases, audit standards should be made stricter than in the past (see Section 4 of this chapter, which deals with the Sarbanes-Oxley Act). External audits should also cover areas mandated by the supervisory authority responsible for oversight. In some jurisdictions, this includes decisions and acts by line managers as well as by those responsible for monitoring and ensuring the effectiveness of internal control.

3.2 Qualification of Auditors and Audit Standards

Sound standards as well as rigorous auditing procedures are prerequisites to obtaining first-class audit results. These two notions should not be confused with one another. *Procedures* relate to acts to be performed, while *standards* deal with

- Ways and means for obtaining results from audit procedures undertaken and
- Deliverables expected from the process of auditing, as well as measures of the quality of performance of audit acts.

One of the issues to which audit standards pay increasing attention is the auditor's professional qualities, including his or her judgment exercised in the conduct of examination and of reporting. In the general case, but not in every instance, the professionalism of internal auditors has been enhanced by standards that offer guidance for effective internal auditing, and these standards reflect some of the most advanced thinking on fraud prevention and detection as well as on other acts.

Apart from the efforts of public bodies, such as the Institute of Internal Auditors (IIA), audit standards in every company can be maintained and improved through a quality assurance program that both trains and evaluates the operations of the internal audit function. Standards must provide guidelines that describe:

- The process of quality assurance in connection with internal reviews and external reviews
- Issues associated with verification of account and management acts
- Criteria for judging the frequency and depth with which audits should be conducted

The qualified auditor is a person who not only knows the standards and masters the auditing tools, but as well possesses personal and technical attributes that range from thorough knowledge of modern accounting practice to knowledge of the business organization in which he or she works. Auditing results risk being faulty without both types of knowledge. Moreover, because the impact of auditing is greatly felt on financial reporting, another prerequisite for the chief auditor and his or her staff is a broad knowledge of finance. Since the auditor is constantly dealing in terms of money, he or she will be so much more effective if well versed in financial matters. Also quite important for internal auditors is knowledge of cost accounting. Incorrectly costed products lead to untrue operating results. Therefore, the auditor should be in a position to determine whether there are biases in the company's cost accounting procedures.

The chief auditor should be an experienced company executive, preferably with a polyvalent background and the necessary business acumen to work effectively with fellow senior executives. One of the professors I had at UCLA taught his students that the chief auditor should be a person toward the end of his or her career, because in this case the auditor is not exposed to career pressures that sometimes induce auditors to look the other way. This is very important, because the effectiveness of a company's internal audit function depends to a significant degree on the objectivity of the chief auditor and his or her staff. Entities must ensure that their internal auditors are free to perform their functions in an objective manner, without inference, and that they are able to report findings to the audit committee for corrective action. Among key factors contributing to independence and objectivity are

- Organizational positioning of auditing,
- Corporate stature of the chief internal auditor, and
- Reporting relationships of the chief internal auditor to the board's audit committee.

The chief auditor should attend audit committee meetings, reporting to the committee at regular intervals on the activities of his function, which is an important in-house source of information for the audit committee. Senior management and the audit committee should ensure that the chief auditor's involvement in the entire financial reporting process is not hindered by company politics.

What has been said about the qualifications of internal auditors also applies to external auditors, who also face requirements for additional skills. An example is mastery of budget preparation and control, as the external auditor often needs to control the ways and means used for the preparation of budgets. If the audited budgets are inaccurate, the company's suppliers and clients may well hold the auditor responsible for significant differences in budgetary elements that filtered into the financial reporting.

There are cases where the full potential of an audit is not realized because the IT auditors lack a financial background. Moreover, on the absence of a consolidated-statement approach to auditing can be a major limitation. It is not uncommon that

- Internal auditors concentrate on review of controls at division, subsidiary, or other business unit level, rather than at the corporate level; in contrast,
- External auditors are generally responsible for audit examination at the corporate level of reference.

Lack of polyvalence in approaching one's work is another example of a limitation. Increasingly, internal and external auditors are required to provide services to the organization that are broader than those relating to accounting and financial auditing. Operational auditing, management ethics, and special investigations are examples.

Legal risk is one of the reasons why auditors should systematically consider the results and potential impact of nonfinancial audits on financial statements. Depending on the CPA firm, training in business law might be a "must." The laws of sales, contracts, agencies, negotiable instruments, bankruptcy, and insolvency are interwoven with accounting practice.

Terrified of lawsuits, many companies let unproductive employees linger, laying off some of their best workers while retaining less valuable ones, and paying severance even to crooks in exchange for promises that they will not sue. A few decades ago, the unable, unwilling, and unnecessary could be easily fired. Today, even the worst employees have reasons to believe that they, too, are entitled to be rewarded on the way out, just as the most disastrous CEOs are awarded with golden parachutes.

The best auditors also have training in taxation. To save money for his or her client, the external auditor must have a thorough knowledge of all taxes affecting the client's operations at home and abroad. In fact, with globalization, taxation is an ever-increasing course of work for the certified public accountant.

Both internal and external auditors must also be computer literate, with a complete mastery of how to use high technology, from data mining to modeling and experimenting, in connection with auditing procedures. The auditor must be fully conversant with new developments in technology, as the day will come that he or she will need to do IT auditing.

3.3 Transparency in Financial Reporting

Whatever the products an entity is dealing with or the markets to which it appeals, the transparency of accounting records and financial reports is at a premium. This is achieved through management policies, auditing action, accounting standards, and supervisory regulations that include industry-specific rules for financial reporting. For banks and other financial services institutions, elements that need both accuracy and transparency are:

- Banking books
- Trading books
- General accounting
- Consolidated financial statements

As we will see in this and in the following sections, new accounting rules and reporting standards require companies to provide comprehensive information about their balance sheets and income statements (profit and loss [P&L]), including their exposure and risk-control practices. Industry-specific risks are to be addressed in special detail, including the nature of existing risk-management systems, monitoring policies, and management's corrective measures. Focal points in regulatory reporting are:

- Capital held to cover risk
- Balance-sheet risk provisioning
- Transparency of financial reporting for market discipline reasons

For instance, in the banking industry, the concept underpinning market discipline is that not only shareholders, bondholders, creditors, and subordinated creditors, but as well correspondent banks and other institutions must have sufficient information, incentives, and clout to influence a bank's behavior *ex ante*. Regulatory action usually comes *ex post*.

For the banking industry, what needs to be done to enhance market discipline is specified by Pillar 3 of Basel II's new capital adequacy requirements. (The other two pillars of Basel II are: Pillar 1, which addresses capital adequacy; and Pillar 2, which enhances the authority and responsibility of national supervisors. Stress testing, for example, recently came under Pillar 2.)

The transparency requirements of Pillar 3 include the semiannual disclosure of risk information. Adjunct qualitative information provides a general overview of risk-management objectives and procedures, as well as information on internal control, compliance, and financial reporting practices.

Seen in a holistic manner, regulatory requirements advanced by Basel II pay significant attention to the assessment of credit risk, not only in regard to the gross credit volume, but also in terms of a more detailed analysis of loans that are past due or impaired, including a description of collateral. Likewise, the evolution of risk provisioning during the reporting period has to be disclosed, broken down by type of loan.

Banks are requested to provide credit details to manage the counterparty's creditworthiness. Crucial factors are probability of default (PD), loss given default

(LGD), risk weights (RW), and exposure at default (EAD) weighted with outstanding risks. Institutions have to disclose information and assessment on their exposure separately for credit risk, market risk, and operational risk. Credit risk disclosure includes information on

- Portfolio structure,
- Impaired and past-due loans, and
- Distribution of exposures.

With the internal ratings-based (IRB) approach for capital adequacy, credit risk estimated through models should be compared with actual outcomes. Retail loans may be disclosed by meaningfully breaking down the portfolio by *expected losses* (EL). In contrast, major exposures can be found at the spikes of the long leg of the distribution in Figure 3.2, where *unexpected losses* (UL) lie.

Information on the securitization of assets and credit-risk-mitigation techniques also needs to be detailed for market participants, according to the rules of Basel II. Additionally, a further distinction is made between qualitative and quantitative information, with evident effects on the job that internal and external auditors should do. Under Pillar 1:

- *Qualitative information* relates to the scope and method of application of Basel's new capital adequacy
- *Quantitative information* includes the disclosure of Tier 1 (equity), Tier 2 (other assets), and total capital ratios of the bank

Regulatory authorities who are worth their salt focus on Tier 1 capital and the individual components thereof. Information requirements cover capital needs for individual types of risk. Capital ratios of the consolidated financial group are just

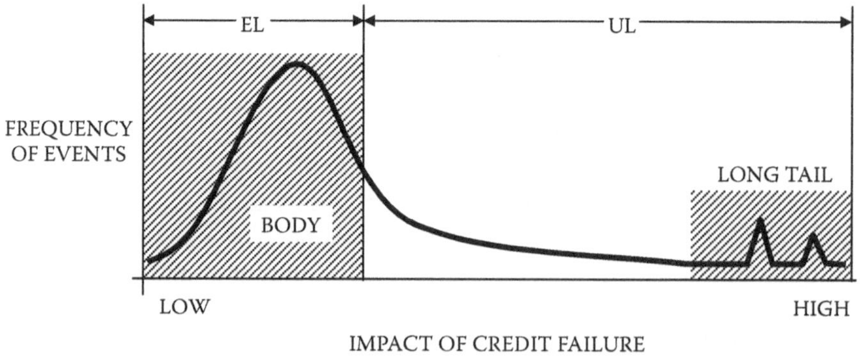

Figure 3.2 Expected losses, unexpected losses and the long tail of the loss distribution.

Table 3.1 Past and Present Requirements in Financial Reporting for the United States and the European Union

Past	*Present*
■ GAAP Accounting Standard in the United States ■ Different national accounting standards in each European country	■ GAAP in the United States ■ IFRS in Europe **Supervisory rules:** ■ Basel II and Basel IA in the United States ■ Basel II in Europe EU Directives 2000/12/EC and 93/6/EEC in Europe Solvency II for the insurance industry in the United States and Europe

as important, because they enhance the actions associated with national supervisors under Pillar 2.

In terms of accounting principles, the law of the land in the United States is the generally accepted accounting principles (GAAP) by the Federal Accounting Standards Board. The recently enacted International Financial Reporting Standards (IFRS) applies under European Union law, with binding effect on the consolidated financial statements of business entities. Table 3.1 presents the past and present financial reporting requirements for both the United States and the European Union.

Like GAAP, IFRS standards are designed to satisfy the information needs of the readers of annual financial statements—regulators, investors, and counterparties, among others. As such, they provide a much greater degree of transparency than statements prepared according to the parochial accounting standards that, until recently, characterized the transparency requirements in each European country. Also, in a way closely approximating U.S. GAAP, IFRS has given priority to information requirements for capital market investors. This requires complete reporting of all assets and liabilities, including derivatives, and specifies that they be marked-to-market if *management intent* is to hold them for trading, as opposed to hedging. Crucial parts of the system include international accounting standards (IAS), such as

- IAS 30, whose themes are disclosures in financial statements made by banks and other institutions;
- IAS 32, which concentrates on disclosure and presentation in financial instruments; and
- IAS 39, which targets measurement and recognition of derivatives exposure.

The intention of IFRS at large, and most specifically of IAS 30, 32, and 39, is to ensure that all players in the financial market can make their investment decisions on the basis of the same information. Marking-to-market corresponds most closely to the IFRS's fundamental premise of fair presentation, but markets do not always exist for all financial instruments.

The role played by accounting standards in financial transparency should never be discounted. On April 30, 2007, U.S. and European authorities signed an agreement in Washington, D.C., to reconcile and bridge the gap between GAAP and IFRS accounting standards. This freed European companies listed in the United States from the need to reconcile their financial reporting under two different standards, and vice versa. Experts look to this agreement as part of a framework for advancing transatlantic economic integration. (The timetable targets 2009 for GAAP/IFRS conversion, but whether this could become the global norm remains uncertain.)

3.4 The Sarbanes-Oxley Act and Its Aftereffects

The focused and effective management of exposure has been conspicuously absent among companies who, in recent years, have become embroiled in scandals and bankruptcies. This highlights the importance of the quality of corporate governance as a crucial consideration for all organizations, with management ethics, internal control, and the audit function being at the kernel of an evaluation. News items in the first years of this century highlighted the problems of poor accountability and of management malfeasance in large listed companies. However, the underlying issues are just as prevalent in smaller listed and unlisted firms. Moreover, because external auditors looked the other way in some of these scams, their role came under public scrutiny.

Conflict of interest has been a particularly touchy point. In many cases, its origins were found in the fact that, for several decades, external audit firms have been performing a variety of consultancy roles for the same companies they audit, thereby

- Becoming too close to the client and
- Losing objectivity in the push for profitability.

The aftermath of such inadequacies is magnified by the fact that companies today operate in a fast-moving environment. Changes in terms of products, markets, and technology present both opportunities and risks, with the result that many firms seize the opportunities but are far less sensitive to the risks, including those of malfeasance and biased judgment.

In the decades before the Sarbanes-Oxley Act (SOX) made it untenable for an investment banker to sit on his or her client company's board, such board seats were much sought after by bankers as a way of gaining the most insight into the client's strategic thinking and its prevailing financial staying power. This practice also helped to ensure that the investment bank walked away with the lion's share of the client's business.

The cases of Enron, Adelphia Communications, and WorldCom in the United States and of Parmalat in Europe—to name just four—are too well known to be described here in detail. The Enron scandal of December 2001 was followed in short order by WorldCom, whose report of $7 billion in fictitious profit dwarfed Enron's concealment of a "mere" $1.8 billion in debt. By the end of 2002, the list of companies with questionable financial reporting included AOL, ImClone, Merck, Qwest, Tyco, Xerox, and Arthur Andersen, a powerhouse certified public accounting firm that was severely weakened following prosecution for its lax practices while auditing Enron and eventually went out of business.

The ripple effect of accounting scandals, auditing scams, and fake financial reporting shook the business community and bent the resistance to tougher legislation by a myriad of lobbyists. In a climate of public mistrust to business because of widespread creative accounting practices, the Sarbanes-Oxley Act was passed in July 2002 by the U.S. Congress.* The act

- Established rigorous corporate governance rules and
- Set specific expectations on the reliability of financial statements of firms whose shares are traded on U.S. stock exchanges.

Section 302 of the act requires CEOs and CFOs to certify the dependability of their firms' financial statements, including whether their entities have (a) effective systems of internal control related to external financial disclosures and (b) procedures capable of notifying both external auditors and their audit committees when significant control deficiencies are detected in these systems. Section 404 of the Sarbanes-Oxley Act demands that a firm's external auditor must report on the reliability of management's assessment of internal controls. Both Sections 302 and 404, however, have raised important questions. For instance:

- How many and what type of control deficiencies can the CEO and CFO not report to external auditors and the company's audit committee without violating the act?
- What is the threshold above which the Securities and Exchange Commission, and civil courts, will act?

---

* Several technical issues of the Sarbanes-Oxley Act are discussed in Chapter 12. Chapter 13 is a "what if": Would things have been different with Enron, Adelphia, Global Crossing, WorldCom, and other companies had the act been passed in the year 2000, after the stock market bubble, rather than in 2002?

There are, as well, complex technical issues connected to SOX that should be well understood to provide a defensible legal course. For their part, certified public accounts must exercise great care in deciding on the need to qualify statements. Lack of qualification will essentially be tantamount to agreeing with the opinion reached by the CEO and CFO when forming the CPA's response on the issue of control effectiveness.

There are good reasons to believe that the accuracy in reporting huge losses for 2007 by Citigroup, Merrill Lynch, Bear Stearns, MBIA, Ambac, and many other well-known financial companies can be found in the rigorous requirements imposed by the Sarbanes-Oxley Act. The act made it mandatory that the CEO and CFO

- Sign the entity's annual financial statements and
- Assume full personal accountability for their figures and contents.

Indeed, no better example of the Sarbanes-Oxley impact can be found than the financial reporting on the aftereffects of the 2007 crisis in the subprime mortgage market, which created a torrent of red ink and brought many of the world's bigger banks against the wall. This was a crisis created single-handedly by the banking industry, rather than being due to an external event like sovereign bankruptcies in emerging markets.

When the bubble of the subprime mortgages blew in July/August 2007, it was revealed that the chief executives of Citigroup, Bear Stearns, Merrill Lynch, Morgan Stanley, UBS, and many others had

- Assumed an excessive amount of credit risk,
- Used irrelevant credit ratings for their judgments,
- Overleveraged their institutions with an inordinate amount of debt, and
- Employed a shamefully low level of risk management.

Through their policies with subprime, "no doc," and "Alt-As" lenders, they also practically brought to bankruptcy millions of U.S. homeowners while also spoiling the capital of their own institutions to the tune of billions of dollars. In the aftermath, the U.S. Supreme Court considered extending liability for corporate fraud to any company that did business with a U.S. corporation that defrauded its investors.*

Back in 2002, many persons suggested that compliance with SOX would be a costly enterprise, although few openly expressed the opinion that business pressure would eventually be instrumental in changing some of the Sarbanes-Oxley provisions. Yet this is exactly what happened in mid-2007, under fire from lawmakers and business groups, who blamed the Sarbanes-Oxley Act for

---

* *Financial Times*, October 5, 2007.

- Driving the costs of compliance higher and
- Pushing firms to relocate to less-regulated markets overseas.

In May 2007, the Securities and Exchange Commission announced new guidelines along with a revised auditing standard from the Public Company Accounting Oversight Board (PCAOB). These guidelines and standards have aimed at ending more than a year of debate over whether the law's costs outweigh its benefits. (PCAOB is an independent panel formed under the Sarbanes-Oxley Act. Its recent guidelines aim to reduce auditor testing by encouraging accountants to rely on work that companies have already done. Established in 2003 in the United States as a regulator to oversee the auditors of publicly listed companies, the PCAOB is one of the items mandated by the Sarbanes-Oxley Act, with the authority of revising standards that CPAs should use when auditing a company's internal controls over financial reporting. In this capacity, PCAOB oversees the U.S. accounting profession.)

One of the new PCAOB auditing standards (AS) established by SOX, specifically AS5, was aimed to ease the burden of Sarbanes-Oxley compliance by making it less prescriptive and more scalable according to size of the company. The SEC, which oversees the PCAOB, wants AS5 to make life easier for the roughly 6,000 smaller companies with market capitalizations of less than $75 million, while most large, publicly listed companies are required to comply with Sarbanes-Oxley. These large companies have

- Learned how to live with SOX and
- Absorbed the law's initial implementation costs.

To maintain uniformity in the application of the law and fence off efforts to create loopholes, Christopher Cox, SEC's chairman, has resisted demands from members of Congress to exempt small companies from the law. Instead, he tried to reduce corporate audit fees by eliminating a requirement that accountants assess how companies review their internal control.

While undoubtedly greater rigor on auditing does not come free of cost, it would be wrong to judge Sarbanes-Oxley in a unilateral way. "What was going on was so twisted and so perverse that more than five months after WorldCom went bankrupt several analysts expressed the opinion that the company would not survive independently in the long term," said a senior executive of an investment firm. "It will probably be spring or summer before it has its books in order."

WorldCom's huge fraud made use of the fact that there are gray areas in accounting standards on how to capitalize expenses for the different financial outlays. Its case, however, is neither the first nor will it be the last case of that nature. Accounting literature lists numerous events of aggressive and improper capitalization of expenses. Among experts, the majority opinion has been that, on two counts, there was no doubt that WorldCom broke the spirit and the letter of the law on accounting principles.

The Sarbanes-Oxley Act not only improved the reliability of financial reporting, but also made it much harder for firms to get private securities fraud claims thrown out of the bankruptcy courts, as used to happen routinely. External auditors are now required to provide opinions on the effectiveness of internal control in a company's financial statement, and had better get more efficient in internal control assessment by employing individuals with a wide range of experience, helping the client company to identify key exposures in the armory of internal controls.

To deal with potential management malfeasance, there is no alternative to critically reviewing the control environment, including organizational and governance issues; human resources; monitoring procedures; and more—covering not only financial, but also operational matters such as authorization procedures and segregation of duties, internal auditing information practices, and information technology policies able to assist management in decision making and in internal control.

3.5 The Auditor's Independence of Opinion

It should never be forgotten that the opinion expressed by an auditor upon completion of his or her work, in the report or certificate, is an expression of professional skill and integrity as well as the independence of his or her opinion. That being said, several considerations are to be borne in mind in connection with the practice of auditing so that there is no misunderstanding of this function.

> The examination made by the auditor is not to be regarded as simply a process of routine verification.

It is uncommon for the auditor to carry out exceptional controls, each one being an important phase of the examination he or she is entrusted with. Alternatively, however, the auditor may choose not to employ the right of professional reliance upon the system of records and representations by management, and proceed instead with exceptional controls.

> While observing generally accepted auditing standards, the auditor must carefully exercise his or her informed judgment as a qualified professional person.

This is the sense of the qualitative appraisal to be given by the auditor in accordance with the Sarbanes-Oxley Act. It is nevertheless possible that conditions of an unusual nature, in cases of collusion, may subsequently indicate error in the judgment taken, since findings were biased by unreliable data.

> Any given individual auditor may not be a valuer or appraiser of goods or properties, or an expert in materials or commodities, but it is part of his or her work to be concerned with adjustments to, or the disclosure of, fair values.

Therefore, in order to be able to provide an independent opinion, the auditor must be versatile with market values, with marking-to-market, and with marking-to-model. Extra professional luggage is necessary when he or she undertakes anything in the nature of passing out of the rules of professional accountant. The auditor must be legally competent to take steps outside the old confines of the accounting profession. In turn, part and parcel of an auditor's legal competence is his or her ability to ensure independence of approach and of opinion. Professional bodies guard against the presumption of loss of independence.

- Intrinsic independence is synonymous with mental integrity.
- Its possession is a matter of personal quality.

Lawyers have developed the expression of "presumption of law," or *inference*, that is sometimes conclusive, but more frequently it is rebuttable. Insofar as a presumption has been enacted as stipulation in the profession's code of ethics, it has the force of professional law for the auditor. Without excluding the bearing of other rules, at the top of the list in matters of the auditor's independence is his or her free expression of opinion:

- On false or misleading statements
- On conflicts of interest in a client firm
- On contingent fees, commissions, and brokerage and other fees
- On occupations incompatible with control activities

In the final analysis, independence of opinion means honest disinterest on expression of his or her findings and qualification of statements. This requires not only unbiased judgment and objective consideration of facts as determinants of the auditor's opinion, but also the strength to put such findings in writing.

In auditing accounting records and financial statements, the course that has just been outlined does not imply the attitude of a prosecutor, but rather a judicial impartiality that recognizes an obligation on his or her part for fair presentation of facts. The auditor owes such impartiality not only to the firm's management and shareholders, but also to the creditors of the business, the supervisory authorities, and those who may otherwise have a right to rely upon the auditor's report.

This is written in the understanding that audit is an indispensable element of every effective system of internal control. Additionally, management audit, as prescribed by Sarbanes-Oxley, is distinct from the function of exercising day-to-day supervision. It is

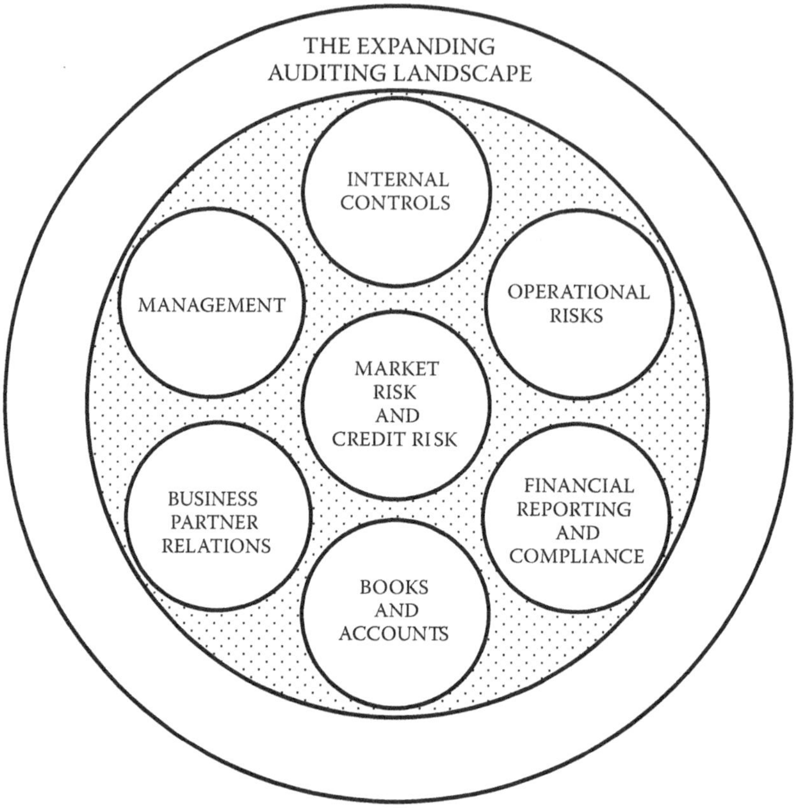

Figure 3.3 The domains where auditing functions are necessary in modern business continues to expand.

an appraisal process addressing the expanding auditing landscape shown in Figure 3.3, and it should be fully assisted through technology.

The board of directors and senior management should be keen to guarantee the independence of internal auditors by having their human resources, promotion, compensation, technology, and budget determined by the audit committee (see Chapter 5), rather than by managers who are affected by the internal auditors' work and by internal control action.

Both the supervisory authorities and every board of directors need unbiased information about the company's financial activities and condition. For this reason, the Basel Committee has underlined that the frequency and extent of internal audit reviews should be consistent with the

- Nature,
- Complexity, and
- Risk of the institution's business.

In contrast to these principles, a fragmented audit approach may result in internal control programs that are poorly structured as a series of discrete steps concerning specific activities without connection to one another. Or it may be the case that there is a lack of a thorough understanding of business processes. Moreover, when the performance of investigations is interrupted midstream, controls become incomplete and substandard.

The Sarbanes-Oxley Act aims to avoid half-baked approaches by specifying that, while auditing looks into accounts, it also searches for personal accountability. This is the only way to make auditing work independent of internal control. The crucial queries to be asked in connection with this approach are Cicero's six evidentiary questions:*

- *Who*, apart from the person who signed off on or contributed to this decision, action, or transaction, was witness to the event?
- *How* did the persons involved, alone or by committee, come to this decision, action, or transaction?
- *Where* was the evidence that led to the commitment being made?
- *When* was this action or transaction made, and under *which* conditions has it been effected?
- *What* exactly are the commitments involved? Were they subsequently changed or manipulated?
- *Why* was the decision, action, or transaction made, and for what precise goal is it targeted or intended to avoid? Was there a conflict of interest?

Effectively translated into modern business practices, Cicero's queries—who, how, where, when, which, what, why—can be instrumental in testing the internal control system of any organization, provided that the answers being given are knowledgeable of both the foreground and background elements of decisions and action, and that the final judgment on what has happened is characterized by independence of opinion.

3.6 Auditing the Bank's Internal Control: A Case Study

The Basel Committee on Banking Supervision strongly recommends that there should be an effective and comprehensive internal audit of the bank's internal control system. This must be carried out by appropriately trained and competent staff, as part of a steady monitoring function that reports directly to the board of directors' audit committee.

Internal control's audit is essentially a management audit, and therefore it is distinct from the classical audit functions such as in-depth analysis of fraud and

* Marcus Tullius Cicero, Roman senator and orator, 106-43 B.C.

other mishaps connected with transactions and operations. On the other hand, all audit functions are an appraisal process to which management audit contributes its own specific characteristics. Take as an example basic questions asked in connection with the information that internal control should provide relative to credit-risk-control reasons:

- Are our credits diversified, or are they connected to just a few names?
- How are our credits distributed? By counterparty? By currency? By maturity?
- Who are the credit officers always dealing with the same counterparty?
- What is the pattern of our credits by branch office, by region, and by foreign subsidiary?
- Where has there been an abnormal number of weak credits? Have the reasons been identified? What has been done to correct them?

The emphasis on steady auditing of internal control is well placed, because the board needs ongoing monitoring and independent assessment of the long-term adequacy of the entity's ability to respond to challenges. Administrative audits include, but are not limited to, organization and structure, procedures and records, management's authorization of transactions, and more. In the case of a credit institution, managers require descriptive information regarding specific functions and activities, including internal control information, on the following:

- Assets and liabilities
- Customer profitability
- Credit risk analysis and evaluation
- Loan pricing models and accuracy of their output
- Loan yields by type, officer, and branch
- Analyses of lost accounts, including background reasons
- Work measurement reports (customers handled, transactions executed, and so on)

Other feedback information includes variance analyses of departmental budgets, service pricing studies, profitability evaluation by product and branch, compliance with rules and regulations by branch as well as at headquarters, control over systems and procedures to avert computer crime, and corrective steps if computer crime is identified.

In a financial institution where I have been a consultant for 15 years, the board and CEO looked at audit and internal control as the cornerstone of the organization's edifice. The CEO had taken the position that if managers are continually the subject of administrative control while at headquarters or at the branches, they are unlikely to have the time to thoroughly analyze, each one on his or her own, the bank's internal control function. As a result, the bank established a policy of formal evaluation procedures for its administrative system, which worked by stages. Management accounting has been one of the first objectives. Questions asked of the auditors by the CEO included the following:

- Is the accounting system producing results compliant with rules and regulations? Relevant to management's needs?
- Has all accounting information been properly accumulated, tested, and distributed to the appropriate executives?
- Is management accounting data arranged in a clear and understandable format so that action can be taken?

Such questions require factual and documented answers that sometimes reveal interesting hindsight. In one of the financial institutions, the internal auditor asked questions very similar to those in the above list while evaluating the firm's accounting books. The evidence pointed to integrity in the accounting system, but toward the end of his work, the auditor examined one of the company's main branch offices and took a look at some key relationships, including those between:

- Branch director and the controller
- Branch director and the area vice president, to whom he reported
- Area vice president and administrative vice president

As revealed by that part of the audit, relationships between the different people were strained, and troubled relationships threatened the overall performance of the branches' operations. On the basis of his perceptions, the auditor was able to diagnose the source of the difficulties as the poor relationship skills of the administrative vice president, whose actions were said to include

- Threatening comments
- Unwillingness to help with problems
- Unsympathetic responses to inquiries
- Failure to keep others informed of changed expectations
- Violation of the values to which he held others accountable

The audit report stated that, although the evidence from the accounting audit was that internal control worked in a satisfactory manner, some of the concerns over relationships pointed to potential problems in operations. These same problems, however, presented opportunities for significant improvements over existing performance, on which the CEO followed up. Auditing should evaluate the ability of the current structure to manage and control operational risk and, as the case arises, prompt operational risk alerts.

3.7 Audit Reports and Audit Trails

One of the challenges with the auditing of internal control is that when auditing staff does not have the necessary expertise, they are often hesitant to ask questions. Or when questions are asked, auditors are more likely to swallow the answer than to challenge it. Here is an example of crucial queries auditors should ask in testing the internal control's functioning in regard to trading activities:

- Is the same dealer following a similar pattern with the same counterparty?
- Is the counterparty a steady user of over-the-counter (OTC) instruments, or are the transactions balanced with exchange-traded products?
- Why is *this* counterparty dealing in billions of dollars in swaps?
- What is the net and gross exposure with the counterparty? Is the account executive aware of such exposure? What has he or she done about it?

Another important auditing activity involves the examination of internal risk measurement models for use as a means of determining the capital charges for market risk through backtesting and testing of hypotheses. The criteria set by these audits include both quantitative and qualitative measures.

One of the qualitative criteria is how the risk model is incorporated in the bank's day-to-day risk management. A quantitative criterion is whether its output is in compliance with capital requirements for the trading activities.

Supervisory authorities are sensitive to minimum-requirements audits, which monitor the organizational framework within which trading transactions are conducted. Such audits must also examine not only risk-control practices, but also the way in which trading activities are set up, operations are organized, and conflicts of interest impact upon the way the risk-control system functions.

Conflict of interest is a frequent background factor in fraud, misappropriation, or plain failures, and the auditors must be able to travel back in time to establish the facts in their original form. In order to fulfill this requirement in an able manner, back in the late 1990s the European Monetary Institute (now European Central Bank) advised in a seminal document* that each transaction be recorded accurately in the proper period

- On a timely and factual basis and
- With an adequate degree of detail.

Going back in time means being able to reconstruct all transactions in their chronological order, supporting the evidence pertaining to commitments with original documents, and accounting for movements in balances from one statement

* European Monetary Institute, Banking Supervisory Subcommittee, "Internal Control System of Banking Institutions," EMI, Frankfurt, July 1997.

to the next. Such policy can be effective only when the board of directors and senior management

- Establish the appropriate policies and
- See to it that they are steadily followed.

Whether they regard internal control, transactions, operations, or specific cases of fraud, audit reports must be factual and documented. A great deal of this documentation is provided through audit trails.

An *audit trail* is a history of activities registered in an accounting book. The objectives are transactions or other events posted because of audit operations and used as evidence to back up conclusions in audit reports. Event description of an audit trail identifies the specific audit activity, references the activity and preconclusion, along with a time stamp.

An in-process audit trail signifies that monitoring and verification of a given function are performed while the process being audited is in execution. In contrast, a postprocess audit indicates that the recording of the audit trail is performed after the process to be audited has been completed. In the case of a transparent audit, the executives in charge of the functions being audited are aware of the audit.

People with experience in audit appreciate that audit trails form an important part of frontline defenses for fraud detection and prevention. The problem is that, in the majority of companies, audit trail systems are not as robust as they should be, and in many cases the surrounding controls are often inadequate, overrun, or simply ignored.

Fraudulent information reporting is even found in scientific environments, with an evident adverse impact associated with it. For instance, it has been reported in the press that, at Bell Labs, superconductor research by physicist Jan Hendrik Schön was revealed to have included falsified data at least 16 times in two years. The large number of papers coauthored by young scientists—80 in 3 years (1998 to 2001)—should have raised skepticism. In the end, the lack of reproducibility of the experiments was the reason that ultimately blew the whistle on the sham.*

In terms of the documentation that supports an audit, the board and senior management must ensure that not only are they themselves satisfied with its quality and completeness, but also that dependable information is available for follow-up reasons as well as for compliance purposes. In some cases, inadequate knowledge and substandard training of internal audit staff are part of the problem rather than of the solution.

The Basel Committee also points out that internal audit can be rendered ineffective when senior management does not immediately follow up on issues

---

* *Communications ACM*, 46, no. 1 (2003); (Schön was fired in September 2002, and six patent applications were dropped by the corporation).

identified by auditors. Delays attenuate the audit's results; additionally, the effectiveness of an audit is impaired when members of the audit committee and senior management fail to acquaint themselves with the fine print of reports indicating critical subjects.

Chapter 4

Internal and External Audit

4.1 Auditing Responsibilities Prescribed by Regulatory Agencies

Auditing must fulfill regulatory requirements. For instance, in the United States, the Federal Securities Law, Regulation §240.17 Ad-13, is quite specific in terms of internal accounting control responsibilities. It states that every registered transfer agent shall file annually with the Securities and Exchange Commission (SEC), and the transfer agent's appropriate regulatory agency, a report prepared by an independent auditor concerning the transfer agent's system of internal control. The auditor's report shall

- State whether study and evaluation was made in accordance with generally accepted auditing standards (see Section 2),
- Describe any material inadequacies found to exist as of the audit date and any corrective action taken, and
- Comment on the current status of any material inadequacy described in the report.

A material inadequacy is defined as a condition for which the independent certified public accountant believes that prescribed procedures, or the degree of compliance with them, do not reduce to a low level the risk that errors or irregularities encountered would have a significant adverse effect on the transfer agent's ability to promptly and accurately

- Transfer record ownership and
- Safeguard related securities and funds.

The occurrence of errors or irregularities encountered more frequently than in isolated instances may be evidence that the entity's control system has a material inadequacy. A significant adverse effect on a transfer agent's ability to promptly and accurately transfer record ownership and safeguard related securities and funds could inhibit the transfer agent from promptly and accurately discharging its responsibilities under its contractual agreement, with the result being material financial loss.

If the CPA's report describes any material inadequacy, the transfer agent is given by the regulators 60 calendar days after receipt of the report to notify in writing the commission and its appropriate regulatory agency regarding corrective action taken or proposed to be taken. For any practical purpose, SEC looks to the *pattern of events* rather than to an isolated event.

An interesting insight is that, in regulation and supervision of the U.S. banking industry (but not the banking industry of other Western nations), there is little connection between bank regulators and external auditors. The examiners of the American regulatory agencies do the hands-on bank inspection.* In contrast, British, German, French, and Swiss regulators depend a great deal on the external auditor's report, which constitutes the basis of their examination of the bank. In brief:

- The United States solution can be compared to a three-tier system of inspection.
- In contrast, the European model is a two-tier system, where external auditors do the examiner's job.

The difference between a two-tier and a three-tier approach to supervision can be significant in terms of auditing results. The Federal Reserve, for example, is mandating more stringent requirements for its examiners than those usually followed by external auditors, an aftereffect of practices established by regulatory authorities in other Western nations. Typically, regulatory agencies

- Develop their own rules in connection with internal and external audit for the industry under their authority, and
- Set appropriate guidelines on how the inspection of an entity's internal control should be performed.

---

* The only exception to this rule is the Federal Housing Finance Board, which uses external auditors for its inspection.

In a way, the work done by external auditors is not only a supercontrol; it is also a supplement to that of internal auditors who are often understaffed. According to the Basel Committee on Banking Supervision, internal audit is not a sizeable activity in most credit institutions, representing on average 1 percent of the workforce. Yet, over the years, its scope has considerably expanded to include

1. *Financial audit*: Assessing the reliability of accounting, information system support (see Part 2), and financial statements.
2. *Compliance audit*: Evaluating the quality and appropriateness of internal control in regard to compliance with laws, regulations, and internal corporate policies.
3. *Operational audit*: Focusing on organizational structures, information technology risk, control methods, systems and procedures, and the way transactions are cleared, registered, databased, data-mined, and followed up.
4. *Management audit*: Targeting the quality of management, its approach to risk, and associated control of exposure from transactions and inventoried portfolio positions. This has to be done in accordance with the bank's objectives and management guidelines, and must include as well the likelihood of management malfeasance.

Among Group of Ten countries, the so-called industrialized nations, practically all regulators require that internal auditors and external auditors should not be the same. This is, however, a soft regulation. In a September 2000 letter, then Enron chairman Kenneth L. Lay said that Enron's use of Arthur Andersen as both internal and external auditor was "valuable to the investing public ... given the risks and complexities of Enron's business," which is, of course, nonsense.

Enron's descent into the abyss is one more piece of evidence that the same auditors should *not* perform internal and external audits. In Enron's case (and in so many others), the best approach would have been an outright ban on the intermixing of internal and external audit functions, but the SEC was willing to accept as a compromise that no company could rely on its independent auditor for more than 40 percent of internal audit services. The facts of life have proven that even that was too much for Enron and Arthur Andersen, who sank together in a deadly embrace.

As the dust settled around the fallen empires of Enron, Global Crossing, Adelphia Communications, WorldCom, and others, Paul Volcker, the respected former chairman of the Federal Reserve, pointed out a basic reason for these megafailures: "The dominance of the investment banking profession corrupted the legal profession and the accounting profession. They were so highly paid that it created pressure on the legal and auditing professions. People in those professions would ask: 'Why are investment bankers being paid so much and why are we being paid what, by comparison, is a pittance?'"*

* *Financial Times*, September 25, 2002.

In Paul Volcker's opinion, such tensions led to catastrophic results because accounting firms felt that auditing was a dead-end job and that their rewards were dependent on diversification. Practically all public accounting firms, and most particularly the big ones (see Section 8), developed a consultancy as well as information technology services sold to the same clients they were auditing—in plain conflicts of interest. The discipline in the auditing side of the firms, if not lost, was certainly attenuated.

4.2 Structure and Standards of Internal Audit

It is not enough for a company simply to declare that "it has an internal audit department." This department must also be provided with an organizational structure, well-trained people, and appropriate authority. In terms of mission, the first question is: Has the board of directors placed the audit function at a high level in the firm? If so, to whom does the chief auditor report? Also, has the board established an audit committee (see Chapter 5)? If yes,

- Does it comprise solely outside directors? (which is positive)
- Are the audit committee members qualified for their particular responsibilities?
- Does the audit committee meet with the chief auditor and review reports issued by internal audit? If so, how often?
- Do the minutes of the audit committee indicate an appropriate interest by the whole board in the activities and findings of internal audits?

This emphasis on the audit department's dependence directly from the audit committee (further explained in Chapter 5) is critical, because organizational and structural contradictions in relation to the audit function have existed in the past. In many instances, the internal auditor takes part in the performance of operational tasks that he or she is later asked to verify for accuracy. In other situations, audit is a part-time staff function intended to fit in after primary line duties are completed. Both cases lead to wrong results in an audit.

In performance of their work, internal and external auditors must be independent of those they serve. Such independence is defined as the ability to act with integrity and objectivity without giving in to organizational pressures. In accordance with the rule on independence, which should always be included in the professional code of ethics, independence is considered to be impaired if, during the period of his or her professional engagement, the (internal or external) auditor

- Had any direct or indirect material financial interest in the audited firm, or
- Had any loan to or from the audited enterprise or any other director or principal stockholder thereof.

All audit work must be done in the sense of a highly professional, multidisciplined approach, with adequate and steadily trained staff. This is necessary inasmuch as the internal auditor and his or her people must be persons who are capable of meeting fairly complex objectives. They should understand the entire scope of management control and the reasons why controls are made. They should also be conscious of procedures that are working well, in addition to negative situations.

Lack of auditor independence leads to reputational risks that could affect an entity in a negative way, hence the need for implementing effective safeguards to protect the company's reputation and that of its management. Additionally, only truly independent-minded auditors can

- Identify, appraise, and report mishappenings in financial reporting,
- Translate key findings into business risks on the basis of the audit program, and
- Extend a system-based audit approach to examine a malfunction in internal control.

Organizationally, it is plainly wrong for the firm's auditing department to report to the senior financial officer. Apart from possible conflicts of interest, this dependency indicates that audit is considered as a purely financial activity. In contrast, modern audit is a general control function, with the auditor being the prime partner in a continuous in-depth sampling control necessary to any and every manufacturing company, financial institution, or other entity. Moreover, nearsighted board and CEO policies limit audit's coverage to "this" or "that" domain in disregard of the fact that, in well-managed firms, the scope of audit responsibility extends into operations, administration, finances, and other staff and line sectors. The internal audit department should conduct functional, organizational, special management, and compliance reviews; its role is not only that of ensuring financial integrity.

Critical questions must be asked and answered not only in terms of functions (see Section 3) and of organizational structure, but also, if not most importantly, in connection with the independence of the audit functions and of those performing them.

- Is the internal audit functionally segregated from operations in the organizational structure?
- Are reporting procedures of the auditor independent of the influence of any operating personnel?
- Does the audit committee review and/or approve budget, salary, and promotion of the chief internal auditor? If not, who does?
- Do the responsibilities of the audit staff exclude any duties to be performed instead by operating personnel, such as preparation or approval of general ledger entries, official checks, daily reconcilements, and so on?

Along with organizational structure, lack of conflicts of interest, and independence of opinion comes the establishment and observance of auditing standards. In the United States, this is assisted by the existence of generally accepted auditing standards (GAAS) by the American Institute of Certified Public Accountants (AICPA), as distinct from generally accepted accounting principles (GAAP).

The existence of generally accepted auditing standards is important because they are concerned with the auditor's professional qualifications, the judgment the auditor exercises in the performance of his or her audit duties, and the quality of audit procedures as well as reports. GAAS rules are grouped into three classes:

- General standards
- Standards of field work
- Standards of reporting

GAAS specifies that audits cover balance sheet, income statement, statement of changes in stockholders' equity, and statement of cash flows. Typically, more accounting and financial records will be involved, and, as explained in Chapter 3, the qualitative audit has now been added to the quantitative audit.

General standards require that the audit be performed by persons with adequate technical training and proficiency, characterized by independence in mental attitude and capable of exercising due professional care in audit. This includes overall performance, the discovery process, and preparation of audit report.

Standards of field work call for the audit to be adequately planned, auditors to be properly supervised, and a proper study and evaluation of existing internal controls to be made to determine the audit scope and the procedures to be performed during field work. Also, sufficient evidence must be obtained to formulate an independent factual opinion regarding internal control, accounting records, financial statements, and other issues being audited.

GAAS *standards of reporting* focus on the matters confronting internal and external auditors, for instance, whether accounting records and financial statements are presented in accordance with GAAP. The application of GAAP in audited accounting records, statements, and reports must achieve the fundamental objective of accounting, which is to provide reliable financial information about the economic resources and obligations of a company.

- Informative disclosures in financial statements must follow GAAP, or
- The auditor must state otherwise in the report.

An important reference to GAAS is that it recognizes that management, not the auditor, has primary responsibility for the preparation of the financial statements and presentations therein (see also Section 4 in Chapter 3 for more on the Sarbanes-Oxley Act of 2002). The auditor's responsibility is to express an opinion on the financial statements. GAAS requires that auditors plan and perform auditing procedures to obtain reasonable assurance that financial statements are free from material misstatement.

In conclusion, under GAAS, an audit includes examination on a test basis and should provide evidence supporting the amounts and disclosures in the financial statements. An audit also includes assessing the accounting principles used and any significant estimates made by management, as well as evaluating the overall presentation of the financial statement.

4.3 Internal Audit Functions

In a nutshell, the goal of internal audit is the analysis of accounting records in search of general malfeasance or specific acts of fraud, evaluation of the quality of performance of the audited staff or line department (or person) in carrying out assigned responsibilities, and, more recently, examination and evaluation of the adequacy and effectiveness of the organization's system of internal control.

- The board of directors should provide general direction as to the scope of work and activities to be audited.
- To guarantee objectivity and independence of opinion, internal audit should report to the board's audit committee (see Chapter 5).

Starting with the latest of an internal auditor's important responsibilities, the purpose of review for adequacy of the system of internal control is to ascertain whether (as established) it provides reasonable assurance that the organization's feedback—and more generally the arteries of communications—have not been clogged. The arteries must be functioning properly for senior management to receive plenty of information on events as they happen. The system of internal control is functioning as intended, *if* it ensures

- Dependability and integrity of feedback,
- Data on compliance with policies, plans, procedures, laws, and regulations,
- Information on safeguarding the entity's assets, and
- Reporting on accomplishment of established objectives for operations and programs or, alternatively, reports on deviations.

In terms of auditing the banking book, trading book, balance sheet, income statement, and other accounting documents, internal auditors should have full and timely access to all general accounting information, including accounting personnel, work papers, work plans, programs, reports, budgets, and risk assessments. Delays in accessing these information sources usually require the internal auditors to

- Widen the scope of their examination and
- Follow up with more generic examination to enable supervisory action by the board.

The board of directors and the audit committee should promote the internal audit manager's impartiality and independence by having the audit manager report audit findings directly to them. The audit committee should also ensure that internal audit functions are adequately staffed and managed to guarantee that

- Audit plans are met,
- Programs are carried out, and
- Results of audits are promptly communicated to interested directors and managers, no matter if there are critical findings.

For their part, the audit manager and his or her staff must promptly respond to identified internal control and/or accounting weaknesses, using rigorous standards when assessing internal control performance, accounting functions, information technology, risk management, and other activities or systems. The work of internal audit must be consistent with the long-range goals of the institution and, at the same time, respond to its short-term requirements. To fulfill these obligations, an internal audit must accomplish the following objectives:

- Review loan originations as part of the client's approval process
- Analyze customer credit information as part of the loan authorization process
- Examine whether transactions have been properly executed and accounted for
- Examine whether there have been creative accounting practices in any part of the organization, anywhere in the world
- Evaluate how well the entity safeguards its assets as well as its source documents and audit tracks (see Chapter 3)
- Report to the board, or the audit committee, on its findings

To a significant extent, this report to the board is not only a quantitative evaluation, but also a qualitative analysis. In *The Memoirs of Sherlock Holmes*, Arthur Conan Doyle described so well what should be the auditor's investigative spirit: "... the curious incident of the dog in the nighttime.... The dog did nothing in the nighttime.... That was the curious incident," remarked Sherlock Holmes.

As the foregoing bulleted items suggest, the mission of internal audit regarding the bank's intermediation activities is to ensure that the rules established by credit policy, trading policy, limits policy, and so on are being followed. The checkup on credit policy is accomplished by

- Statistical sampling of credits,
- Reviews of credit ratings, and
- Interviews with account managers as well as credit officers.

With the exception of cases of fraud, malfeasance, or serious mishandling, results of audits are typically summarized into process ratings and portfolio quality ratings. Poor ratings reflect failure to comply with established rules and may lead to curtailing a business unit's authority in dealing or even shut it down until it gets its house in order.

Audit reports must be presented to all members of management, with defects properly identified so that they can be remedied systematically and promptly. Follow-up audits should describe defects that have been remedied and recommendations that have not yet been implemented, and this list must be brought to the notice of the CEO and senior vice presidents.

A sound practice will see to it that internal auditors are required to examine the limits system, functional separation of duties, the degree to which prices and rates are in line with market conditions, and other crucial issues. The auditors must also have the skills to check positions, evaluate the results of and changes in information technology, and examine issues related to organization and structure. This is not as much of a general practice as it should be.

4.4 Failures in Auditing Internal Control

In its conclusion of a study of failed banks conducted in 1991 by the General Accounting Office (GAO, renamed as the Government Accountability Office in 2004), the authority auditing the U.S. government stated that weaknesses in internal control lead to banks filing inaccurate financial reports. GAO indicated that one aspect of the importance of internal control to the health of the banking system is to ensure that accounting principles are properly applied in the preparation of bank reports and financial statements.

The same GAO study also found that internal control should provide an early warning of practices affecting the safety and soundness of banks as well as breakdowns in the systems of corporate governance in credit institutions. These findings are significant, inasmuch as they have been instrumental in shaping up the definition of missions that entered the Federal Deposit Insurance Corporation Improvement Act (FDICIA) of 1991.

One of the failures in auditing internal control is that of paying only lip service to risk assessment and risk management. Yet, as documented in Chapter 1, internal control and risk management correlate. To build confidence in the firm's internal control system, senior executives must decide which tools and mechanisms will serve both internal control and risk management, particularly in connection

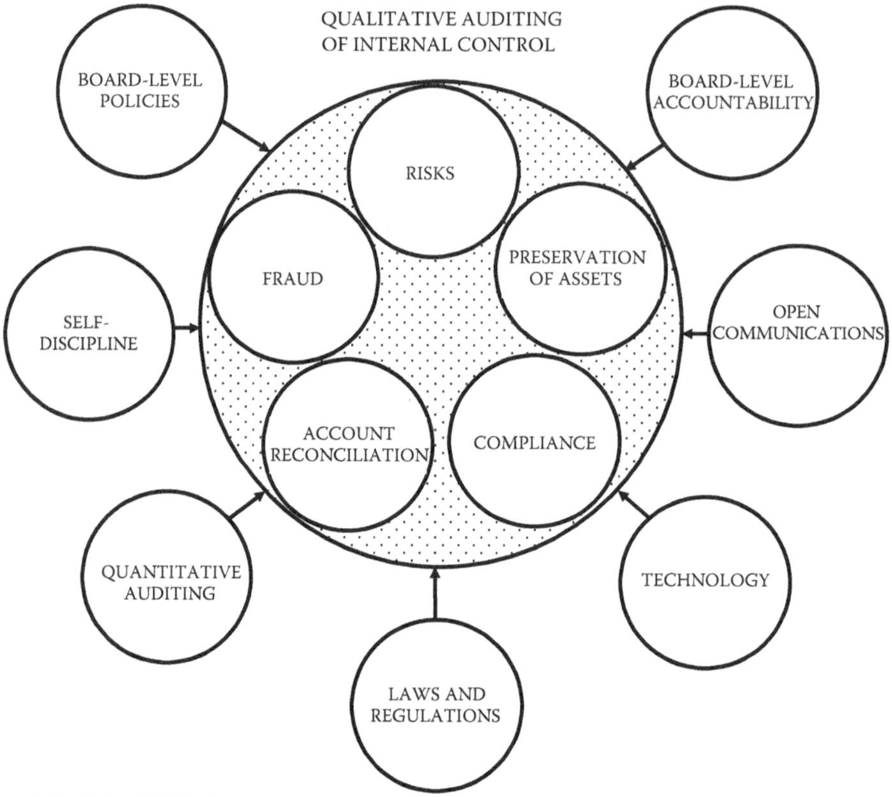

Figure 4.1 Focal areas of internal control and the impact of internal and external key factors.

with the organization's mission-critical processes. This approach complies with the fact that internal control is the bigger framework, integrating every type of risk faced by the entity, as shown in Figure 4.1. Therefore, it integrates methods and tools employed by risk management, such as statistics and models, even if the top criteria in internal control are qualitative, examples being

- Accountability and
- Due diligence.

Additionally, both risk management and internal control make use of information elements and procedures that help in increasing their sensitivity or assist in documenting the need for corrective action. Years of personal experience in internal control and risk management suggest that if one of the two is defective, the other will also be substandard.

The 1997 crisis in East Asia, for example, was caused by inadequate internal controls and very poor risk management in massive short-term bank-to-bank international capital movements. As several operators began exploiting the resulting market anomalies, the Asian economies were penalized by a gross devaluation of their currencies affected by the markets. In currency terms, the dominant refuge in 1997 became the American dollar. A lack of appropriate control and risk-management policies and procedures saw to it that the magnitude of the downturn in East Asia caught the majority of market operators by surprise, because most people do not realize that today's global economy is much more integrated than it has ever been.

- The freedom of capital and currency movement cause a great deal of volatility in the markets.
- The main players have been greatly exposed to this volatility without benefit of the compass provided by risk management and internal control.

As a reminder, the 1997 financial meltdown of Thailand, Indonesia, and subsequently South Korea was not due to fraud but to panic; fraud, however, may be another reason for unrest among market players. In early 2006, in an apparent total lack of internal control, Livedoor, a Japanese Internet company, saw its CEO Takafumi Horie indicted on charges of falsifying profits and creating a false market in company shares. These acts brought his $6-billion entity crashing down.

The crash had aftershocks, causing chaos on the Tokyo Stock Exchange (TSE), and other events, too, had an aftereffect. Another Japanese company that rapidly fell from grace was Misuzu Audit, formerly ChuoAoyama PricewaterhouseCoopers. Once Japan's third-biggest audit firm, it used to count Sony and Toyota among its clients. But in late February 2007, Misuzu asked other leading auditors to take on its remaining clients as a prelude to its liquidation. The Japanese auditing firm's problems began in earnest in 2005 when several of its accountants were arrested for allegedly conspiring with executives at Kanebo, a cosmetics firm, to falsify the firm's accounts. ChuoAoyama had also audited Ashikaga Bank, a big regional bank in trouble with Japan's Financial Services Agency (FSA) for cooking its books to conceal its insolvency.*

- Scams with financial reporting and creative accounting practices flourish when there is a combination of lack of transparency and poor internal control.
- Eventually, a not-so-ethical external auditor conveniently agrees to mask the facts, and this works to the detriment of all stakeholders.

Only the best-managed organizations are willing and able to appreciate that internal control is an integral and important part of sound governance and

* *The Economist*, March 24, 2007.

that every stakeholder gains from financial transparency. Internal control can catch a sophisticated crook only when standing policy obliges him or her to be at least partly transparent.

A principle taught by experience is that many financial institutions, merchandising organizations, and industrial companies that are "not so transparent" are, indeed, not transparent at all. This greatly diminishes supervision, and it practically wipes it out when top management is at the origin of the scam.

Creative accounting—in the absence of effective management control and risk management—helps the firm earn high profits over a period of time, but nobody should ever think that this would continue forever. For evidence, look at Enron, WorldCom, and Parmalat; all three are examples of what should not be done.

4.5 Outsourcing Internal Audit

Outsourcing arrangements for an internal audit are far from uncommon. Such arrangements are often referred to as "internal audit assistance" or "extended audit services." However, these are misnomers, as such activities are unfit for an institution or other entity that is

- Properly structured,
- Prudently managed,
- Carefully conducted, and
- Vigilantly guided by a responsible board vested with final authority.

In the United States, the federal bank supervision agencies have concerns that the nature, scope, and characteristics of some internal-audit outsourcing arrangements do not truly contribute to the safety and soundness of the supervised institutions. Therefore, supervisors want to ensure that internal-audit outsourcing arrangements do not leave directors and senior managers with the impression that they have been relieved of their responsibility for

- Maintaining an effective system of management control and
- Directly overseeing the quality of internal audit functions.

The Basel Committee on Banking Supervision says that, regardless of whether an internal audit is outsourced, the board, the CEO, and senior management remain ultimately responsible. The CEO, CFO, and other responsible executives are accountable for ensuring that the systems of internal control and internal audit are adequate and that they operate effectively.* In its directives to commercial

* Basel Committee, "Internal Audit in Banks and the Supervisors' Relationship to Auditors," BIS, Basel, August 2002.

banks, the Basel Committee also underlines that internal audit is a *core function* of all credit institutions and, in principle, core functions should not be outsourced. Still, even if a bank outsources the auditing work, it can never outsource the auditing responsibility.

Down to basics, the type of outsourcing arrangement discussed in the preceding paragraphs is a contract between a company and a third party to provide internal audit services. Such arrangements can take several forms. For instance, the contracted services can be limited to helping internal-audit staff in an assignment for which they lack expertise; alternatively, the whole internal audit function can be outsourced, or the contract can specify a solution that rests between these two cases.

Limited outsourcing arrangements are typically under the control of the company's internal audit department, with the outsourced vendor reporting to the company's chief auditor. When outsourcing arrangements require the vendor to perform virtually all internal audit work, the company would be well advised to maintain a manager of all internal audits with the support of a small internal audit staff. In this case, the vendor

- Assists the internal audit staff in determining risks to be reviewed,
- Performs audit procedures as approved by the internal audit manager, and
- Reports all findings to the company's audit committee jointly with the internal audit manager.

In the case of financial institutions, to help bank management appreciate its responsibilities, U.S. regulatory agencies have set forth some characteristic criteria of sound practices for internal audit function. These include how to use insourcers for audit activities. In addition, the regulators provide guidance on how outsourcing arrangements may affect their examiners' assessment of internal control.

If the regulatory agency's examiner's evaluation of an internal audit outsourcing arrangement indicates that such outsourcing has diminished the quality of the institution's internal audit function, the examiner will adjust the scope of his or her examination, as well as

- Bring that matter to the attention of the bank's senior management and board of directors, and
- Consider it in his or her evaluation of the institution's management and composite ratings.

When an examiner's initial review of an outsourcing arrangement raises doubts about the external auditor's independence, the practice is that he or she would ask the institution and insourcer auditor firm to demonstrate that the arrangement has not compromised the auditor's independence of opinion.

- *If* the examiner's concerns are not adequately addressed,
- *Then* the regulatory agency follows up on this matter.

Cornerstone to senior management's responsibility is the fact that even when outsourcers provide internal audit services, members of the board of directors, the CEO, and senior managers of the bank are responsible for ensuring that internal controls, including audit, operate effectively. Therefore, when negotiating the outsourcing arrangement with an insourcer, an institution should proceed with care:

- Setting the scope and frequency of work to be performed by the vendor
- Establishing the manner and frequency of reporting to senior management and directors about the status of contracted work, and
- Elaborating the protocol for changing the terms of the service contract, especially for expansion of audit work if significant issues are found in the course of the inspection.

Internal rules and regulations should see to it that all work by the insourcer should be factual and well documented, and all findings of accounting or control weaknesses should be promptly reported to the institution's manager of internal audit. Furthermore, prior to entering an outsourcing arrangement, the institution should perform enough due diligence to satisfy itself that the insourcer has sufficient staff qualified to perform the contracted work.

Because the outsourcing arrangement is a personal services contract, the institution's internal audit manager should have confidence in the competence of the staff assigned by the insourcer, and receive prior notice of staffing changes. In spite of this, it should be appreciated that when an institution enters into an internal audit outsourcing arrangement—or significantly changes the mix of internal and external resources used by internal audit—it increases its operational risk (see Chapter 2).

Finally, because the arrangement might be suddenly terminated, the entity outsourcing its audit function should have a contingency plan to mitigate any significant discontinuity in audit coverage. Planning for a successor to the prospective insourcer should be part of negotiating the latter's service contract. Contingency planning goes further than that by requiring that the outsourcer have on hand a skeleton of internal resources capable of tracking the outsourced functions.

4.6 External Audit Functions

A bank's internal audit function is controlled (and sometimes supplemented) by the skills of *external auditors*. Typically, external auditors are certified public accountants who act as an extension of the supervisory authorities of a given industry sector. Because of relative independence from the company's management, external auditors can play an important role in the maintenance of an effective system of internal controls, assisting in avoidance of the weaknesses examined in Section 4. As part of their mission, external auditors usually perform the following functions:

- Evaluate the work of internal auditors
- Examine the client's accounting principles and its compliance with them
- Analyze financial reports and disclosures
- Test the assets, liabilities, revenues, and expenses
- Pay particular attention to high-risk areas, such as derivatives exposure
- Appraise the performance of internal controls and their adequacy under stress conditions

The work of external auditors requires a mindset tuned toward patterns that exist in accounting books, financial transactions, and, more generally, in the audited bank's database. The external auditor capitalizes on his or her status as an outsider whose work is required by supervisory authorities. The challenge that the auditor faces is the diversity of responsibilities toward the client, including:

- Consulting
- Performance analysis
- Operational review
- Organizational duties
- Information technology assistance

These five examples go beyond the areas of financial control and certification, which are the reasons justifying the services of an external auditor. They also overlap with one another and create opportunities for conflicts of interest. Supervisory authorities have a different vision of the external auditor's mission. They want the auditor to

- Analyze the bank's internal control structure and
- Report all findings over and above the report on financial statements.

In jurisdiction after jurisdiction where the auditing of internal control has become mandatory, external auditors have reported that this is an uphill battle because not all career auditors have been trained in the qualitative evaluation of internal control and other functions that now have to be audited (see Section 4 in Chapter 3 on the Sarbanes-Oxley Act). Such analyses go beyond the classical assessment of whether or not the financial impact of a company's business has been correctly reflected in its financial statements.

Classically, external auditors have been interested in the bank's system of internal control only insofar as it plays a role in the correctness of accounting records and financial statements, since they need to rely upon the firm's controls to form their opinion of what is written in the books. That is the basic principle, but its implementation varies between countries and, sometimes, by the client company, the CPA firm, and the auditor's personality and skill.

In several countries, this emphasis on auditing internal control has been the aftermath of a report written by the International Auditing Practices Committee of the International Federation of Accounts, after consultations with the Basel Committee on Banking Supervision. By 1998, in Germany and in other European Union countries, external auditors were required by supervisory authorities to provide a specific assessment of the

- Scope,
- Adequacy, and
- Effectiveness

of the bank's internal control. This must include an opinion on internal audit as a system. In other jurisdictions, such evaluation is not part of the analysis of a company's annual accounts, but constitutes a specific task. However, whether or not the connection between financial statement issues and internal control is direct, the goals are very similar.

For instance, in the United States, the Securities and Exchange Commission says that the external auditor must provide an opinion on internal control that is satisfactory. This extension of the external auditor's mission is consistent with the concept that external auditors can and should provide an important feedback to senior management and the regulators on the effectiveness of the entity's internal control.

Many people say that conducting an evaluation of internal controls in order to assess the extent to which the auditor can rely on this system is an extension of already existing external audit procedures. But there is a difference, which comes from the fact that, with the new rules by supervisory authorities, external auditors tend to become subject to special requirements that specify the way they evaluate and report on internal control. Furthermore, through the 1996 Market Risk Amendment by the Basel Committee on Banking Supervision, external auditors are included among the parties who are entrusted with the task of ensuring the validation of internal models used for measuring market risk, although supervisory authorities still retain the overall responsibility. It is reasonable to think that with Basel II, this duty will be extended to credit risk models.

4.7 Unqualified and Qualified Reports by External Auditors

External auditors generate different types of reports and supporting documents in the aftermath of their examination. Typically, these include the *standard audit*. This is a *management letter* in which the auditor confidentially presents detailed findings and recommendations to the client firm's management. Also, in some cases there are reports addressed by the auditors to *regulators* during the auditing period, or at its end.

Major types of standard audit reports will never have a heading or other statement in the report that identifies which type it is. Rather, the type of report is specified by certain terminology used in the text of the report, as we will see in the following examples. Major types of standard audit reports are:

1. The *unqualified report*, or clean opinion, which states that financial statements are presented in accordance with rules and regulations and that the necessary audit work has been completed.

In an unqualified report, the external auditor will typically state that: "In our opinion, the accompanying consolidated balance sheet(s) and related consolidated statements of income, cash flows, and changes in common stock equity present fairly, in all unilateral respects, the financial position of (the audited firm and its subsidiaries). Therefore, they are in conformity with accounting principles generally accepted in (the country the audit took place)."

Usually, in an unqualified report, the external auditor will further state that: "We conducted our audits of these statements in accordance with the standards of (for instance, the Public Company Accounting Oversight Board in the United States)." Such standards typically require that the external auditor plan and perform the audit in such a way as to obtain reasonable assurance about whether the financials are free of material misstatement. An audit of financial statements includes:

- Examining, on a test basis, evidence supporting the amounts and disclosures in the financial statement
- Assessing the accounting principles used and significant estimates made by management
- Evaluating the overall presentation of the entity's financial statements

If the results of all exams are positive, *then* the external auditor will state in its unqualified report that: "We believe that our audits provide a reasonable basis for our opinion."

In regard to internal control over financial reporting, in an unqualified statement the external auditor will add that: "Also, in our opinion, the client's management's assessment included in Management's Annual Report on Internal Control Financial Reporting, that the company maintained effective internal control over financial reporting as of (date), is documented and based on criteria established in 'Internal Control—Integrated Framework' issued by the Committee of Sponsoring Organizations of the Treadway Commission (COSO)."

The point made by COSO is that the external auditor must give a firm written opinion on whether what the client's management stated is fairly stated, in all material respects. Such opinion must reflect the aforementioned criteria. Furthermore, the external auditor must confirm whether, in his or her opinion, the client company maintained, in all material respects, effective internal control over financial reporting. This opinion too should be based on the aforementioned criteria.*

2. The *qualified report* may use the same language as the unqualified, but it will add *except for* or some other indication of a problem, or a certain qualification suggesting that there is a problem.

What the qualified external auditor report targets may be a lack of sufficient evidential material, restrictions imposed on the scope of the audit work, departure from accounting rules, or other issues having to do with financial statements. The *except for* indicates that the supervisors should ask additional questions of management.

In the case of a qualified report, the external auditor will carefully notice that the audited company's "management is responsible for establishing and maintaining adequate internal control over financial reporting," further adding that "internal control over financial reporting is a process designed to provide reasonable assurance regarding the reliability of financials, and preparation of financial statements for external purposes, in accordance with generally accepted accounting principles."

In a large number of cases, the external auditor's report will also state that, under the supervision and with the participation of management, including the chief executive officer and chief financial officer, an evaluation was conducted of the effectiveness of internal control over financial reporting based on "Internal Control—Integrated Framework," and identify the issues that were found to be wanting.

3. The *adverse report* usually concludes that the financial statements are not presented in conformity with rules and regulations. This type of report is issued when auditors and the firm's management cannot work out their differences.
4. A *disclaimer* expresses no opinion on the financial statements. The external auditor may issue it when he or she has concluded that substantial doubt exists about the ability of the entity to continue as a going concern for a reasonable period of time.

The disclaimer is intended to indicate that the external auditor is not assuming the responsibility for the bank's statements. Sometimes the reasons for assuming such a position are not too clear and, because the external audit is a major

---

* D.N. Chorafas, *Reliable Financial Reporting and Internal Control: A Global Implementation Guide* (New York: John Wiley, 2000).

component of supervision, many regulatory bodies conduct their own review about the external auditor's independence.

The reader should notice that no disclaimer and no report waives the external auditor's responsibility, as plenty of cases document. In several instances, external auditors have been sued by creditors of failed companies, and in others they sought out-of-court settlements with creditors of companies that went bankrupt after having been audited by them. The creditors claimed that auditors were guilty of intentional misconduct by

- Failing to qualify the accounts of the failed firm or
- Failing to blow the whistle on long-standing fraudulent deals by the audited companies.

For instance, supervisors, investors, analysts, accountants, and auditing experts asked themselves how it happened that PricewaterhouseCoopers, the external auditor, did not see the scams at Tyco. Did the certification it provided as external auditor fail to probe Tyco's accounts, or were there other reasons? Why did PwC not catch wind of the massive loans and self-dealing that CEO Denis Kozlowksi (now serving a prison term) and others allegedly engaged in?

One would think that if the auditors could spot anything, it would be the loans to corporate executives, but it did not happen that way. Beyond that, given the potential for abuse, the outside auditors "should have reviewed all transactions between the company and its officers," said Philip Livingston, CEO of Financial Executives International, a professional association of chief financial officers.* Such a review should have uncovered how these loans mushroomed far beyond anything the board had authorized.

In 2003, the bankruptcy of Parmalat, the overleveraged Italian hedge fund with a dairy food outfit at the side, caused an uproar. The scam mushroomed to about Euro 14 billion ($18.5 billion) in vanished assets, putting to shame Enron's scam. This resulted in a payout of Euro 115 million by auditor Deloitte to Parmalat's receivership to settle claims relating to the company's collapse.

Worst hit were the banks that played occult financial games with Parmalat and, therefore, with fire. In mid-June 2007, three and a half years after the Italian dairy company/hedge fund's collapse, a judge in Milan indicted four big banks—Citigroup, Deutsche Bank, Morgan Stanley, and UBS—on charges of concealing Parmalat's financial woes from investors.† The trial was scheduled to begin in January 2008.

As we have seen, CPAs, too, are not immune to prosecution. Typically, in the majority of cases, they initially reject the creditors' allegations and refuse to enter talks about damages and compensation. But eventually the facts of the case become

---

* *BusinessWeek*, September 30, 2002.

† *The Economist*, June 16, 2007.

public knowledge as creditors provide evidence that the external auditor had not shown due diligence.

A major inducement for out-of-court settlements is the enormous complexity and volume of material for certain cases. Both creditors and CPAs realize that court proceedings would be extremely costly and could last for years. An interesting case dates back to the mid-1990s, where an 875-page charge sheet alleged that the audited firm was patently fraudulent, having used a chain of interconnected frauds to evade the scrutiny of its creditors for a period of some years.*

4.8 Challenging the Dominance of the Big Four

In the early years of this century, many people and institutions began criticizing the dominance of the so-called Big Four globally certified public accountants: PricewaterhouseCoopers (PwC), Deloitte, KPMG, and Ernst & Young (E&Y). Critics point to a monopoly, or at least at an oligopoly, in terms of

- Market choice,
- Audit quality,
- Dependability of reports and, therefore,
- Financial stability of the firms hiring the Big Four.

Part of the criticism is that the number of global accounting firms continues to shrink. Ten years ago they were the Big Six, but Price Waterhouse and Coopers & Lybrand merged. Then Arthur Andersen went bankrupt, further reducing the available options of well-known CPAs. The shrinkage of big players also created problems of compliance.

Theoretically at least, after the merger, Coopers partners and staff had to divest shares they owned in companies audited by Price Waterhouse, and vice versa. Practically, some of the required divestitures never took place. At the SEC's insistence, PwC hired a special counsel to conduct an internal investigation, which uncovered 8,000 violations involving half of the firm's partners. Some were significant infractions. For instance, the heads of major PwC divisions and top managers in charge of enforcing the conflict-of-interest rules owned stock in audit clients. Rumor had it that even James Schiro, the chief executive officer of PricewaterhouseCoopers, owned forbidden stock. I have seen no documentation to that effect.

Critics claim that oligopoly creates its own risks, and these can be major. In June 2006 the Association of British Insurers (ABI), which represents shareholders controlling about 20 percent of the British stock market, stated that it was not always appropriate or necessary for companies to select an auditor among the remaining Big Four. Audit committees, ABI suggested, should periodically examine the case for appointing a new auditor, and do so by considering all possible contenders.

* *European Accountant*, May 1995.

Also in Britain, the Financial Reporting Council (FRC) has taken a lead among global regulators by launching a discussion paper on Big Four dominance. Regulatory and supervisory authorities everywhere were reminded of the risks inherent in the current state of affairs in July 2006, when the Japanese authorities suspended PwC for two months. By 2007, critiques against the Big Four had intensified. At the core of these critiques lies the fact that, as audit companies, PwC, Deloitte, KPMG, and E&Y do the vast majority of audit work for listed firms around the globe. The Big Four audit all but one of the FTSE 100 companies and 97 percent of the FTSE 250. According to the United States General Accounting Office (GAO, renamed as the Government Accountability Office in 2004), the Big Four's corporate clients account for 99 percent of the country's listed companies.

The aforementioned reasons apart, this concern about an oligopoly in external audit is fed by fears over a financial crisis that may ensue if one of the Big Four auditors were to be put out of business. Unlike banks, auditing firms do not have a big treasury to face adversity, and the European Commission is actively considering the option of placing a legal limitation on a CPA's liability in cases where it is found to be negligent.

Charlie McCreevy, the European Union's internal market commissioner, headed off that kind of a move in January 2007, stating that this sort of legislation would probably be unworkable. Moreover, EU member states are split on the matter. In Britain, companies, investors, regulators, and academics agree that the status quo with the Big Four is not ideal, but they add that, as far as change is concerned, options can be divided into three classes:

- Bringing more firms into the blue-chip audit market
- Reducing the risk of a big firm failing, as a result of costly litigation, criminal indictments, or disciplinary penalties
- Minimizing the disruption caused should one of the Big Four go under, as happened with Arthur Andersen

A solution is fairly urgent, as information in the public domain suggests that each of the Big Four firms has had a brush with mortality in recent years. E&Y faced down a challenge from its former audit client Equitable Life in British courts, and eventually emerged in one piece. But in 2005, KPMG paid $456 million and narrowly escaped criminal action by the U.S. Department of Justice after admitting to selling "fraudulent" tax-avoidance schemes.

Memories of these and other troubles loom large, and it is notable that the Financial Services Authority (FSA), Britain's influential chief financial watchdog, has suggested that accounting firms must be subject to the same corporate governance and internal control rules as those that apply to listed companies. A different but fairly stringent rule of CPA supervision has been enacted in the United States in the aftermath of the Sarbanes-Oxley Act.

Chapter 5

The Board's Accountability for Audit

5.1 Membership of the Board of Directors

When selecting outside members for their boards of directors, the nominating committees of well-governed companies looks for individuals who, if elected, will best serve the interests of the firm and its stockholders. Being mindful of the overall board composition, the chairperson and the nominating committee members typically target in each candidate a balance of skills, as well as some of the following characteristics:

- Personal maturity and leadership
- Integrity and a commitment to ethics
- Independence and diversity of thought
- Existing commitments to other boards
- Absence of past current or potential conflicts of interest (as such, it is a characteristic)
- Willingness to deal directly with difficult issues
- Management accomplishment practices and expertise relevant to the company's products and markets
- An understanding of business practices, financial affairs, and complexities inherent in stock exchanges.

While exact criteria guiding the choice of outside directors vary from one company to the next, and in many cases (but not always) also include the representation of major shareholders, these eight bulleted items describe a more general perspective that can be found in business and industry.

It needs no explaining that intelligence, perceptiveness, good judgment, and maturity are sought after. Outside, or independent, directors may feature in their CV (curriculum vitae) accomplishments in current or past jobs such as chief executive officer, chief operating officer, legal counsel, university president, executive director of a major unit of government, or professional advisory services.

Sometimes, nominating committees of the board engage a third party to assist them in identifying and evaluating director-nominee candidates to replace current members of the board who are not standing for reelection. The committee gives to the third party the characteristics, skills, and experience that it prizes, and the headhunter submits recommendations for nominees.

Board members are also inside directors, who work for the company at senior management level. Examples are the company's president, and often the chief financial officer, chief technology officer, or other top-level senior executives, with the choice often depending on the firm, its business, and its history. In principle, there should be many more *outside* directors than *inside* directors.

The duties and responsibilities of board members are to supervise senior management, watch over the affairs of the company, safeguard its assets, and act with a view toward the best interests of all stakeholders, including employees and shareholders. In addition to this personal statutory accountability, the board is collectively responsible for:

- Reviewing and approving the entity's strategic plans, including its products, markets, human resources, IT, and financial strategies
- Scrutinizing major financial commitments and actions by management, including resource allocation, annual budget, capital budget, and other chapters of expenditures
- Monitoring operational performance of the company, such as execution of strategies, effectiveness of management policies and decisions, and standards of deliverables
- Overseeing the results of critical management control processes, like auditing, internal control, and risk management
- Assuring the quality and integrity of the entity's accounting practices, financial reporting system, disclosure control, and compliance

An integral part of the last bulleted item is the board's accountability in ensuring that the company's business is conducted in accordance with high standards of ethical behavior and in conformity with applicable laws and regulations. This should happen in all jurisdictions where the company operates.

Further responsibilities of the board include developing and implementing appropriate policies and procedures for communicating with shareholders and other stakeholders; selecting, monitoring, and evaluating the performance of senior managers; choosing the CEO and fixing his or her compensation; and developing and approving succession plans for the chief executive, senior management, and members of the board.

Every board has a *chairman* whose primary role is to lead as well as to ensure that the collective responsibility of the board is clearly understood by all members and the firm's senior management; that the boundaries between the board and executive management are understood and respected; and that the board functions effectively. The chairman presides at meetings of the board and shareholders and leads the board in monitoring and evaluating the performance of the chief executive officer (CEO), except in cases where the chairman and the CEO are the same person.

The key role of the *chief executive officer* is to manage the firm in an effective, efficient, and forward-looking manner; to fulfill the priorities, goals, and objectives determined by the board in the context of strategic plans, which he or she helps to develop; and to lead in the establishment and execution of the entity's financial plans, product plans, market plans, and human resources plans.

Indeed, among American and British companies, sometimes the chairman of the board is the CEO, while in other cases the CEO is the company's president. More rare is the case where the chairman, CEO, and president are one and the same person. This does not happen among companies in western Europe, particularly Switzerland and Germany, where the external board is more or less limited to supervisory duties and where there exists an internal board, often known as the *board of management*, which carries the strategic functions outlined in the preceding paragraphs.

The CEO's decisions should promote shareholder value. Other responsibilities include maintaining and developing the entity's role as a leading company, providing quality leadership to the staff, and acting as an entrepreneur and innovator within the context of the firm's objectives.

5.2 Legal Responsibilities of Board Members and Senior Management

As Section 1 has explained, membership to the board of directors carries with it responsibilities, some of which are not unlike those of internal levels of management, but broader. These responsibilities have well-defined legal consequences. In the United States, for example, board members' and senior management's responsibility for the accuracy of a credit institution's financial report is established under both federal statute and common law.

Precedence was specified in 1938 in the *Atherton v. Anderson* case, when the Sixth Circuit Court of Appeals held a bank's directors liable because the CEO had falsified the institution's financial reports. More recently, during the last two decades, the Federal Deposit Insurance Corporation (FDIC) has brought to court a number of suits against directors of banks that failed because of their negligence in supervising the

- Conditions and
- Statements

of their institutions.

Although not all court suits brought by supervisors have been successful, the penalties applied by the courts saw to it that jurisprudence has been reinforced. Additionally, Congress has passed legislation that strengthened the control of illegal practices by bank management. Recent examples are the:

- Federal Deposit Insurance Corp. Improvement Act (FDICIA)
- Financial Institutions Reform, Recovery and Enforcement Act (FIRREA)
- The dreaded Racketeer Influenced and Corrupt Practices Act (RICO)
- Sarbanes-Oxley Act of 2002 (detailed in Section 4 of Chapter 3; see also Chapters 12 and 13)

Each one of these acts has had an important effect on malpractices. For instance, with FDICIA, external auditors have been directed to attest to management's assertions regarding the effectiveness of internal control as well as compliance with safety and soundness laws. External auditors have no specific duty to regulators in the execution of their duties, as is the case in Britain, Switzerland, France, and other countries, which increases the external auditor's accountability in the United States. However,

- The external auditor's opinion on the financial statement is heard by the supervisors, and
- The legal infrastructure compels the external auditor to be inquisitive while studying the bank's financial reports.

Additionally, the legal responsibilities of board members and senior management mediate for reinforcement of internal audit and control functions. Irregularities involving members of the board of directors, CEO, CFO, and other senior management on material differences,* established at any level in the organization, should be reported by internal auditors directly to the audit committee (Section 5).

In regard to the regulatory environment and fiduciary responsibilities confronting the board of any organization, its members have an immediate and deep interest in ensuring that sound management practices are widespread in the entity under their watch. Risk control in the financial industry provides an example.

---

* See footnote on page 32.

- Banks are primarily in the risk business.
- Therefore, the better-managed banks have, over the decades, developed processes to control and monitor their risks.

But with the globalization of banking and finance, and the advent of derivatives, many institutions find that their board members do not understand the risk embedded in leveraged global instruments. At the same time, traditional tools for monitoring exposure no longer suffice, which tends to increase a bank's exposure.

This is well known to many national regulators and international regulatory committees, who have issued a number of pronouncements and recommendations to enhance existing risk-management policies, practices, tools, and systems. Such enhancements have included

- Proactive use of the board's audit committee and
- Redefining of responsibilities in internal control functions.

For their part, American regulators (and Swiss regulators for big banks) have a body of bank examiners who, as contrasted to external auditors, tend to take a deeper and more skeptical view of assets, liabilities, and financial reports, as well as of management quality. Examiners are also more inquisitive when they feel that they might be confronting an institution of questionable financial condition.

If the members of the board are to effectively exercise this greater responsibility in terms of soundness of financial statements, internal control, and risk management, they must have mastery of *compliance* with rules and regulations, as well as the development and implementation of a rigorous system of internal control.

The supervisory authorities themselves must be audited for their compliance with the rules. The General Accounting Office (GAO, renamed as the Government Accountability Office in 2004), which is the auditor of all government agencies in the United States, of Congress, and of the Executive Branch, controls the Federal Reserve Board. GAO also has a practical veto on new methodologies. For instance, it did not endorse COSO (Committee of Sponsoring Organizations of the Treadway Commission)* until it had an assertion that a clause was inserted on the safeguarding of assets.

For its part, the Federal Reserve Board audits the 12 regional Federal Reserve Banks. A group of 20 to 25 examiners spends a month each year with each regional Fed bank, looking into issues such as electronic funds transfer (EFT), the automatic clearinghouse, check processing, and other selected operational areas and then coming up with an opinion on whether the bank is qualified or unqualified. This examination is "a kind of hybrid between internal audit and external audit, but it is done in a cost-effective manner like a management consultant's work," said David L. Robinson of the Federal Reserve Board in a personal interview. The Federal Reserve

* D. N. Chorafas, *Reliable Financial Reporting and Internal Control: A Global Implementation Guide* (New York: John Wiley, 2000).

Board also uses the same external auditor for each of the 12 regional banks. Auditing statements must be accurate and well documented because their audience is the Congress and the public. What the auditors say immediately reaches the public through the media. There is as well an oversight by the Fed's Board of Governors.

5.3 Committees of the Board

In many companies, bylaws typically outline the committees that directly originate from the board, as well as their duties. No two firms have exactly the same board committees or give the same responsibilities to these committees. The only general rule is that the board discharges some of its functions through a selected number of committees.

- Typically, each committee meets at least once a year or more frequently as deemed necessary by its chairman and members.
- A majority of the members of a committee constitutes a quorum for the transaction of business at all committee meetings.

A committee chairman may invite executives of the firm to attend committee meetings to assist in discussion and consideration of specific types of business. A board committee may, from time to time, require the expertise of outside experts. Usually, at the next board meeting, the committee chairman will report to his or her colleagues on activities of the committee. Minutes of committee meetings are typically available to all directors.

Among the more frequently encountered committees are finance, governance, nominating (see Section 4), audit (see Section 5), compensation, human development, corporate responsibility, environmental impact, health, safety, pensions, and risk management. It is rather current practice that

- The audit and finance committees are composed entirely of independent directors, while
- Membership to the other committees consists of both inside and outside directors.

The *finance committee* reviews financial and fiscal affairs and also makes recommendations to the board of directors regarding dividends, financing, and fiscal policies. It reviews financial exposure; scrutinizes strategies related to the company's overall portfolio and its impact on earnings; watches over major transactions related to mergers, acquisitions, reorganization, and divestitures; and recommends policies that enhance the firm's financial staying power.

Some boards have a *values and human development committee*, with the mandate to provide guidance to and oversight of the company's management in its development and articulation of core values for personnel and for social responsibilities. Other missions include maintenance of a safe work environment, establishment of a strategy for the company's human resources, monitoring and measuring of individual performance in advancing the firm's goals, and development of policies for ensuring the firm's involvement in the communities in which it does business.

Duties and responsibilities of the *compensation committee* of the board of directors are more homogeneous among different companies than the examples the reader will find in Sections 4 and 5. Briefly stated, its mission is to review and make recommendations to the board regarding the company's compensation policies. This includes all forms of compensation to be provided to executive officers and directors of the entity involving, among other things,

- Annual salaries and bonuses,
- Stock options, and
- Other incentive compensation arrangements.

This committee also makes recommendations to the board on compensation for outside directors. Some firms endow their compensation committee with broader responsibilities, such as establishing and reviewing the entity's overall compensation philosophy; approving the salaries and other compensation of high ranking employees, including all executive officers; and reviewing the effectiveness of, and approving changes to, the compensation program.

Often, though not always, it is the duty of the compensation committee to administer the company's discretionary option-grant program and stock issuance, particularly with respect to executive officers and board members. If the CEO reserves such decision for himself or herself, then this committee at least formulates and periodically revises the option-grant principles. By deliberate choice, some companies see to it that their executive compensation program consists of four elements:

- Base salary
- Short-term incentive compensation
- Long-term incentive compensation
- Stock options

Altogether, the objective of a compensation program is that of creating a closer relationship between business aims and management performance by encouraging the creation of value for shareholders. It is, however, also true that compensation plans with bonuses and stock options lead to excesses that are

- To the benefit of management, and
- To the detriment of shareholders.

Many compensation committees want to show consistent application of the company's compensation philosophy for all executive officers, with variations based on differences in the level of responsibility or the nature of the functions performed by particular individuals. Critics, however, say that not every compensation committee is keen to ensure that the management people are rewarded for their initiative in identifying and developing business opportunities for the firm, and that there are many loafers among those lavishly compensated with options.

A far better definition of compensation committee responsibilities is that practiced at Lazard Frères New York. When George Blumenthal passed the reigns of the bank to Frank Altschul after World War I, he retained for himself three functions as a one-man compensation committee:

- Negotiating annual partnership percentages
- Reprimanding of partners who were deemed to be lazy or underperforming
- Proper accounting of costs among the three houses* (of Lazard: New York, Paris, and London)

In most businesses there is no more absolute power over employees than the authority to set their compensation and determine if they will have a job. But a compensation committee of the board of directors that only distributes goodies—from lavish stock options to golden parachutes—without reprimands for laziness and underperformance is a paper tiger and is hardly worth its name.

Depending on the industry to which they address themselves, companies may also have special board committees, some of them being highly technical. For instance, the board of a power production firm I have in mind has instituted a *nuclear oversight committee* that provides oversight of nuclear safety, guidelines for operational and financial performance, and development of long-term plans and strategies for the entity's nuclear power program. In this particular case, the committee's oversight role is one of review, observation, and comment, but in no way does it alter management authority, responsibility, or accountability in nuclear energy production matters.

5.4 The Corporate Governance and Nominating Committee

Sometimes a board committee executes more than one function. This is frequently the case with the *corporate governance and nominating committee*, which is responsible for identifying and recommending director nominees to the board, ensuring that the board committees have qualified independent members, choosing a successor to the CEO, and developing corporate governance policies and procedures.

---

* William D. Cohan, *The Last Tycoons* (New York: Doubleday, 2007).

In some firms, specific functions of the corporate governance and nominating committee include:

- Studying corporate governance matters and advising the board on its conclusions
- Ensuring that policies regarding corporate governance matters are implemented
- Reviewing independence of the directors and their qualification standards
- Conducting annual performance evaluations of the board and its committees
- Evaluating nominee suggestions received from stockholders, other interested parties, and headhunters
- Recommending candidates at the annual meetings of stockholders to the board as nominees for election
- Making recommendations regarding director orientation and continuing education

The foregoing bulleted items are descriptive, but they do not necessarily provide a universal definition of such a committee's goals and responsibilities. In a company where I served as a consultant, the corporate governance and nominating committee assisted the board in overseeing the implementation and monitoring the effectiveness of measures regarding not only corporate governance guidelines, but also a code of ethics and a policy to avoid conflicts of interest. This same committee was also involved in developing and recommending modifications or additions to corporate policies to the board. Additionally, the corporate governance committee had the following objectives:

- Ensuring board independence
- Supervising processes and practices that foster solid decision-making by both management and the board
- Balancing the interests of all stakeholders: investors, customers, suppliers, employees, the communities where the firm operated, and the environment

On significant issues, following a recommendation of the corporate governance and nominating committee, the board adopted guidelines and set forth procedures that executive management should carry out. Such guidelines usually address areas like structure, governance principles, responsibilities, qualifications, and functioning of the enterprise.

In another entity I was associated with, company bylaws specified that the corporate governance committee must comprise three or more members, all of whom qualify as independent directors under the listing standards of the exchange as well as other applicable rules and regulations. This particular firm also had a separate nominating committee whose responsibilities included:

- Assessing the board's membership needs and recommending nominees
- Recommending to the board those directors to be selected for membership on, or removal from, the various board committees

- Advising the board of directors on who should be designated as chairman of a board committee
- Sponsoring and overseeing performance evaluations for the entity's senior management, including chief executive officer

Furthermore, the company's rules stipulated that both the corporate governance committee and the nominating committee could conduct, or authorize, investigations into matters within the scope of their duties and responsibilities, and each committee could retain external advisors at the company's expense. Each of the committees also conducted an annual self-evaluation of its own performance.

One of the interviewed companies said that the objective of its corporate governance and nominating committee was to review the size, composition, individual performance, and level of compensation of the board of directors; to recommend changes thereto; to evaluate and suggest candidates for chief executive officer and for election as directors; to assess the performance of the board of directors; and to review the company's corporate governance profile and make suggestions for improvement.

As the reader can easily appreciate, the duties and responsibilities of corporate governance and nomination committees are not the same in all firms, but among the range of firms, there is a discernible pattern.

5.5 The Audit Committee

During the last two decades, in a large number of cases, boards have added to their range of responsibilities an *audit committee*, which exercises plenty of authority not only on auditing but also over financial reporting and accounting functions. Therefore, the better-governed firms see to it that each of the audit committee members is independent, under exchange listing standards. In the United States, committee membership must also satisfy the Security and Exchange Commission (SEC). Moreover, it is highly advisable that each member of the audit committee

- Qualify as a financial and accounting expert, under applicable rules and regulations, and
- Understand and appreciate financial auditing and risk-control requirements.

In several instances, but not in every case, company bylaws require that an audit committee member be able to participate in all committee meetings held in connection with review of management practices, audit findings, financial statements, and other reports filed with supervisory authorities.

Since about a decade ago, executives who see further than the immediate issues confronting their firms are the first to say that the audit committee of the corporate board of directors must take a strong leadership role. "We rated the different units, and those that were not up to par were summoned to an audit committee meeting and asked for a report and then follow-up reports. That gets attention," said CFO Frank J. Borelli, of Marsh & McLennan.*

In the majority of cases, the audit committee serves as a direct channel to the bank's internal audit department, to whom internal auditors submit their findings. In this capacity, it assists the board in fulfilling its oversight responsibility of accounting and financial reporting. The audit committee may also function as a safekeeper of internal control duties and as a supervisor of other control systems. The audit committee also serves as the gateway through which the independent certified public accounting firms contact the company, as it selects the CPA, receives its reports, discusses with external auditors their findings, and renews the CPA's mission. Or, alternatively, it changes the external audit firm when such change is warranted.

Similarly the audit committee reviews the appointment and replacement of persons responsible for internal audit, most particularly the chief audit officer. Moreover, the committee oversees and monitors the company's procedures for the receipt, retention, and treatment of complaints regarding accounting, internal accounting controls, and auditing matters. In some companies, the audit committee also handles the confidential, anonymous reporting by employees who question accounting or auditing practices.

All of the functions outlined in the preceding paragraphs are necessary because, in the general case, the authority of the audit committee expands beyond the review of professional services provided by external and internal auditors. Material changes in accounting policies and financial reporting practices, and material developments in financial reporting standards, are part of its remit.

Audit committee responsibilities also include the definition and revision of accounting principles and auditing practices to be used as well as evaluation of the structure and presentation of financial statements, including making demands about and approving such matters that are consistent with financial policies as determined by the board of directors, accounting standards bodies, and regulators. This may include:

- Financial reporting and internal/external audits of the company
- Internal control functions concerning results and scope of audits and other financial controls
- Compliance with legal matters that have a significant impact on financial reports and may present legal aftereffects

Some companies have a separate risk-management committee, but in others the audit committee is also responsible for risk management, a duty that goes beyond financial statements but has to do with the company's financial staying power. In a way not dissimilar to that of other board committees, studied in Section 3, each company tends to assign audit committee duties in its own way.

* *BusinessWeek*, July 13, 1998.

A pharmaceutical company stated in its annual report that its audit committee is responsible for assisting the board in its oversight of the integrity of financial statements, compliance with legal and regulatory requirements, internal control over financial reporting, disclosure controls and procedures, and financial reporting practices as well as internal audit function and performance.

The annual report of another company emphasized that the audit committee meets several times over the year. It also brought in perspective that it meets separately with both management and certified public accountants to discuss and review issues associated with audited financial statements as well as interim reports prior to issuance of an external audit. In several cases, these discussions also address

- Quality, not just acceptability, of accounting principles,
- Clarity of disclosures in the financial statements, and
- Reasonableness of significant judgments made by internal and external auditors.

With new, more-stringent regulations enacted by legislators in the 21st century, audit committees oversee management's documentation on testing and evaluating the firm's system of internal control. For instance, this has become a "must" in response to requirements set forth in Section 404 of the Sarbanes-Oxley Act (SOX) of 2002 and related regulations (see Chapters 3, 12, and 13).

To help itself in performance of functions associated with this broadening area of oversight, audit committees request and receive periodic updates provided by management, internal auditors, and external auditors at each scheduled committee meeting. This information enables audit committee members to express an opinion on

- Management's compliance with rules and regulations and
- Management's assessment of the effectiveness of internal control over financial reporting.

In conclusion, if one looks for a common ground among descriptions of audit committee duties in different firms, the most frequent reference is to assist the board in carrying out its financial oversight and compliance responsibilities. This is followed by the detailed examination of financial information pertaining to operations, duties connected to SOX, supervision of internal auditors, choice and supervision of external auditors, and assurance that critical financial questions receive proper attention.

5.6 Situations That Escaped the Audit Committee's Watch

Section 5 made the point that the audit committee enhances the board's ability to be in charge in matters concerning the control of accounting, financial, and other operations where money plays a key role. Essentially, this is also a protective and constructive service to executive management. As the audit committee's role is expanding, internal and external auditors are measuring and evaluating events with much broader aftereffect than financial records alone. For instance, some major financial events are connected to the assumption of credit risk. In the classical banking business of intermediation, practices are aimed at gathering information about the counterparty, thereby avoiding major loan losses. Screening of creditworthiness includes the following:

- Repayment history of each borrower
- Analysis of loan losses according to management-established criteria
- Examination of likelihood of poor loan mix and overconcentration of credit risk
- Estimation of profits and losses from loans by customer class and loan type
- Unearthing of unwanted practices, such as bending of internal control and failure in cost accounting

Each one of these bulleted items can have an impact on counterparty risk by influencing the criteria for extension of credit. Limiting exposure is the business of risk management, but checking on whether such limits are observed is that of the audit committee. The same is true of

- Fraud cases connected to financial intermediation,
- Inadequate credit records, and
- Light-handed decisions on risk criteria by line management.

Technology should be drafted to effectively assist this expanding role of internal audit. Since practically every loan officer is connected to a computer, expert systems and agents should track all loans transactions as well as the basis on which credit decisions are made (see Chapter 12). Other expert systems should be used to analyze the profile of each loan officer, counterparty, type of loan, money bracket, country and town where the loan was granted, etc., in search for exceptions.

One of the most valuable criteria for this pattern analysis is the counterparty's overindebtedness because of leveraging and/or accumulated business losses. In October 2002, Fiat, the Italian auto manufacturer, which today is a prosperous enterprise, had accumulated net debt of Euro 5 billion ($6.7 billion), which was huge for its size. By the end of June 2002, Moody's had cut Fiat's long-term senior unsecured debt rating, citing the continuing weak performance of the company's core motor business. Shares in Fiat fell, with its bonds, after the Italian motor group suffered a credit ratings downgrade that left its debt at BBB–, one notch above junk.

Neither were investors impressed by the Italian carmaker placing a 35 percent stake in Ferrari with Mediobanca, the Italian investment bank and Fiat's long-term ally. In fact, Mediobanca had formulated a plan to push the company into bankruptcy and force its banks to accept a debt-for-equity swap. This was one more piece of bad news for General Motors, which had taken an option on Fiat.

In Detroit, GM announced a third quarter 2002 loss of $804 million, blaming it to write-down of its 20 percent Fiat stake from $2.4 billion to $220 million. Eventually, GM paid a high price for its inability or unwillingness to follow up closely what was happening at Fiat and opt out of its option without losing more feathers. This provided evidence that:

- GM's safeguard of its assets was not at its best.
- Its internal control functioned poorly in some parts of the empire.
- The company's audit committee was looking rather inward in Detroit, while its top management assumed major credit and financial risk abroad.

As negotiation after negotiation between the top brass of GM and Fiat failed, GM had to put on the table a cool $2 billion at a time its losses on its automotive business were huge. What happened with management control at both companies was beautifully paraphrased by Dr. Antonio Fazio, then governor of the Bank of Italy, who suggested that

- There were deficiencies in Fiat's bookkeeping and
- Such deficiencies blinded management to looming financial problems.*

It needs no explaining that deficiencies in bookkeeping are squarely an audit committee responsibility. They are also a bad omen whose effect is magnified by a nonfunctioning internal control system. Even had Fiat had at that time an audit committee (it did not), its chairman and members would have been incapacitated by what Fazio called "deficiencies in bookkeeping." GM, however, had an audit committee which, as the above evidence suggests, was not functioning.

Another example of audit committee malfunctioning and a lack of internal control is restatements. First quarter and second quarter 2002 losses by Swiss Life, Switzerland's biggest life insurer, were originally stated to be CHF 386 million ($314 million). But in late October 2002 they were restated as CHF 578 million. Through auditing, PricewaterhouseCoopers had discovered an error just prior to a stockholder assembly.

The company said it had incorrectly valued some maturing bonds because of a "programming error" (an often-used excuse). Swiss Life also stated that its internal control was deficient, but that it was being strengthened. At the same time, it restated its 2001 results, suggesting it had "incorrectly booked an unrealized investment gain." The aftereffect was that

- Instead of a gain of CHFF 253 million ($211 million),
- Its 2001 accounts were restated with a loss of CHF 1 billion ($830 million).†

---

* *The Economist*, October 19, 2002.

† *Les Echos*, October 22, 2002.

There is a long list of reasons why executive management, the board, and its audit committee may be blinded when it comes to appreciating the problems that exist in the firm's financial accounts. Additionally, the new financial instruments available today increase this list at the side of greater leveraging and exposure, to the point that the failure of a major derivatives dealer could trigger the bankruptcy of other entities, if not a global financial crisis.

This was the case, for example, in early-to-mid-2007 when, apart from the huge subprime crisis shaking the housing market and its banks, a couple of the best-known investment banks were shaken because of astronomical losses by hedge funds that they had created, financed, and promoted. As these events demonstrated, the audit committees of these institutions were not at the level of their mission. The assumption of huge exposures by these investment banks was not part of a business plan; it was the business plan itself.

At the end of the day, in most organizations, corporate governance committees and audit committees can go only as far as executive management wants them to go. What the Fiat/GM, Swiss Life, and banking cases have in common is that highly paid individuals, members of the board and CEOs, who were supposed to be skilled pilots of their firms' fortunes, have been asleep at the wheel. They were not in charge of the entities whose control they were entrusted with.

5.7 Cultural Change

Some years ago in a seminal document on internal control and audit, the Basel Committee underlined the notion that a bank's board of directors should have responsibility for understanding the risks run by the institution, setting acceptable levels for all types of exposure, pressing the need for limits, and ensuring that senior management take the necessary steps to

- Identify,
- Monitor, and
- Control

the bank's exposure.

This thesis conforms to the principle that the board of directors must provide governance, guidance, and oversight to senior management on a permanent basis rather than in a spotty manner. Moreover, the board is also responsible for setting broad strategies and major policies in a steady manner. In a globalized economy, however, permanence requires focus, concentration, and a cultural change.

The term *cultural change* is widely used these days without appropriate definition. Let me therefore explain in a nutshell its meaning. By *culture* are meant the inner values and attitudes that guide a person, a company, or a market. In this context, *change* is a term that is identified with evolution and adaptation to rapidly developing new perspectives. Change must be managed, and *cultural change* is a term that stands for the orderly evolution of values so that the entity lives within its times. The management of change is not easy because we are targeting at the same time

- Continuity and
- Adaptation to the environment.

Deregulation, technology, and rapid innovation see to it that a company must reinvent itself in order to survive. Culture makes much of the difference between success and failure in doing so. Yet, it is not a concept economists like because it is inherently unquantifiable, and it frightens scholars because it looks as if its concept clashes with their inheritance of legacy procedures.

What has been stated about cultural change at large is definitely applicable in the context of accounting, auditing, compliance, internal control, risk management, and the technology designed to support them. According to the position taken by regulators in the Group of Ten countries during the last 10 years, a bank's board of directors ultimately bears a nearly unlimited responsibility for ensuring the establishment and maintenance of

- An adequate management-control culture and
- Policies and procedures promoting cultural adaptation.

Being a leader in cultural change requires far-sighted views and opinions, as well as an appropriate level of competence and sufficient time to be adequately informed about changes taking place in the market, including those that are latent but have a chance to show up. The change in risk appetite characterizing the late 1990s and early years of this century provides an example.

In a way commensurate with its mission, the board not only has to approve risk policies, but also must outline appropriate risk measurement procedures, exposure control mechanisms, and means for corrective action. Policies need to be established that are capable of mitigating vulnerability to new types of risk as well as to old risks that have become more menacing. Examples are credit risk, market risk, liquidity risk, operational risk, reputational risk, and legal risk.

Additionally, as we will see in Part 2, an integral part of the board's responsibilities is to ensure that the bank's information system is at the state of the art; that it is designed to effectively support the company's business strategy; and that it is regularly audited, including specific audit reasons—for instance how well it serves as the engine of real-time risk management. At the board level, this requires

- Adequate evaluation of the impact of new technological advances and
- Prompt identification of any breaches of the board's policy that IT must, first and foremost, serve the requirements posed by strategic business opportunities and business risks.

As we have seen on several occasions in this book, information technology, the practice of audit, and internal control are all correlated. The impact of audit and internal control can be magnified through high-tech models, simulation, and experimentation. Their usage is a cultural change, and the board must see to it that the company's technology is regularly assessed in terms of its effectiveness in relation to the aforementioned duties.

To help in describing the board's role in connection with the responsibilities outlined in the preceding paragraphs, the term *high-level control* has been coined. This includes all controls instituted and exercised at the initiative of the board of directors in its capacity as the body elected by the general meeting of shareholders to watch over all of the company's operations.

High-level control is necessary, inasmuch as the lack of adequate board oversight and accountability, or failure to develop a policy of cultural change, can lead to a state of decline: hurting the institution, swamping its creative powers, increasing its costs, and bending its market standing. Most often, major financial losses and eventually bankruptcy reflect management inattention to, and laxity in, high-level control.

II

CASE STUDIES ON AUDITING A COMPANY'S INFORMATION TECHNOLOGY

Chapter 6

Auditing the Information Technology Functions

6.1 Snapshots of IT Audits

First, let us briefly talk about the information technology (IT) auditor. To do a proper job, he or she must be a flexible thinker who can act quickly when needed (more qualifications are described later on). What is not so often said is that the IT auditor should, as well, be able to handle *company politics* because IT, and therefore IT auditing, involves an inordinate amount of politicking.

As for the job itself, Chapter 5 made the point that information technology, audit, and internal control correlate among themselves and with sound governance. Advanced IT can be instrumental in assisting auditing functions and internal control, but at the same time, IT must be audited for:

- Conformity to the company's strategic plan
- Efficiency of its operations
- Fraud and other mishappenings
- Whether it is ahead of the curve compared with the IT of competitors

All four bulleted items can serve as guidelines for the IT auditor. A few years ago, in a joint IT policy statement, the four main regulators of U.S. banking—Federal Reserve, Office of the Comptroller of the Currency (OCC), Federal Deposit Insurance Corporation (FDIC), and Office of Thrift Supervision (OTS)—stated that internal control, internal audit, and the technology supporting them must be

- Correctly monitored and
- Properly controlled.

"Responsibility cannot be transferred to somebody else, even if certain activities are delegated or outsourced," said two executives of OCC during our meeting. "Whether it is internal control or information technology, whether it is done in-house or it is outsourced, it is the board's responsibility to assure quality." This statement is absolutely right because, in the 21st century, IT has become an efficiency tool that, properly used, can be instrumental in

- Enhancing management control,
- Promoting business opportunity, and
- Helping in making the control of exposure more effective.

The downside lies in the fact that, as far as the majority of companies are concerned, "enhanced management control" is not a keyword characterizing IT expenditures. Every year, companies are spending billions of pounds, euros, and dollars on information technology, even though few boardrooms know the value of the hardware and software their firms acquire or the contribution that IT investments make to their businesses.

This is the finding of a study published on October 1, 2007, and based on the survey of 250 chief information officers (CIOs) and chief financial officers (CFOs) from companies in America, Britain, Germany, France, and Italy. Fewer than half the interviewed persons had ever tried to value their IT assets, and 60 percent did not know the worth of their software. The sample of firms with such dismal references included businesses with revenues from $100 million to more than $1 billion, across all industries.

Despite this absence of cost/benefit analysis and profitability evaluation, or even a basic understanding of IT's contribution, U.S. corporate spending on hardware and software rose 4.7 percent in the second quarter of 2007, according to the U.S. Department of Commerce. Yet, MicroFocus, the software developer who did the aforementioned study, estimated that

- 30 percent of respondents did not know how much money their companies spent on software each year, and
- Only 37 percent of CIOs have tried to quantify their IT assets compared with 60 percent of CFOs.*

Another interesting finding has been that 56 percent of respondents thought that the financial value of software was ignored or poorly evaluated compared with

* *Financial Times*, October 2, 2007.

other corporate assets; as far as costing is concerned, the main emphasis was placed on hardware. One of the conclusions that can be derived from these statistics is that technologists focus on new IT developments rather than on cost/effectiveness. CIOs and their people pay little attention to the benefits, and even less to (badly needed) better management of legacy IT assets.

The fact that technologists focus more on new IT developments than on costs has a silver lining: The sophistication of applications has been improving over the last 15 years, and several end users have become aware of this fact. As the president of a company commented during our meeting: "What can be done through sophisticated information technology solutions can never be achieved through traditional data processing." Another CEO added that much of what has been achieved in his company is due to the findings of IT audits.

IT audits are not a one-time affair. They are a steady business whose deliverables must be brought without delay to management's attention. To perform his or her duties, the auditor of a modern information system should have good knowledge of basic and applications software, expert systems and agents (see Chapter 12), databases and data mining, servers and workstations, and communications nodes and links.

Moreover, a great deal of modern IT auditing must be done mostly online. In contrast, traditional audit approaches have placed all their reliance on hard-copy audit trails, with verification of separation of duties subject to various approval levels. With online interactive systems, however, hard-copy records do not exist, nor would they make sense if they existed.

For relatively simple issues, audit is now done around and through the computer. Auditing *around the computer* consists of examining input transactions and all outputs to ensure that the inputs are correct, the outputs are timely, and that all the transactions were processed correctly. The auditor can also use expert systems for audit, following each transaction through every step of the processing cycle—a process known as tracing.

In contrast, the audit of complex issues requires human judgment. For instance, as the case study in Chapter 7 will demonstrate, auditing around the computer is not suitable for a top-management view of the company's information systems and communications networks. The answer is personal interviews assisted through the results of auditing *through the computer*, thereby

- Making maximum use of expert systems and
- Performing a series of substantive tests to prove that the company's current information technology is sound and competitive.

Well-managed credit institutions do not need to be convinced about the necessity of using high technology in their operations—from analysis of business opportunities to the control of exposure—because they have already experienced the benefits of high tech's contribution. The board and CEO of successful companies appreciate that it is no longer enough to know assets and liabilities only in average or with reference to yesterday's data.

- The CEO and senior management must always be provided with real-time data.
- Such information should be available ad hoc, with a fast response time (see Chapter 10), to enable decisions as market factors change.

It follows that one of the crucial issues to be addressed by the IT audit is whether the firm's technology, its systems solution, and its IT applications are ahead of the state of the art or at the bleeding edge of laggards. Getting the pattern of management thinking requires a statistically valid sample of interviews conducted person to person with the company's executives and professionals.

An IT audit that limits itself to operating between the walls of the information technology department is nothing more than a half-baked effort that states the obvious. In contrast, the guide of an IT audit that examines the state of the art of company application must definitely include the best examples that can be found among competitors. For instance, in an effort to control integrated risks, one of the high-tech U.S. banks ran a three-dimensional matrix with the following dimensions:

- Counterparty risk
- Market risk
- Liquidity risk

At the time, this was an avant-garde implementation that was providing fairly accurate, timely, unbiased, and unfiltered information to senior management. Other commendable applications have been developed to bring management's attention, in nearly real-time, the effects of volatility and liquidity, violations on observance of trading limits, as well as virtual balance sheets (V/BS) and virtual income statements (V/IS).

6.2 Tuning the IT Audit to Regulatory Requirements

An IT audit should pay full attention to whether the company's information system provides ways and means for the observance of the letter of the law and prevailing regulatory requirements. Such an IT audit strengthens management's hand and benefits the company. An example would be a system solution capable of producing—for any important issue and at any time—responses needed by the company's executives in regard to the regulators' queries. Lack of this service is a handicap (see Chapter 7).

Regulators are well aware that the governance of top-tier banks has been improved through technology. A few years ago, in a meeting at the Federal Reserve Board, the executives I was talking to saw two major advantages connected with real-time IT implementation and intraday follow-up positions:

- Visualization of observance of margins
- Better management of intraday exposure

Another crucial issue that the IT audit should monitor is the speed at which system solutions and their applications are updated. Computer and communications technology continue to change rapidly, and such changes have an impact on management style. In turn, this affects audit requirements. For instance, in today's computing environment, moving data across a distributed network requires more emphasis on security than centralized operations (see Chapter 11).

What is the experience of regulators regarding real-time systems and other advanced technology in commercial banking? Executives at the Federal Reserve Bank of Boston answered that the banks themselves appreciate the need for advanced technology, with one of them stating: "We struggle to keep up with the sophistication of systems installed in commercial banks."

This in no way means that all commercial banks are ahead in technology. There always exist leading-edge and bleeding-edge institutions. Year after year, my research has documented that in any industry, and at any time, companies betting their future on innovation theoretically have the upper ground, but only a few firms qualify practically as high tech.

- Only 5 to 10 percent of all companies are on the leading edge.
- About 20 percent are followers who eventually may be catching up.
- The other 75 percent are laggards, and many find themselves on the bleeding edge.

Reading between the lines, this means that the state of a firm's technology affects the auditor's work. There is no one-size-fits-all in the examination of information technology's status. Therefore, the toolkit of IT audits must be flexible and adaptable.

Precisely because the rate of progress in IT is different in different firms, and because it is uneven, the level of experience that is required for IT audit continues to increase. On the one hand, positive developments add their weight to the need for new approaches in IT audit; on the other hand, for companies at the bleeding edge, old approaches can still be used because the newer ones will be out of place.

This statement is evidently true for both system solutions and applications. The auditing of credit-risk and market-risk models, over and above the more classical audit of credit-risk and market-risk files, provides an example that impacts both on the institution's internal auditing policies and on the regulators.

The more clear-eyed regulators appreciate the need for a dual approach in judging an institution's state of the art in IT. In a meeting in Washington, D.C., the executives of the Office of the Comptroller of the Currency said that, from a supervisory standpoint, they do not think that OCC wants to go fully mathematical. Prudential supervision still needs judgment. However:

- The use of models helps in fleshing out weaknesses or negative trends.
- Models are very helpful in experimenting to evaluate different courses of corrective action.

The faster technology advances, the more demanding become the different stages of IT audit. Technology audit was straightforward enough with the old electronic data processing (EDP), but this is no longer the case for the new systems. To evaluate technology solutions in the company for which he or she works, the auditor must be familiar with a golden horde of subjects, including mobile and wireless networks in practically every major wireless market segment:

- Wireless local area networks
- Cellular and wide-area networks
- Personal data networking
- A range of emerging next-generation mobile technologies

This task is challenging because every one of these markets is in transition. For instance, the cellular handset market is in transition from pure voice to broadband multimedia, with these changes transforming the traditional cellular phone from a voice-only device into a multimedia gateway.

From mathematical models to nomadic computing, IT solutions are a never-ending process of adaptation, because to remain competitive, both the manufacturers of IT gear and the users must keep pace with rapid change and evolving industry standards, developing and implementing

- New cost-effective technological solutions or
- Better functionality than their competitors.

Additionally, IT auditors should pay full attention to the fact that, in an effort to push banks toward a more effective use of IT, since the late 1990s, some regulators no longer accept paper documents. But technology can also open Pandora's box in terms of risks connected to security. Therefore, while U.S. regulators look very favorably at usage of high technology by the banking industry, they also carefully examine the problems that might come up, thereby requiring a new focus in supervision.

Financial fraud in cyberspace is a growing concern as the Internet becomes the medium for conducting commerce and electronic banking (see Chapter 11). While the majority of entities on the Internet are legitimate, some try to take advantage of the Web's anonymity to engage in unauthorized and possibly illegal activities. This likelihood is placing new emphasis on the IT auditor's search for breaches in the security of information systems.

6.3 Procedure of an IT Audit

It is redundant yet important to say that in order to perform an effective audit of information technology, the auditor must have not only first-class knowledge of what information systems are and are not, but also plenty of experience in IT practice. Lack of such knowledge and experience makes it impossible to tell how advanced the applications are, how well the IT systems are being used, whether they are cost effective, and what sorts of results must be expected from them.

Speaking from personal experience, when an IT auditor confronts suboptimal technological plans, the most frequent excuses heard from the chief information officer (CIO) are that he or she did not have the freedom of designing the information system from scratch, or that top management does not sufficiently appreciate that advanced IT solutions are a big factor in the firm's competitiveness.

While there is truth in these statements, it is as well an inescapable fact that the CIO is not only a department head but also an advisor on information technology to the CEO and the board. Advantages to be derived from high-technology implementation have not escaped the attention of the independent rating agencies. "We look at technology indirectly and focus on relative efficiencies for conducting the business," said Clifford Griep of Standard & Poor's, during our meeting. "We also examine the internal accounting management information system and customer service levels."

In Standard & Poor's credit rating methodology, IT is not at the same level as financial statements, profitability, and capital base; however, the company does specialized reviews of certain parts of a commercial bank's IT to establish if it has a technological advantage. For example, its analysts look into customer-oriented knowledge-based systems (see Chapter 12) capable of

- Utilizing customer behavior patterns and
- Incorporating their findings into risk management.

Internal auditors of IT would be well advised to keep this reference in mind, because it talks volumes about the dynamics of an audit. It also distinguishes modern approaches to IT audits from traditional approaches, which have been a periodic function limited to what has been seen as "normal checks" of an IT system.

While necessary, under currently prevailing conditions, tests limited to fraud and to programming errors are only a small part of an IT audit. Knowledge engineering must be both audited and used to help the IT audit. The need is for concurrent auditing with expert systems that are used to perform, through sampling inspection, continuous control in critical areas such as:

- Transaction execution
- Observance of risk limits
- Avoidance of wrong-way risk
- Compliance with regulations

Special-purpose audit languages and audit software are available and should be employed. The capabilities provided by knowledge artifacts extend beyond the mere extraction of information. Interactive software can furnish an effective method of obtaining data for audit purposes, rather than having to rely only on existing reports.

Expert systems are enabling the auditor to extract and analyze pertinent information in a manner almost independent of IT's operations management, which is being audited. At the same time, it is necessary to ensure that live data and the information content of the audited system is unaffected by the audit's performance and by its requirements for tests and experiments.

This task must be properly planned, because the information upon which a large part of fact-finding associated with the IT audit is based is not only accounting data. Also, IT strategies, policies, plans, and deliverables are seldom established without some reference to accounting records and reports feeding into a system of accounts.

Audits taken to measure efficiency or analyze IT's contributions to different parts of organizational activities are almost always based upon data accumulated and presented through the information system. This is *internal data*, the kind of information seldom, if ever, reported to creditors, investors, and the general public, and it is basic material with which the auditor must work.

The internal IT auditor is, therefore, dearly interested in the accuracy, timeliness, and precision of the information elements with which he or she is dealing, including quality standards characterizing the systematic collection of facts and figures about operations. Also subject to IT audit are procedures related to internal control and those having to do with compliance with rules and regulations.

In the background of this discussion lies the fact that careful procedural planning is necessary if the IT audit tests are to be meaningful and thorough. The principle of materiality must always be kept in mind. The more-material side of IT operations and their deliverables, including financial reporting and accounting systems, must be prime parts of the audit. To take a constructive view, the content, objectives, and procedures of an internal IT audit must be considered from at least two standpoints:

- Auditing serves to analyze, record, and document the wrong impact of an obsolete IT system on transactions, records, and reports.
- Auditing's outputs, and the procedures guiding them, are intimately connected to the management of the bank at all levels of the organization.

That is exactly the reason why, in the bottom line, IT auditing is a responsibility associated with sound management. To do this job in an able manner, the auditor must be given the authority to access all of the firm's databases. The contents of banking book and trading book are no sacred cows, and managers who consider them as such have something to hide.

6.4 Why IT Audit Impacts a Firm's Technology

During the research for this book, one of the more interesting opinions expressed about the extent and impact of an IT audit is that it should start making itself felt during the preliminary design stages of the information system's life cycle (see also Chapter 2 on design reviews). If they start by examining the design stage, internal IT auditors get closely involved with the concepts in the minds of the system designers, while the latter project the system with check points and controls to ensure ease of validation.

Examination from a cause-and-effect viewpoint bears fruit when IT audit requirements are not an afterthought but a precondition in system development. Auditing that starts at the level of design reviews is better positioned to cast its shadow as the system evolves. Additionally, the auditors will be involved in the system's testing phase and in verification of the users' response to deliverables. Here are a few examples on what can be expected from this approach:

Increase in depth and breadth of system analysis, without increase in costs

Figure 6.1 provides a snapshot of what is achievable in different phases of information handling through sophisticated solutions, in contrast to what low technology has been delivering so far. Notice the most significant improvement in analytical capabilities.

Identification of apparent weaknesses. System design should be audited to determine whether it can efficiently and economically achieve its objectives. Weaknesses should be noted and brought to attention.

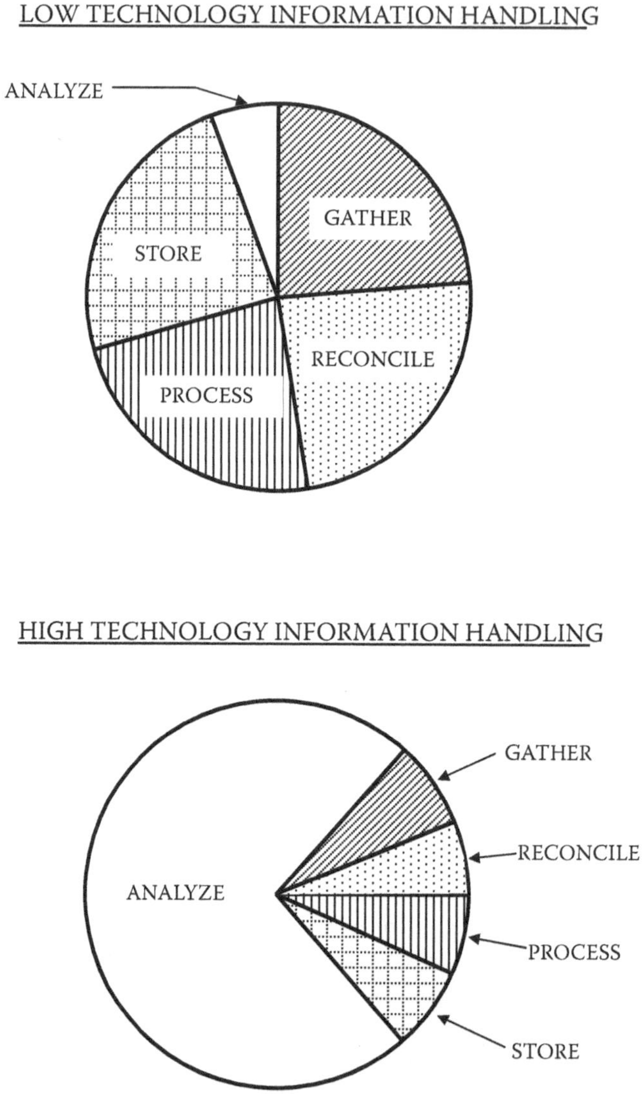

Figure 6.1 Increasing the depth and breadth of analysis through high technology without increasing costs.

By means of identifying and testing a system's weak nodes and linkages, the IT auditor can reach a decision as to whether (following specific adjustments) the adopted solution is adequate, or there exist major flaws that will handicap performance. The audit's findings should be discussed with management along with any recommendations for changes.

Execution of design compliance tests. The aim is to evaluate whether the IT system is operating as intended. Such tests should range from observation and inspection to detailed comparison with alternative designs.

Design-compliance tests are targeted to identify possible deviations from original specifications. Stress tests provide an input on where deviations most likely reside, with subsequent experimentation helping to identify the nature of such deviation.

The vendors of information technology hardware and software face similar challenges. This is easy to understand because of the fact that both perceive a business opportunity and a risk when developing new products. For the producer, the sophistication of modern technological products could result in unforeseen delays or expenses due to undetected defects that may

- Damage the firm's reputation with current or prospective customers,
- Result in significant increases in costs and claims, and
- Adversely affect the market's broader acceptance of the firm's products and services.

For the user organization, for instance a credit institution, the challenge posed by a complex technology is that of having first-class designers and knowledgeable auditors capable of ensuring that design or material weaknesses are caught and reported by internal control, while problems are solved before their aftereffects become a torrent of trouble.

For companies that have chosen the strategy of being leaders in technology, management depends on external IT experts and on well-trained internal IT auditors. The former provide the big picture, and they sometimes suggest a 180-degree change (see Chapter 7); the latter have to determine whether the system meets "this" or "that" design specification and whether it supports specific services that have been required.

- System changes can be a costly issue and should be handled with care.
- On the other hand, implementing a poor system design for fear of incurring change costs will end up being a disaster.

In contrast to the approach taken in the design phase, once the system is operational, the primary function of an IT auditor is to perform periodic examinations not only of the entire system but also, if not primarily, of its component parts. Furthermore, various operational controls must be reviewed on an ongoing basis.

Other things being equal, the better focused is the control a company has over its IT projects, the better are its chances to lead them successfully. Joint projects involving different companies with diverse objectives do not benefit from management focus. Here is a short list of four examples that ranged from uncertainty to chaos:

- *Westpac with IBM.* Computer System for the 1990s (CS90). The project was characterized by split management and split goals. After seven years of accumulated costs, it crashed.
- *Banco di Roma with EDS.* The project kept going in time, and it was terminated when new management took over at the bank.
- *J. P. Morgan with a consortium.* IT was outsourced, allegedly because it was a bother to Morgan management; eventually the project was dropped.
- *American Airlines/Hilton/Marriott/Budget Rent A Car.* All four companies sent their less capable people to the common effort; the project landed in court.

In all four cases the project was subverted, albeit for different reasons. There is no project that cannot be subverted, and so-called common IT projects have a greater likelihood of failure because of a cacophony of clans and tribes carrying them out. Just like lack of leadership, the absence of IT audit is damaging. Eventually the deliverables will come late, cost too much, and be worryingly inadequate. (See Section 7 on auditing the overall IT system concept.)

6.5 Auditing Fraud Cases

The fact that IT audit today pays a great deal of attention to factors that were not in the limelight 20 or even 10 years ago in no way diminishes the importance of uncovering fraudulent activities. Information technology is particularly vulnerable in that respect because so much information about money is stored in databases.

In one of the banks where I was a consultant, we were confronted with what was by all evidence a petty crime, but one that had provided a nice nest egg for its instigator. A young programmer had inserted a small routine that

- First rounded the client's accounts to the nearest dollar, then added a few cents to it;
- The routine then credited the difference to an account his wife had opened with the bank, in her maiden name.

Each fraudulent transaction made the programmer a relatively small profit of 40 cents, on average, per client account statement—but there were millions of client accounts.

Other types of IT fraud are more damaging to both the bank and its clients. A decade ago, on November 12, 1998, ABN Amro admitted the loss of Fl 178 million ($94 million) as a result of what was alleged to have been a systematic fraud carried out by employees handling the accounts of rich nonresidents. This is the worst fraud the bank seems to have suffered in its home market until then, or since. According to the bank's announcement, the fraudulent system was built on a shadow bookkeeping that, over five years, had allowed the embezzlers to milk a significant number of some 800 "dear client" accounts held at the so-called diamond branch of the financial institution.

- These were largely Swiss-style numbered accounts for which privacy-minded customers did not wish to be sent regular statements.
- The bank employees involved in the scam were said to have opened additional accounts on behalf of existing clients. While they debited the true accounts, they simultaneously credited the fake accounts.

Connected to this case, there was legal risk (see Section 9). For many years, Dutch law has required cash transactions of unusual size to be reported to the authorities; that law was breached. The scheme had escaped detection by internal and external auditors, and when management got wind of it, a new firm of certified public accountants was brought in to undertake a special audit. Correctly, senior management wanted to know *everything* about the irregularities.*

Bookkeeping scandals have been known for centuries, but computers provide fraudulent people with a new set of "opportunities." All books and all accounts may suffer from fraud, and in many cases the fraud may go unpunished even if it is reported by whistle blowers.

Not all fraud concentrates on altering the a bank's books. Trading is one of the fields that, at least in some institutions, has become less secure because of technology. One of the executives participating in the research that led to this book mentioned a trader who put false deals into the system to see if it could catch them—sitting back and observing *if* and *how* the IT system responded. It took two days for the bank to catch the false trades.

New systems are particularly vulnerable to fraud perpetrated by sophisticated operators, because even if the system has undergone testing, its weaknesses show up rather slowly a long time after it is in use. Embezzlement is rare in the world of high finance for an obvious reason: The people who want more money know that there are legal ways to get it. But that is no assurance that embezzlement will not occur.

In mid-1987, Stephen Sui-Kuan Wang, Jr., a Morgan Stanley employee, was induced into insider trading by Fred Lee, a Taiwanese citizen operating in Wall Street. For over a year, from July 1987 to August 1988, Wang gave Lee tips on 25 pending deals. Armed with this information, Lee earned $16.5 million in the elapsed months (big money at that time).

Morgan Stanley had no criminal involvement, but this case showed that its internal control was in poor shape. Then the U.S. district attorney, Rudolf Giuliani

* *Financial Times*, November 13, 1998.

said: "You would think there would have been better controls, better procedures." In October 1988 when Federal District Judge Kevin T. Duffy sentenced Wang, he told him: "You had a brilliant future and you blew it in greed.... The first time you could have been a crook, you were."*

"We are all responsible for internal control," said the CIO of a New York broker. "The self-assessment we used to do was mainly manual. Now it is assisted through online database mining." The information technology system that this securities firm has developed is extensively used by the firm's auditors in their work. Among other applications, they analyze patterns of

- Trade limits and
- Daylight overdrafts.

Financial institutions have started to capitalize on the fact that they have access to a technology they could not have dreamed of 10 years ago, even if the majority of them do not take advantage of it. "Technology can help the banker so much more if all transactions are online and they are supported through secure digital signatures," said the chief information officer of a well-known credit institution, "but there are also things technology cannot do. Corruption at government level will not be stopped through technology." (For more on security, see Chapter 11).

6.6 Auditing Technology Risk

The cases we have examined in the preceding section illustrate different phases of technology risk. Section 4 discussed risks of a strategic and engineering nature that could damage a company's competitive standing by causing it to fall behind in its IT. In contrast, the risks outlined in Section 5 are of a tactical and accounting nature, and they have mainly to do with security. But there is more to be said on this subject.

In an advanced industrial society, a company's operations are highly dependent on the integrity of its technology system. Its success depends, in great part, on its ability to mine increasingly rich distributed databases and make timely decisions in anticipation of client demands and industry changes. Moreover, a company needs advanced technology to be in control of risks assumed in the environment in which it operates.

Business operations are negatively impacted if the firm experiences system interruptions, input and other errors, or downtime. Operations are also hindered if the business falls behind its competitors in the information technology that it uses and the ways in which that technology is used. Therefore, the board and senior

* Ron Chernov, *The House of Morgan* (New York: Touchstone/Simon & Schuster, 1990).

management must be committed to an ongoing process of upgrading, enhancing, and testing the entity's technology to effectively meet

- Sophisticated client requirements,
- Market and regulatory changes,
- Evolving internal needs for information and knowledge, and
- A growing range of operational risks (brought to the reader's attention in Chapter 2).

Technology risk also includes the failure to respond to these prerequisites, as well as many other issues such as human error, obsolescence of applications and machines, reliability issues (see Chapter 10), mismanagement of IT capital expenditures, and the effects of natural disasters as well as of riots. Technology risk is manageable, but it takes a significant amount of *will* and *skill* to do so.

Of all operational risks connected to IT, *mismanagement* at large may well be the more deadly, and it is widespread. When it comes to computers, communications, and software, many industrial companies and financial institutions just throw money at the problem rather than doing a rigorous IT audit and refocusing their effort (see Chapters 7 and 8). The money thrown down the drain goes to buying "more computer power," and the job is often done haphazardly. The difference between red ink and profits from investments in technology is made by astute IT management, both in terms of policies and decisions at corporate level and of the IT operations themselves.

- Top-tier companies benefit from advanced, highly competitive computer applications.
- The laggards pay the costs, but they get meager results because they mainly think of the past, not of the future.

The message the reader should retain from this discussion is that, while practically all companies spend large amounts of money on computers, communications, and software, only the leaders derive real profits from their investments. Spending big money on technology without the corresponding return on investment (ROI) speaks volumes about poor management at large.

- One of the major flows in current practice is the continuing use of legacy applications as a basic frame of reference.
- The use of legacy applications limits the implementation bandwidth and keeps the company in a technological backwater.

From the viewpoint of growth and survival, therefore from a strategic perspective, enterprises succeed or fail based on the speed with which they can respond to changing customer demands and market conditions. What many boards fail to realize is that, properly chosen and correctly used, information technology is a vital ingredient of rapid response; similarly, the swift development of sophisticated software is a cornerstone to competitiveness.

There is practically no market "secure" from international competition. Globalization and deregulation have greatly increased the number of competitors worldwide. Ten years ago, who would have predicted that Mittal Steel buys Arcelor and Tata buys Corus? Business solutions need to be put in place faster than ever before, but ironically:

- In many cases, it is no longer practical to build new business applications from the ground up.
- Neither is it always viable to deploy a packaged solution, as packages do not keep up with new, specific company needs.

Where business competitiveness is at stake, the answer is *rapid prototyping* and a fast track to implementation (see Chapter 2). Assembling a business application from software components is like using ready-made parts to build a car or house. The fast track offers a competitive solution to the dual problem of

- Speed of response and
- Flexibility in adaptation and upkeep.

Rapid prototyping also helps in another criterion of good management: IT costs must be contained. Rapid software development is a good way to swamp costs, because a huge chapter in the IT budget is personnel. Another vital ingredient in cost control is the avoidance of duplication of effort in regard to data capture through a policy of one entry, many uses. In classical electronic data processing (EDP), the same information element is entered up to seven times. Recently, the average number of reentries was between 3 and 4. Even today, the average is 2.4, which is still way too high, as is its associated cost. An IT audit that downplays the duplication of effort in data input is not worth the money it costs. Another downside is that repetitive inputs of the same information element are characterized by an inordinate amount of errors coming into the IT database. Typically, these entries are made in multiple incompatible formats and they address heterogeneous files, usually corresponding to discrete islands of applications, which represent another major technology risk.

It is no wonder that, in many companies, data entry costs, including subsequent clearance of embedded errors, have been consuming 20 to 25 percent of the IT budget. The best policy is: one entry, many uses, but its implementation demands lots of organization and self-discipline. Both are lacking from a significant number of IT operations, with the result that operational risks are booming. Therefore, this is an area where the IT auditor must pay a great deal of attention.

6.7 Auditing the Overall System Concept

Another fertile area for the IT auditor, one that can be instrumental in restructuring the company's information technology culture, is that of the overall system concept and its evolution. This starts with system design and extends over the entire applications domain. Its main phases of activity, which should be subject to IT audit, are

- Planning
- Analysis
- Design
- Implementation
- Maintenance

Planning is a largely conceptual activity. *What* do we want to do? *How*? *When*? With what resources? In which timetable? Behind these queries lies the fact that planning is done for a specific purpose. Both the purpose and the plan itself must be audited. To appreciate the importance of auditing an IT plan, one should realize that, contrary to what was generally believed for five decades—that reduction in paperwork and automation of clerical operations were IT's goals—the *main* objects of computing are

- Foresight
- Insight
- Analysis
- Design

As we have seen in Chapter 5, in connection with the board's responsibilities, the IT auditor should clearly keep in mind that the most urgent need to be fulfilled by information technology are changing over time. What does the end user want? When? What does he or she have today? How can IT be made more responsive to user needs? How can the timetable of deliverables be significantly shortened?

Much can be learned by studying what the best IT installations have obtained as well as by examining lessons taught by past experience. What have we learned over five decades of experience with computer applications, databases, and communications networks? The knowledge gained can be phrased in these three observations:

- The able usage of information systems is a matter of *culture*, not of machines.
- We get little from our investment unless we have *clear goals* and effectively use technology to reach them.
- Without challenging the "obvious," the results of an IT audit will be minimal, while operational risks will continue to run high.

For the IT auditor, these three observations emphasize the importance of abandoning old structures that limit our ability to obtain results and cost too much for the service they provide. The computer, as we have known it for over the past five decades, is dead. The new master of the technological domain is flexible and evolving *system solutions*.

System *design* is creative work that can be best examined when an auditor is experienced in system development and integration. A similar statement is valid about auditing the *implementation* process, with the added challenges of developing the timetable for installing the new system, training the user, and fulfilling babysitting requirements.

Maintenance has its own prerequisites in terms of IT auditing: What provisions are in place for system upkeep? For steady tuning? For expanding and restructuring? For attaining at least 99.9 percent reliability? For shortening the response time (see Chapter 10)? All of these IT audit functions can be simpler and better focused *if* the auditor

- Has a goal and a plan,
- Acquires the proper know-how and experience, and
- Properly informs himself or herself of alternative ways of doing a first-class job

This can be stated in conclusion: To study, confront, and be in charge of technology risk, the IT auditor must first have a plan. This will help the auditor identify and inventory the current state of the available computer applications, databased information, basic software endowments, applications software libraries, physical networks, and so on. The auditor's references must be user oriented, and this goes beyond the classical definitions of software and hardware.

6.8 Testing Existing Auditing Procedures

Because technology risk should be audited in no uncertain terms, we must have in place auditing procedures that themselves have to be regularly controlled. Evaluation and testing of existing IT audit procedures requires that they be properly described and documented. Their effectiveness must be evaluated with regard to what they unearth in a number of issues, including

- Risk of falling behind in information technology
- Risk of cultural backwater in system design
- Project management risk
- Quality and sophistication of software risk
- Risk of slow applications development
- Risk of internal and external fraud

- Vendor failure risk
- Risk related to third-party outsourcing

Many people say that, aside from the risk of fraud and vendor risk, the objective evaluation of technology exposure is difficult, and that some reasonable legacy risk must be accepted because applications software libraries are so big and difficult to wholly redo. This is nonsense.

What is important in an IT auditing process is that all major activities be identified and specific control objectives be properly defined. These form the framework of an effective IT audit and of appropriately applied management controls. Failure to adequately define corporate IT objectives typically leads to the identification of weakness in the firm's information technology system and makes the work of the IT audit that much more frustrating. Furthermore, while IT audits are necessary, year-long monitoring of IT activities and deliverables is just as valuable. In fact, aside from interviews and ad hoc tests, an IT audit also depends on a monitoring record to express a factual opinion. The same is true of logs, which in the course of an IT audit will provide a basis for cost/benefit analysis.

Are the IT auditors properly evaluating IT cost? Return on investment? The effectiveness of IT services as seen by the end user? Several principles help in safeguarding the auditor's ability to do the assigned job. One of them is that the auditing of information technology requires questioning of the end users: managers, professionals, and clerks (see Chapter 7). Another principle is that, if handled correctly, IT audits should produce a working partnership between end users and internal auditors as well as between the latter and IT professionals, since all parties are interested in effective utilization of information technology resources. Such relationships will also be beneficial to internal control because of the amount of feedback information transiting through the information system.

Another principle is that—because by all likelihood internal IT audit will be done on a sampling basis, at least at the end user's side—the sample should be statistically significant. Once the sampling method is selected, the auditor must establish two parameters:

- Confidence level
- Precision factor

An easy way to explain the confidence level is that it represents the proportion of times that a given sampling plan will yield the correct conclusion when it is applied over and over again to the same population.* A bit more complex is the notion of a Type I error, or producer's risk, shown in Figure 6.2. The operating characteristics curve in that figure provides the likelihood that a manufactured piece will be

* D. N. Chorafas, *Statistical Processes and Reliability Engineering* (Princeton, N.J.: D. Van Nostrand Co., 1960).

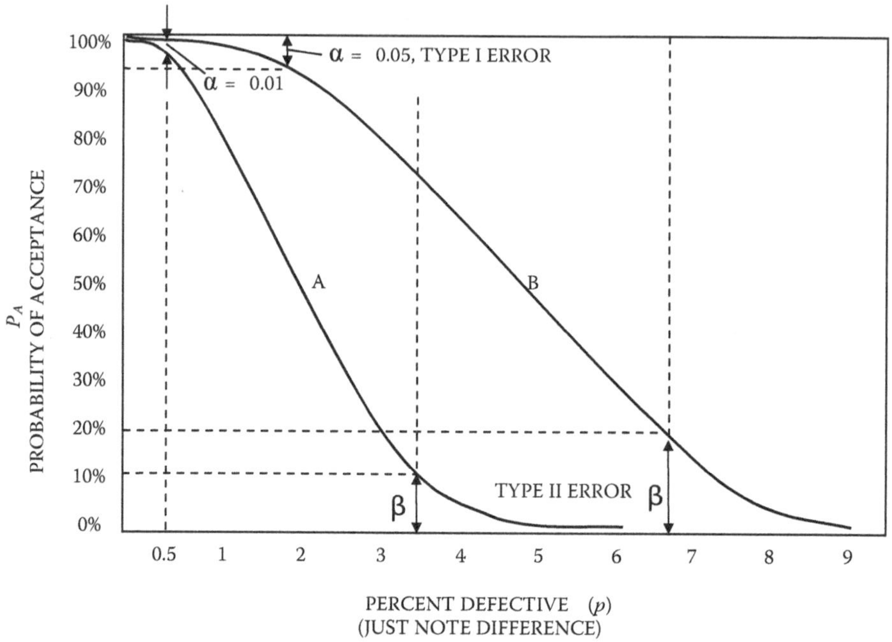

Figure 6.2 Operating characteristics curves for sampling plans.

rejected even though it conforms to tolerances or, in the field of finance, that a loan will not be given to a borrower who has good credit because this is not apparent from his or her documentation.

The use of sampling plans is a powerful statistical tool with a wide range of applications. It is essential that persons familiar with statistical sampling techniques be involved in developing IT auditing procedures, so that the results provide adequate assurance to those who receive them. Statistical verification through sampling is a straightforward activity, once one knows how to do it. It is a discipline well established in manufacturing, and it has found its way into the banking industry. For instance, the performance of the traditional trust-vault count consists of five basic components:

- Selecting securities to be counted by sampling
- Establishing and maintaining vault control
- Physically counting securities selected
- Researching differences, if any
- Evaluating sample results to reach a decision

Statistical verification provides better, more dependable results than 100 percent inspection, despite the possibility of a Type I error (the probability of rejecting a good risk) or a Type II error (the probability of accepting a bad risk). The decision to use audit procedures based on sampling is managerial, and in this particular case, it rests on the shoulders of the audit committee. As a matter of fact, the use of statistics in all types of investigation, examination, and audit provides the internal audit department with an important means of analysis not only in IT matters, but in all of its activities. The traditional audit, which is basically accounting oriented, can make as much use of statistics as a technology audit does.

In addition to knowledge of statistical analysis and sampling methods, the effective IT auditor must have knowledge in areas such as cost accounting, qualitative inference, and quantitative methods as well as economics, return on investment, and managerial finance. Such skills should be given due weight in the selection, training, and know-how of all internal auditors.

6.9 Auditing IT's Legal Risk

The origins of legal risk are infinite, and each case has its own characteristics. Most legal risks are connected either to current mistakes or to errors of the past that are amplified over time. Legal risk is an operational risk that can grow by leaps and bounds.

Globalization and deregulation have significantly increased legal risk. Experts say that many of the current transnational agreements will not stand if tested in court. If so, this will have disastrous effects on business confidence, and confidence is at the heart of the financial system. This is important to a discussion of IT audit because technical glitches and diverse interpretations of signed contracts in different jurisdictions are an integral part of legal risk. The untested acceptance of IT vendor or insourcer promises can lead to cases being brought to court. This is further promoted by the fact that, in many instances, legal risk is not an exceptional event but, rather, the means for solving differences of opinions regarding IT contracts.

Existing evidence suggests that legal risk often amplifies other risks, something that many people and companies fail to appreciate. With litigation, the guiding principle should be that, unless you are getting into it with thorough knowledge of the law *and* your eyes wide open, it is not the right process for you. On the other hand, it may be forced upon you, and therefore you must be ready for it.

The Y2K (Year 2000) problem of the late 1990s was a major source of litigation in the area of technology risk. While original projections for Y2K legal costs proved to be exaggerated—lawyers' fees for Y2K were projected to exceed $1 trillion—the ingredients for big legal cases were present, and many experts spoke of "a decades-long litigation against technology companies."

In the late 1990s, Andrew Grove, then Intel's chairman, and many other experts predicted that "the United States will be tied down in a sea of litigation, and Y2K problems will put the asbestos litigation to shame." Lawyers on both sides of the issue were attending seminars on how to bring and defend Y2K cases. In fact, some cognizant people predicted that there would be more lawyer-driven cases than customer-driven legal actions.

It did not happen that way because the U.S. Congress took the right step at the right time, tapering off the potential fallout from Y2K litigation. This relegated to second and third place an expected torrent of breach-of-contract suits against corporate officers of publicly quoted companies. It also put off a projected third wave of litigation expected to involve insurance firms, with defendants seeking to force their insurers to cover

- Legal fees and
- Runaway damages.

Today, Internet-related uses and abuses are the source of many technology-oriented legal challenges. One example is *cyber-squatting*, where the name of a person or business is registered as an Internet domain name by someone who has no connection with the person or business. This practice of warehousing domain names for sale can be very profitable. Another legal risk with the Internet is infringement of copyright law, whether accidental or voluntary.

Many experts believe that the threat to copyright on the Internet has not yet been properly addressed, and the potential threat of legal action for copyright infringement is greater today than ever before. This impacts on the work of IT auditors, who should account for the fact that the Internet has made it possible to replicate and distribute online multiple copies of copyrighted material to any number of companies and people around the world.

- In the past, typical infringements on the Internet tended to focus on copying of information or of software.
- More recently, Internet-connected legal actions in the United States underline the extent to which copyright infringement is rapidly becoming a serious concern for all industries.

IT auditors should also be aware of legal actions originating from electronic mail. A decade has passed since the week of July 14, 1997, when a pace-setting libel judgment in Britain was delivered against the insurer Norwich Union. This was the first case in which a British company received damages for an e-mail libel; the High Court ordered Norwich Union to pay £450,000 ($900,000) in damages and costs to Western Provident Association. The reason for this court action was based on e-mail messages that were written by Norwich Union staff spreading unfounded rumors about their business rival. These messages were posted on Norwich Union's internal system and ultimately reached brokers and clients.* The

* *Lloyds List*, July 25, 1997.

ruling spread the message that, in the eyes of the law, anyone communicating or disseminating information on the Internet is deemed to be *publishing.*

- Both companies and individuals using the Internet are becoming exposed to libel and defamation risks as electronic publishers.
- This legal risk is growing. Previously, such cases (wherever they existed) faced only the traditional civil responsibilities of the media industry.

At the root of the problem is the fact that people and companies tend to be rather casual in their use of e-mail compared with other forms of publication. They operate under the mistaken belief that e-mail messages disappear after they are sent. To the contrary, internal messages between friends and colleagues can be spread across many organizations in just a few hours or a few days.

Chapter 7

Strategic IT Auditing: A Case Study

7.1 Goal of a Strategic Audit

This is a real-life case study based on the strategic audit of a credit institution's information technology, done at the request of the chairman and CEO and of the board. The IT audit was part of an effort to put a system in place that would facilitate effective implementation of the bank's strategic plan and position the institution against market forces.

The fact that chief executives and members of the board ask for independent opinions about the firm's IT is good news for business at large. The way an article in the *Financial Times* had it, industry research suggests that at least 70 percent of projects involving implementation of new information technology systems run into problems, and end up delivering fewer benefits than expected, because top management takes a hands-off attitude. This is happening because too many initiatives become a sad compromise that

- Delivers a "little more automation" or
- Does not even come close to a truly innovative solution.

The rules governing a sound project management are known, but they are not applied. As the *Financial Times* article states, real collaboration between stakeholders and technologists is the only way to manage an ambitious, complex, and demanding IT project.* To this should be added the need for board members and CEOs to be in charge—and, as the foregoing references suggest, a first-class tool for doing so is an independent IT audit.

A crucial part of this IT audit was to develop an understanding of the institution's culture, which required a significant number of personal meetings with cognizant executives. Such working meetings helped to identify a number of problems and, therefore, of opportunities for corrective action. The report prepared for members of the board, the CEO, and his immediate assistants was organized into four parts, each focusing on a specific topic.

- The first provided a strategic perspective of the role IT should be playing and of the IT risks confronting the bank.
- The next two brought to management's attention the findings of the audit, including acts of insourcers (the theme of this chapter).
- Per the CEO's request, the fourth part contained the recommendations on restructuring and reorientation of the bank's IT (see Chapter 8).

The point made in the first and fourth parts is that a changing market orientation requires constant reassessment and possible recasting of strategic plans and, therefore, of IT's goals. The chief information officer must be alert to the impact of changes in the strategic plan on operations under his authority and be ready to revamp his or her own plan of action.

The recommendations advanced by this strategic IT audit centered on necessary revamping of the institution's information technology and, most importantly, on the orientation and management of its projects. The audit also outlined the milestones characterizing the major job of restructuring and reorienting IT operations, which it characterized as an urgent and complex mission.

IT's reorganization and rationalization was a complex issue because the obsolete current applications software had brought to a virtual standstill the business initiatives taken by practically all departments of the bank. The obsolete software also made it impossible to manage the client base. The external IT auditor identified the salient problem confronting the board members and senior executives.

The general conclusion was that the board members and the CEO could not afford to take lightly the need for major changes in IT, and neither could the bank afford to stay put with its current medieval IT approach. Part of the audit addressed specific questions the auditor was asked to examine, such as the requests to determine whether

- System controls were adequate to ensure the integrity of databased information (They were not. The importance of databases under the corporate memory facility is discussed in Chapter 12.),

* *Financial Times*, October 17, 2007.

- The processing procedures (most of them still being batch) could be considered as adequate, and
- The applications' documentation was dependable. (It was found to be either nonexistent or incomplete.)

When commissioning the study, the CEO also asked the IT auditor to evaluate the administrative procedures used to request new applications, and to determine how effectively these applications were screened by the CIO. For his part, the external IT auditor asked the board to notify all bank executives that they must collaborate with the IT auditor. (Indeed the collaboration of all operating departments proved to be perfect.) The external expert also asked for (and obtained) access to previous audits and to information on changes to the IT system since the last audit. Questions posed to operating executives included:

- Are they satisfied by the IT support they are currently obtaining?
- Is IT support covering all of the bank's strategic areas of operations?
- Do they find the current use of computers and communications to be cost effective?
- Would they like to have expert systems and agents (see Chapter 12) to help them in their daily work?

A long list of personal interviews was needed to respond to these and other queries, because audit reports should never be based on hearsay. They should be factual and fully documented through personal responses. And while all pertinent information must be included, only points based on substantiated fact should be reported. Rumors and guesses have no place in an audit. A good rule to work with is: "If you cannot prove it, do not say it."

Audit practices themselves came under the magnifying glass. One of the problems in past internal IT audits was that the objectives were so broad and general that they did not lead to applicable audit results. Another problem was that specific priorities were not observed. Auditing security, for example, was given only lip service (see Chapter 11). The external auditor explained that while computers and communications are valuable tools of banking, they are also potentially weak points for attacks on privacy and security.

Other questions discussed in management meetings and end-user interviews were report-distribution procedures; the timeliness and accuracy of outputs in regard to their final use; and postmortem walk-throughs to analyze critical aspects of each application and of specific topics, some of which concerned regular use and others an exceptional use.

Still, of all the challenges confronting the IT audit, the most controversial has been that of examining whether IT policy and IT investments did or did not provide any support to the bank's strategic planning. As in the majority of similar cases, the challenge was both cultural and political (see Chapter 6).

On the cultural side, not every board member or senior executive appreciated that banking has come to the point where evaluation of principles, goals, investments, abilities, and achievements of the IT department is very important to the whole institution's survival. On the political side, there was resistance in accepting that an evaluation of the CIO and his assistants was to be based on how well their deliverables responded to the following queries:

- How are the strategic and tactical needs of the bank being met?
- Have the IT personnel been trained in new technology to do a first-class job now and in the future?
- What is the quality of the analysis and the programming tools the bank is using? Of the equipment?
- What is the return on investment of IT? Are there major exceptions to a ROI of at least 20 percent per year that should be corrected?

Additionally, it had to be explained that the coordination between strategic planning and information technology should reflect both market forces and the bank's goals, providing the answers to such questions as: Are all operations supported by advanced technology as they should be? Are the various IT services being effectively managed from the end user's perspective?

In conclusion, the competitive advantage of an external audit, like the one in the background of this discussion, is the independence of opinion that it provides. Precisely for this reason, the board gave the IT auditor the needed latitude to properly examine all areas of information technology and of strategic planning, including their influence on the organization at large. But internal political clans came into action at the very moment it became evident that *this* IT audit was not going to rubber stamp what the IT department was doing.

7.2 Strategic Analysis of the Bank's Business

Starting with the fundamentals, no strategic plan will be worthwhile unless it answers, in the best possible way, top management's image of the enterprise, focusing on execution of the goals the board sets forward. Along this frame of reference, the first major questions the IT auditor posed to the board were as follows:

- What is the bank's current position?
- Where would management like it to be?

Positioning the bank is the responsibility of the board, the CEO, and senior management. The strategic IT auditor's advice was that positioning against market forces should target not just the current situation, but also the forces that will come into play in the near future. This was particularly relevant in this case because the country in which this bank operated was confronted with two business plans at the government level:

- Plan A: Join the European Union (EU)
- Plan B: If this does not happen through full membership, consider how the bank should prepare for some sort of an accommodation, for instance, between the EU and Switzerland.

For the CEO and the board, either alternative meant a new kind of competition from the banking world outside the country's current status quo. Plan "A" would have brought into play not only the more aggressive European banks, but also higher-technology American banks with operations in the EU.

One of the strategic challenges under both hypotheses was a takeover by a foreign institution. Assuming that the bank whose IT was being audited would like to maintain its independence, one of the scenarios this study briefly considered was *what if* its immediate competitor fell under foreign control. (A more detailed study had to be undertaken by the bank's strategic planning department. Strategic planning also had to work together with marketing to focus on the stratification of the bank's client population according to Pareto's Law.*)

Because the foreign credit institutions most likely to enter the audited bank's market for financial services would be some of what the CEO called "the big boys," management had an interest in forging alliances *not* with money-center banks but with other medium-sized institutions, particularly the federations of small European banks. These were, for instance: in Germany, Kredit Genossenschaften and Raiffeisen Banken or the Sparkassen; in Holland, Rabobank (agricultural banks); in Austria, Raiffeisenkassen; and so on.

An idea about alliances was discussed with the CEO and members of the board, involving the European postal banks, which have taken a new and higher level standing since the privatization of telecommunications. The underlying concept of these suggestions was that retail banking could be promoted through a two-way approach aiming to capitalize on:

- The tourist trade, which was an important income source for the audited bank's resident country
- The bank's aim to expand abroad through its overseas division, a move that made sense only as a deal between equals

As the CEO stated, his aim was "the evolution of his institution's banking services from retail banking to more sophisticated financial products." In fact, the bank had started to move in that direction with life insurance and with its highly profitable real estate loans subsidiary.

---

* D. N. Chorafas, *Strategic Business Planning for Accountants: Methods, Tools and Case Studies* (London: Butterworth-Heinemann, 2007).

From the viewpoint of potential counterparties, when European popular banks, agricultural banks, and savings banks see their higher-net-worth customers move part of their assets to Switzerland or Luxembourg, they know that they lose control of these assets. As the number of offshores multiplies, an alliance with the audited bank might assure them of retaining partial control of the funds through joint management. Other product lines that the strategic planning department was studying, and that also needed IT support, included

- Private banking, targeted by the bank's overseas subsidiary but not yet exploited inland
- Derivative financial instruments, a market that the bank contemplated entering but rejected because current technology did not permit effective risk management

Not only had risk management been a major preoccupation of the governor of the central bank where the audited institution was resident, but also its CEO appreciated that it is better not to enter any new business, particularly in derivatives, if the bank does not have a tier-1 risk-control system. Indeed, the audit identified the bank's three greatest weaknesses.

1. The bank's No. 1 weakness was its *lag in information technology.*
2. The bank's No. 2 weakness was seen as *risk management.*

The strategic choice of the No. 1 and No. 2 salient problems was defined in consultation with the CEO halfway through the IT audit. This choice was based on the fact that, for both the bank and its clients, a complete portfolio of financial products should address all four investment domains identified in Figure 7.1. At the same time, however, a sophisticated level of information technology is indispensable for success in the more sophisticated and exposed lines of activity.

- IT alone will not guarantee effective risk control, but
- The lack of high-technology support will see to it that the law of unwanted consequences comes into play.

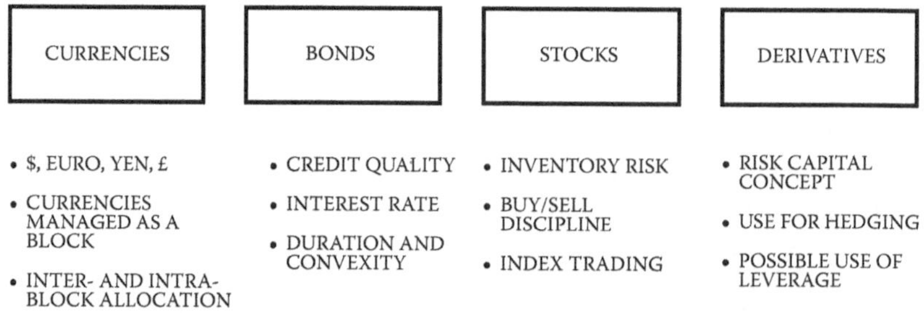

Figure 7.1 The top risk factors affecting an investment portfolio.

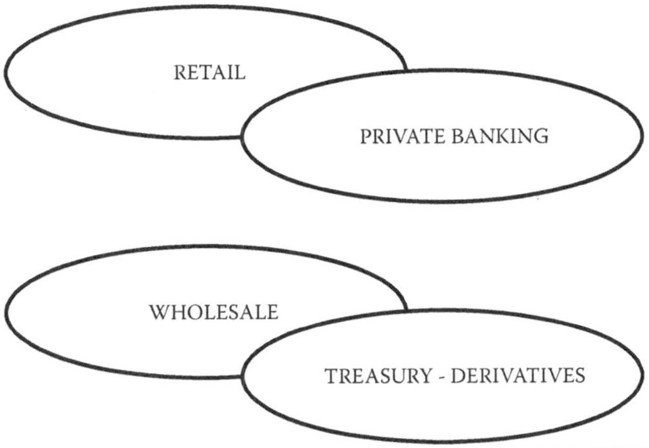

Figure 7.2 Strategic planning should avoid fuzzy answers to the question: "what sort of bank?"

The members of the board were reminded of a statement by Walter Wriston, the former chairman of Citibank, who once said: "Information about money is as important as money itself." Financial products and services, as well as able management of the client base, must be planned, and the same is true of supporting information technology.

The strategic audit documented why *technology planning* should be part of the institution's strategic planning, rather than being a sort of day-to-day IT administration. The IT auditor also advised that, prior to establishing an IT policy, strategic planning should be requested by the board to provide a factual answer to the question: "What sort of bank should we be?" The board was then asked to deliberate over the answer and either confirm or modify it.

Fuzzy answers to the query about the bank's future are not welcome. Choices and courses of action should be clearly stated; business opportunities and risks must be outlined; and synergies between different product lines should be exploited, as suggested in Figure 7.2.

3. The bank's No. 3 weakness was its *lack of profit centers* (see Chapter 8).

This was true of both its customer-oriented operational activities as well as its support services. The external IT auditor presented evidence that, among top-tier banks, every operation is a profit center, whether the fees come by billing customers, hence from the market, or billing internally the operating departments and subsidiaries.

If IT were a profit center, *then* it would have been more cost conscious and more market sensitive. The previous statement came as a response to a query by senior management: Can technology help to contain costs? *If* IT cannot contain its own

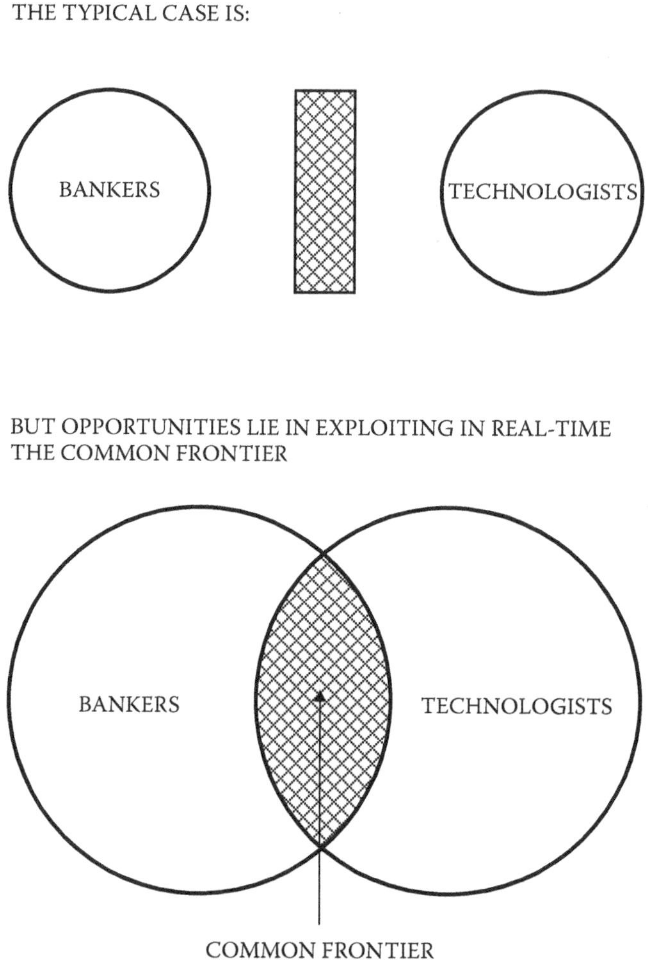

Figure 7.3 The best results are obtained in cases where banking and technology have merged.

costs and show a return on investment, *then* it cannot contain costs in the other departments.

The keyword is synergy. In the Paleolithic age of information technology, IT operations were introverted. The bankers and the technologists were separated by a wall, as shown in the upper half of Figure 7.3. That is what *used to be*, but things have changed. In the better managed institutions, bankers and technologists work closely together along their common frontier (second half of Figure 7.3). At a time when innovation in banking products is king, this is the only reasonable and logical answer.

7.3 Snapshot of IT's Status Quo

As Sections 1 and 2 have explained, the concepts defining a modern bank's operations are indivisible from the development and use of advanced technology. With financial products increasingly becoming high tech, banking products and services that are short of sophisticated software cost too much and have only elementary market appeal. Moreover, if the banking products lack the flexibility provided by new technology, then

- The bank's marketing plans risk being half-baked, and
- Risk management remains substandard, as it cannot be exercised in a comprehensive way in a bankwide sense without the help of high tech.

In a nutshell, this is the conclusion that was provided to the board of the audited bank (for a constructive view, see Chapter 8). The IT auditor also pressed the point that there is no standard answer on how much money IT should cost. The money that banks allocate to information technology varies significantly, from about 6 percent of the noninterest budget to 15 percent or more.

The external IT auditor also noted that the higher level of IT expenditures is closely tied to four criteria that must always be present prior to authorizing an IT budget. To its misfortune, the audited bank lacked every one of them.

1. A guaranteed return-on-investment (ROI) for IT expenditures (Chapter 9)

CEOs who are computer-literate, and who seek results rather than glamour, demand answers prior to proceeding with budgetary approval—and the answer of the CIO must be factual. There was nothing like that at the audited bank. The concept of ROI for IT expenditures was not even present.

2. A very fast time to deliver sophisticated software products

This culture of fast delivery of applications software was totally alien to the bank's IT operations. The concept of delivering software in a matter of two days, a couple of weeks, or at maximum two or three months was absent; typical timetables were at the level of two to three years at best (a situation still encountered in many cases).

3. Increasing use of high tech in software, like knowledge-engineering artifacts

The bank did not have even one operating expert system; indeed, the concept of an expert system was unknown. Worse still, there was no will among the IT department's top brass to even consider knowledge engineering. Instead, everything was in so-called legacy IT, which had been dropped by tier-1 banks in favor of highly competitive systems solutions in the late 1990s.

4. Effective distribution of IT support to the end-user level, with the computer center acting as a large database backup and as a communications switch

This notion, too, was absent. Indeed, the lack of a corporate database was a glaring weakness of the bank's IT, and a significant portion of the complaints formulated by end users during the interviews focused on the fact that IT operations were still based on old-style file management.

Additionally, instead of providing end users with interactive access to databases, the audited bank was still printing an inordinate amount of paper reports whose supposed users had no time to read. This was a legacy of a bureaucratic IT environment that spent too much money on sundry items. Other failures were unearthed while auditing the files of

- Hardware procurement,
- Software procurement, and
- In-house software development.

Decisions were taken without adequately analyzing whether new expenditures made sense, without the benefit of evaluating the cost effectiveness of alternatives, and without concern for end users' needs or for cost control. Each of these failures translated to poor performance and major budgetary overruns.

What these references tell to the trained eye is that the audited bank was *not* in charge of its technology. Because the concept of cost efficiency was alien to the bank's IT people—and because these people had their backs covered by internal politics—there was no drive to yield the greatest efficiency in relation to the incurred cost. Yet, as stated in an old adage, economy does not consist of hiding a piece of coal, but of effectively using the heat while it burns. That is a fine criterion for judging whether a company (or a person) is in charge of what happens. The implementation of cost-effective solutions should be examined by considering their rationale, which is sometimes unclear or misunderstood. As the IT auditor's report stated:

- The option to accept or reject development work, new equipment, or other expenditures is open *before* commitment is made.
- After commitment, the role of cost control is to measure the money spent and the derived benefit, bringing the result to management's attention.

Being in charge of an IT or any other project requires monitoring and measurement of resources committed as well as evaluation of their costs compared with the derived benefit from the completion of the project. Projects become (and remain) useful if there is a surplus of value over cost, and it is to this end that the discipline of cost effectiveness has grown and is used today.

When the management of IT, or any other operation, is not in control, even aggressive cost cutting may be ineffectual. Prior to Chrysler's sale to a private equity firm, the company had sharply cut costs on new-car development. Therefore, it could not use innovation to attract clients. Faced with stiff competition, it had to rely on models that were visibly aged and sales suffered. The same principle of management control applies in banking, in technology, and in any other business where innovation is king.

7.4 What Bank Executives Thought of IT Support They Received

The principle guiding every audit is that both good news and bad news should be reported to top management, because both are important. During the working meetings held with bank executives, one of them said: "When you love somebody you don't just tell him nice things," and he was perfectly right.

In an IT audit, bad news comes from both technical findings and complaints. In this case, the most consistent complaint was that practically every department's operations were greatly handicapped because of a lack of information technology support. The only (and evident) exception to this statement were remarks made by the IT people, who also thought the IT budget was not enough. True enough.

- If a company underfinances its IT operations, it cannot expect to get significant results.
- But throwing money at the problem does not solve it. If anything, it makes it worse.

Judging from the unhappiness of staff and line executives regarding the technology support they had been receiving, throwing money at the problems was exactly what the bank was doing with its information technology budget. Not surprisingly, it got no results. (More on the technical aspects of what was wrong with IT is presented in the following sections.)

This particular institution was one of many I have audited where IT was endowed with a rich budget, but the deliverables were poor. Two of the board members had seen this, and they suggested that their bank could not become a low-cost producer and distributor of financial services *if* the Gordian knot of IT was not cut. Moreover, participants in the first working meeting, and those that followed, pressed the point that lack of IT support to the bank's managers and professionals reduced their productivity and made their work less effective. It also made it very difficult to conceptualize risks assumed with new financial products. Here are some of the remarks that were heard:

- "There is nothing as distressing as losing the bank's money on stillborn projects."
- "Investing involves decision making under uncertainty, and we need tools to analyze risk and return."

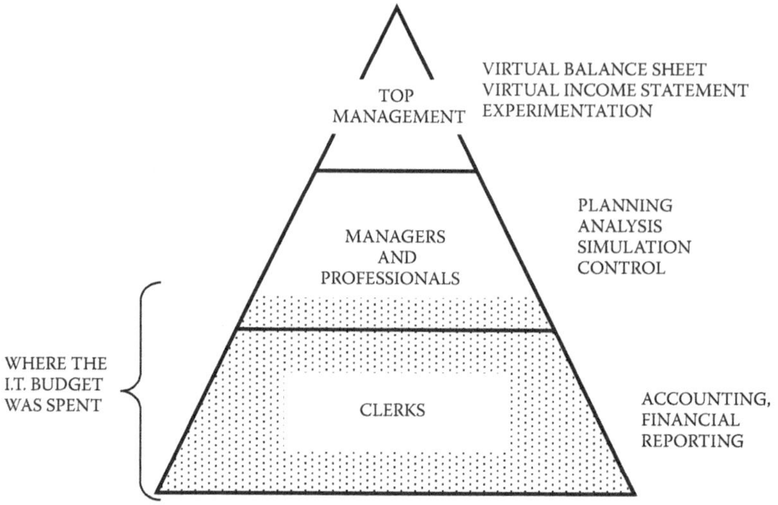

Figure 7.4 Knowledge and information requirements are deterministic at the bottom, but stochastic and possibilistic at the top.

- "If all uncertainty is eliminated, we have no opportunity; hence we need analytics to support our study."
- "If no uncertainty is eliminated, we have only risk."

The more versatile managers and professionals asked for algorithms and models to be used for purposes of analysis, evaluation, and experimentation—prior to making commitments as well as postmortem. Figure 7.4 explains the background of this complaint. The bulk of the IT budget was spent on clerical and administrative functions, while front-desk professionals and most managers were thirsty for IT support.

Headlines at the right-hand side of Figure 7.4 suggest the type of IT support that senior managers wanted but did not get. The sophisticated decision systems needed in modern banking must be tuned to respond to an unstructured, ad hoc information environment. In this case, however (as in many others I have found in my professional practice), the bank's IT resources were some light years from that goal:

While the clerical level absorbed an inordinate part of the IT budget, the more highly paid individuals were starved of IT assistance. In contrast, a modern bank's IT solution sees to it that clerical duties should not receive more than 35 percent of the IT budget, with 30 percent being the next goal. The rest of the IT budget should target the support provided to professionals and senior management. During the audit, many executives stated that

- IT is totally absent from their domain of activity, and
- The absence of IT complicates their task while reducing the effectiveness of their mission.

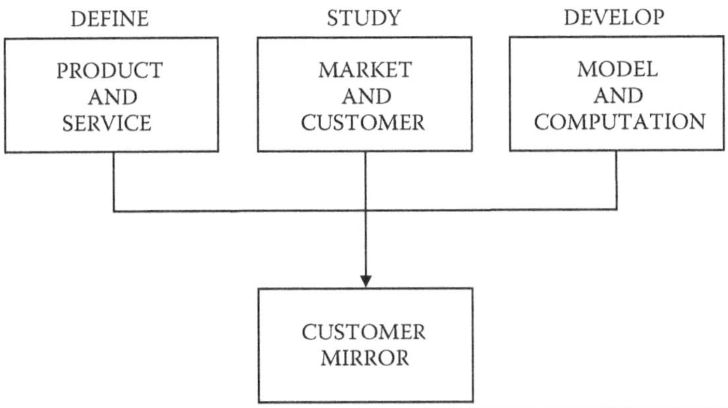

Figure 7.5 Modules contributing to the evaluation of customer profitability.

At the branch-office and head-office levels, IT support to managers and professionals was defective, as attested by an often-heard statement: "We have lots of data, but no information." Said the director of asset management: "Our portfolio has doubled in three years. Therefore, we have lots of IT requirements, but we cannot even retrieve dependable data from the files." Another executive suggested: "When the central bank's inspectors come, we have to retrieve most information manually." The point was as well made that

- The bank could not answer requirements by its more sophisticated customers without changing its current computer culture, and
- Under current IT conditions, even the skills of some of its key personnel risked degradation because there was little by way of computer-based support.

Time and again, interviewed executives stated that they badly needed interactive customer-centered services and a customer mirror to help in their efforts to evaluate customer profitability. Figure 7.5 presents the main components of a customer mirror, an example of what this requirement means in practical terms. Another point raised by the CEO and members of his staff concerned the containment of costs, as costs tended to rise year after year.

Closely connected to this subject of rising costs was the broader issue of human resources development and productivity improvements associated with managers, professionals, and clerks. In this matter, the IT audit found good news and bad news. The good news was that, with the exception of IT, the bank's employees had a fairly good background and understanding of their work. The bad news was that personnel costs were rising. Hence the CEO had a double problem:

- Technical and
- Cultural.

A couple of the directors said that a change in employment conditions was not in the cards because of resistance by labor unions. However, a discussion with union leaders gave evidence that they were very cooperative in cultural change and in restructuring, *if* this meant upgrading personnel skills. In other countries, too, there are tough labor unions, but a personnel development strategy makes it possible to establish a collaboration that is beneficial to all parties.

7.5 High Back-Office Costs, Low Marketing Punch, and Treasury Department Woes

A direct result of IT's failure to answer the requirements at headquarters, regional, and branch levels was that back-office expenses had skyrocketed. According to statistics obtained during the audit, the back-office to front-desk ratio in personnel requirements stood slightly over 2.1. Other banks had reduced this ratio significantly, and they had done so through technology. What this meant was that, despite all of the IT money spent on clerical work, not only were a great many back-office chores not yet automated, but the major cost items themselves also were not followed individually. Costs were booming because

- The organizational work was wanting, and
- IT depended too much on batch operations.

For starters, one of the reasons banks fall behind in IT-based restructuring of their back office is that computer-based approaches are done piecemeal, without a holistic system view. This impacts all the way from data capture (see Chapter 6) to processing, databasing, and reporting. In the case of the audited bank, both front desk and back office suffered from inadequate technology. In contrast, this is changing in other institutions. As a recent study has found, over the next few years, between 40 to 60 percent of fund managers will

- Change their IT and
- Reengineer their back office.

In the bank whose information technology was audited—apart from the back-office managers in the branches and administrative director at headquarters, who were concerned about errors, call overs, and some unbalanced accounts—an executive who claimed that his requests for information technology support were never answered was the marketing director.

The concept of providing marketing skills to subsidiaries through a headquarters unit was good and necessary. But this operation had not been so effective because it was not linked online to correspondent marketing functions at major branch offices. The branch manager was supposed to spend some of his time on marketing without being effectively assisted by a properly designed IT system, which permits marketing action without inordinate spoilage of time, including:

- Market segmentation
- Customer profiling
- Follow-ups on marketing results

Whatever little was available in terms of marketing software was obsolete. Some new marketing routines had been developed, but old and new approaches to exploitation of client information resided in two different machines and would not handshake. (The audited bank's database problems are discussed in Section 7.)

Similar statements about lack of appropriate IT support were made by the bank's treasurer. Much of his operation was still manual, even though packages providing sophisticated computer assistance to treasury duties were readily available in the market. "When I ask a query about exposure in currency options and forex forwards, I want an answer in 5 seconds, not in 5 hours," said the treasurer, underlining the need for *real-time response*. Correctly, he also added that derivatives are a game of risk, and he who manages risk in real-time wins.

Had the treasury department asked for an IT solution to effectively serve its needs? Had it described what it wanted in black and white? "Yes!" said the treasurer. "I was told in the next couple of years, but since then two years have passed by, and nothing has been done." A major worry in his mind was the lack of real-time risk control. He put it simply: "If there is no risk management, there may be no bank," adding that:

- Half computer-based/half manual systems provide no way to control exposure.
- With no risk management effectively supported through real time, the bank was sailing without a compass.

The IT audit also made the reference that it was quite interesting that the issue of real-time risk management had gained a great deal of support among staff and line. The treasurer had also asked for *simulators* to help with marking-to-model inventoried positions, and for a couple of *rocket scientists* to develop new models as well as expert systems. He had gotten neither.

For his part, the chief credit officer said that, some time ago, a study was undertaken at headquarters to speed up credit appraisal through computer support. This involved analyzing and clearing loan requests as well as their subsequent administration. Credit management had also asked IT for models to assist in experimentation on interest rates, credit rating, and exchange control. This was an excellent opportunity for IT to make a move into the future, but it did not.

"Technology is the crux of the problem. Therefore, we have been talking to the computer people to proceed with this application, but they have their priorities. This delay costs money to the bank," said the chief credit officer. Another of his priorities had been some form of computer-based securities documentation, particularly in connection with pledges and policy guarantees, as most of what was available was on paper. "Paper makes it difficult to effectively manage credit risk," the chief credit officer pointed out.

A similar remark was made about *compliance* (see Chapter 12) by the audit department, which was unhappy about the IT facilities put at its disposal. The chief auditor also noted that properly used technology significantly increases the bandwidth of the auditor's reach without increasing auditing costs because of its impact on the auditor's productivity.

The external auditor's conclusion was that, since practically every bank executive and professional being interviewed complained and nobody was found to be happy, something was wrong with IT. The more the audit progressed, the more it became evident that—while the bank had spent lots of money on obsolete and ineffectual IT, and a radical change in policy implied writing off much of this investment—failing to act and implement change could be more costly by an order of magnitude.

7.6 Conversion Problems Created by Legacy IT

Giving the benefit of the doubt to the people running the audited IT operations, the external IT expert hypothesized that at least some of the current problems were due to legacy IT hangovers. As happens with so many audits, there could be several reasons why previous IT managements had limited the reach of the current one.

In a snapshot, the audited bank first started with computers in 1962 when it installed a small mainframe to do accounting, current accounts, and savings, all in batch mode. Several of these very old programs—maintained by people who were born several years after they were written—were still alive at IT audit time, although it was planned to terminate them within the next few months (a very optimistic estimate).

During the 1960s, 1970s, and 1980s, the bank operated an increased configuration of newer versions of the old machines. Only in the late 1980s did it transfer its application to new equipment. Like practically all transfers of applications software from "this" to "that" hardware, this job was done in a rush, and

- It contributed nothing to the quality and functionality of the programs; to the contrary,
- It added to costs and inefficiencies, as software translation from one machine to another always does.

Having learned no lesson from this experience, seven years down the line, a new computer system was installed, and the legacy programs were reconverted at great cost with plenty of bugs to yet another operating system.

- This clearly proved to be a mistake.
- It is one of the reasons for the IT audit.

Deceived by the results of the two applications software conversions, IT management started a new applications development project that was still far from completion when the audit took place. Because the auditing of this project included some confidential information, the findings cannot be discussed in detail. What can be said is that

- Its progress was too slow, and
- The adopted approach was, at best, ineffectual.

Furthermore, the IT audit documented that the new project did not make much sense; its goals were too limited; it had been advancing at a snail's pace; and its documentation was awfully incomplete. For these reasons, the external expert suggested that the project should be killed immediately. However, the management of IT was a protected species, and so were its projects.

In connection with the more recent decisions made prior to the IT audit, it was deemed to be more important to altogether change the software by purchasing a package. However, as it frequently (but wrongly) happens with purchased software, the IT people thought that they should "improve" this package. Not unexpectedly, the "improvement" ran into major difficulties.

This, too, was a very poor IT decision. Prior to the audit, package "improvements" had cost over 100 man-years spent to rediscover the wheel and make it less round. Skill, budget, and time could have been used in a much better way by fixing some gaping holes in internal procedures and plenty of other smaller but urgent improvements (more on this later).

Because the CEO of the audited bank had doubts about where the package "improvements" were going and what could be expected from them, a consultancy had been asked to study the state of this IT project a couple of years prior to the audit. In its recommendations, the consultancy suggested

- A minor change in IT structure and
- The institution of a steering committee (another IT legacy).

The external IT auditor was most surprised that, in the late 1990s, the consultancy advised instituting a steering committee, because steering committees had fallen out of favor in the banking industry more than two decades earlier. For the first 20 years of computers in banking (1955–1975), steering committees served a purpose, given that centralization of what was then electronic data processing (EDP) operations obliged many departments to cooperate in a way they had never done before. However, by 1972, minicomputers provided the possibility for system design based on distributed data processing (DDP), with each department practically having under its authority its own IT resources. With decentralization of processing as well as the advent of corporate databases and of X.25 (packet switching) communications—where the network became the Christmas tree of computing resources—the need for steering committees waned.*

Apart from all this, the audited bank had adopted a poor practice with its steering committee because the user departments were poorly represented, and where such representatives existed, they were people with lower standing in the organization, and therefore with little clout. Hence, it was not surprising that, as the IT audit revealed, the bank's steering committee never really functioned as intended.

What had happened, in fact, was that the steering committee had become a center of company politics, fencing off requests for IT services. Many senior bank executives complained during the IT audit that, in the time since the formation of the steering committee, the IT deliverables were neither on-time nor of acceptable quality, but they were unable to change this. Additionally, it was the steering committee's initiative to buy the aforementioned package and to allow the chosen commodity software to be steadily massaged—a wrongheaded policy that guaranteed that intended applications did not come onstream.

The independent expert advised that the time had come to dismantle the steering committee and, instead of spinning the IT department's wheels in rewriting the package, to pay attention to some more-pressing issues. There has been, for example, a decades-long discrepancy in accounting standards, organizational norms, and IT support between

- The financial group to which the bank belonged and
- The credit institution that was being audited.

The month for the bank closed on the 30/31 of each month, after which, with some delay, consolidated figures were available, although value adjustments were made quarterly, which is too sparse. In contrast, accounts for the Group were prepared (by the same IT center) only twice a year, a fact that Group executives found unacceptable but for which they were not ready to set up a fight.

- An old reason for such a discrepancy was the type of financial disclosure, but
- Its perpetuation provided precious little help to Group-level management planning and control.

* D. N. Chorafas and Heinrich Steinmann, *Intelligent Networks: Telecommunications Solutions for the 1990s* (Boca Raton, Fla.: CRC Press, 1990).

Back to the IT chores, another major weakness with the project in reference was its very long, always elastic implementation timetables. No attention was paid to the fact that interminable delays *effectively kill* a computer project, even if it is kept artificially alive by throwing money at it. Design review was still another issue totally missing from project management (see Chapter 2).

7.7 Database Culture and Software Development

When the early phase of the IT audit revealed that the bank had no database worth talking about, the external auditor asked the chief information officer and his people to comment on this situation. Their muddled answer was followed by a request for a factual and realistic evaluation of

- What is immediately needed in database support, and
- What size the database might become during the following five years, after end users get a taste of data mining.

The IT department had difficulties in answering these queries because it did not know how to size up the requirements of a new database structure. Its estimate was based on very elementary statistics, like the number of clients and the fact of having 2.28 accounts per client. The CIO said he could also offer statistics on accounting files, but since the IT operations were still under file management, this did not mean much.

The way things stood at IT audit's time, guesses had to be made about the online memory bandwidth necessary to accommodate all information elements regarding clients and accounts as well as trading activities and other professional requests. For clients and accounts, the CIO's opinion was that the database size would have to be about 450 percent bigger than what was then available, which proved to be a huge underestimate.

Using similar applications at tier-1 banks as a proxy, it was proven that online support for sophisticated banking products would require significant database bandwidth, plus storage for marketing and relationship banking. To keep costs lower, the installation of redundant arrays of independent risks was suggested rather than augmenting the size of the mainframe-based current solution.

Some people found excuses for the lack of data on which to base their estimates. "We have no clear bank strategy telling us where we are going in banking sector services," said the person who figured in the organization chart as database administrator, even if the bank had no database worth talking about. This statement was funny because one of the units under the CIO was called "IT Strategy," which is, incidentally, a function that does not belong there in the first place.

The IT auditor was puzzled that the information technology people did not see the lack of attention to a design (or at least projection) of a corporate database as being a major weakness of the bank's operational support. Therefore, we had to explain to the IT professionals that the database is a precious corporate resource, as precious as the money in the bank's vaults.

In fact, the audited bank provided an example of what happens when the concepts of the corporate database, and the fact that it is a major asset, are absent. Against all logic, crucial client information and accounts records were thrown away in what the audited bank's IT people called a "gradual roll-out." (I had seen this case only once before with the files of a U.S. company, but at least this was back in 1961.)

The external expert also noted that, despite all of the questions asked, it was not clear why IT management and the steering committee had permitted this to happen. At best, it demonstrated incompetence; at worst, it revealed a possible conflict of interest in keeping an obsolete system alive, whose limited storage capacity had led to throwing away important files.

This being the prevailing condition, the bank could make a virtue out of necessity by adopting the principle that its new database had to be projected from scratch. It had to be designed, the external expert suggested, as an object-oriented dynamic entity

- Accessed online by all authorized executives, professionals, and clients;
- Able to respond to ad hoc queries by users; and
- Enriched with knowledge artifacts to facilitate online search by end users and to guarantee accuracy in response.

Another salient cultural problem in the bank's IT requiring immediate action was that of breaking the software bottleneck created by slow delivery of applications. There was also a need to alter the fact that these applications were not precisely what end-users wanted. Because the release of new applications demands an order of magnitude more time than high tech could provide in software (which is a frequent happening), the users were disenchanted with IT.

The IT audit further documented that an inordinate amount of time was demanded by a relatively recent accounts and savings application. IT people characterized the delays as the result of a "strategic partnership with suppliers" (which merely meant that certain suppliers had looked at the bank as a cash cow), but this and plenty of other excuses fell on the external expert's deaf ears.

Finally, still another negative was the politicking and infighting in connection with IT goals, budgets, and deliverables. To cover their own shortcomings, members of the steering committee (see Section 6) and some of the senior IT people accused the users—managers and professionals of operating departments—as being "nonreceptive of IT" and "noncollaborating." The audit underlined that this was not true, and that politicking should stop immediately—through appropriate top management action if necessary.

7.8 Conclusion: A Lopsided System Design

It is a basic principle in engineering that, when a design looks awfully complex, it means that it has been badly studied. As a result, the projected solution is full of weaknesses and there exists a great number of potential failure points. Therefore, it should be brought back to the drawing board to be completely recast.

In one short paragraph, this statement characterizes quite accurately what had been happening at the audited bank in respect to its computers and communications solutions. It was not only a matter of very slow implementation timetables and of missing services that rang alarm bells. The whole system design was in shambles.

Chapter 6 has explained why the whole system concept has to be audited. Whatever the software development demerits might be, they are worsened by the almost steady jingling around of hardware boxes in an effort to fit the (by then obsolete) vendor's architecture. This led to a totally defective system solution that

- Lacked a unifying concept;
- Was overcentralized, with stiff hierarchies in contradiction to modern trends; and
- Required a lot of interfaces—a frequently encountered deficiency that results in a complex but weak overall system.

The IT audit provided the board and CEO with evidence that the only way out was to scrap the lengthy list of abbreviations that for years had been used to label diverse and incompatible computer components, and to start anew with a streamlined design and a quick implementation timetable. Provided this was authorized, the goal should be to produce a first-class integrated system within six months.

As evidence that this was doable, the external expert presented the case of the Swedish financial company SECURUM, which in September 1992 received from the government the mission to develop its IT from scratch and have it operational within five months. *It met the challenge.* Why should the audited bank put as its objective to do less than that?

With clear goals, good project management, and top skills, as well as the will to succeed, fast timetables were a realistic proposition. In any case, the current situation was no longer sustainable. The existing collection of incompatible platforms did not make sense not only systemwise, but many of them were also incapable of communicating with each other without extensive add-ons, which was a bad policy. To put it bluntly,

- No money should have been authorized for this mismatch, and
- No human resources should have been devoted to develop software for it.

It was indeed surprising that, since the time it was set up, the steering committee had not deliberated on these issues but had, instead, given the go-ahead for the prevailing system confusion. The most favorable opinion that could be ventured on the obtained results was that the whole bank suffered, and continued suffering, from that particular unfortunate decision.

Another puzzle with this steering committee's decision to go ahead with a lopsided system design was that there had not even been a half-decent system analysis of user requirements presented in written form. Yet, this is a most basic element of any sound IT project. Neither were computer-aided systems engineering (CASE) tools considered prior to the "go ahead."

Besides this, as the IT audit documented, money was thrown at the problem on a number of occasions, with no consideration given to return on investment (ROI). Even the consultancy, which proposed the establishment of a steering committee, had asked to spend more money "here" and "there" without any mention of ROI. In fact, in a couple of cases, the consultancy's memorandum stated that this was just "seed money" for "an excellent value idea" which, when audited, proved to be counterproductive. Contrary to the advice it had received from the consultancy, which was still standing, the audited bank had every interest in closing down this chapter of unsatisfactory approach to IT, and starting anew with an efficient and properly designed solution, under different management.

For reasons of cost effectiveness, this had to be a client-server system with modern state-of-the-art software purchased from a reliable vendor, thereby avoiding a repeat of the previous experience where programming products had to be massaged. In this case, and plenty of others, a most relevant a quotation can be found in a report by the U.S. State Department, in Washington D.C., which condemned its own computer system in no uncertain terms: "The outdated system's slow speed impedes the speed at which national security decisions can be made."

Why had things gone astray? Quoting from another report by a major New York institution: "The reason banks spend so heavily on IT is because they are trying to mate outdated, incompatible computer systems." As the client bank's IT audit pointed out: "The prevailing situation could be made worse by authorizing even more technological balkanization." Chapter 8 presents a constructive approach on how the audited bank could deal with its IT problems.

Chapter 8

A Constructive View: Suggestions for IT Restructuring

8.1 Capitalizing on the Strengths of the Institution

When the bank's board authorized the information technology (IT) audit, it also requested that the audit be followed by a constructive proposal on how to bring the bank's technology into the 21st century. Concomitant to this request was the CEO's demand that emphasis also be placed on internal control, organization, cost control, and return on investment in connection with information technology, with the ensuing advice to be focused on

- Exploiting the bank's strengths and
- Taking a strategic view rather than just emphasizing tactical improvements.

That the audited bank had strengths was beyond doubt; without them it would not have survived and prospered over the years. Its loans officers, investment advisors, and traders were in fact capitalizing on the bank's strengths and trying to starve its weaknesses, an effort in which they were handicapped by the institution's Paleolithic IT.

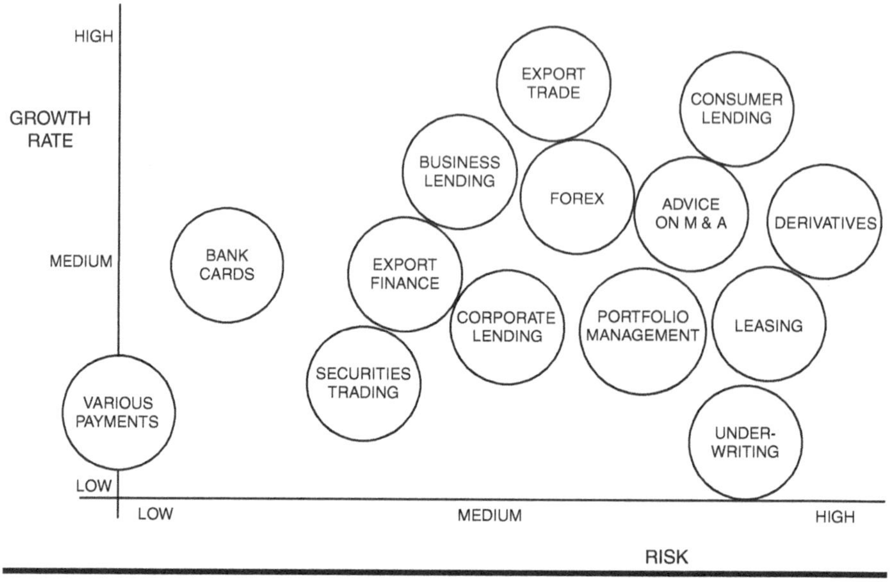

Figure 8.1 Growth and profitability of banking products as seen by asian banks.

The first strength evident to the external auditor was the bank's financial condition. Its core capital satisfied more than twice the capital requirements outlined by the Basel Committee. At IT audit time, the bank had a 16.28 percent ratio in contrast to the 8 percent minimum capital adequacy threshold, the balance being economic capital.*

The second strength was the bank's human capital. The evidence provided in Chapter 7 has shown that the audited bank's professionals and managers were above average, and some were excellent. The only exception to this statement was the IT people and the members of the steering committee.

The third strength was the bank's hold on the local retail market, characterized by a comfortable share of both corporate and personal accounts. Management, however, was becoming aware of the fact that the credit institution needed to use better technology to get more mileage in terms of market impact. Therefore, marketing was instructed to proceed with a reclassification of customer accounts and product lines along a dual frame of reference:

- Growth in business with each client
- Profitability of each counterparty and of each banking product

Figure 8.1 provides a snapshot of a preliminary study by the bank's strategic-planning group focusing on the growth rate and profitability of 14 different channels. As the central bank deregulated, new products were in demand, with derivatives

* D. N. Chorafas, *Economic Capital Allocation with Basle II: Cost and Benefit Analysis* (London: Butterworth-Heinemann, 2004).

starting to play a key role. Money was available for trading, as were investments in more lucrative (but also more risky) financial instruments than those the bank had classically promoted. At the same time, the board appreciated that

- Service and product innovation cannot be propelled until a thorough system of internal controls is in place, and
- A thorough effort to restructure the bank's technology, while moving it forward by 30 years, should be given priority over other goals.

The CEO stated that a first-class risk management system (see Section 7) was necessary to preserve the predominant perception in the local market that the institution was a secure and reliable banker. Therefore, he would not risk the bank's reputation by entering into ventures that the institution could not control.

One case that was contemplated called for vertically expanding the client base by increasing the range and content of financial instruments that the bank offers to the market. Responding to a question posed by one of the board members, the external expert advised that financial products should be chosen on their ability both to satisfy customer needs and to increase the current return on shareholder funds—but shareholder value would be damaged without the support of a strong risk-control system.

In individual discussions with board members, the IT auditor also underlined that moving up the value chain in products and services was a necessary step in positioning the bank against the market forces of the new century. This, however, was both an aggressive and a defensive position, with the latter aimed to retain the more lucrative of the bank's clients in the likely case that foreign financial institutions tried to decream the market.

The reason for outlining these individual positions is to present a pattern of how sound management thinks. An entity's strategy is rarely written in black and white; rather, it is expressed by word of mouth, and it is observed by the company's thoughts and actions. The bank's new strategy, which was awaiting the development of a better infrastructure, could be expressed briefly in terms of:

- Top customers
- Income from services

The CEO, who had worked for several years in the United States, took as an example the key income source of the Bell companies: The top 1 percent of clients, said he, accounted for 25 to 35 percent of total revenues. And for (the former) AT&T, the top 4 percent of business customers made 62 percent of all long distance calls. He then added that similar statistics characterize the best performers in the banking industry, even if such statistics are not widely published.

This is true. But the external expert reminded that, at the same time, these top clients would be asking for products and services that are tough to provide without high tech. And dealing in such products and services would create exposures that require appropriate fencing—hence the need for a reliable risk-management solution assisted through knowledge engineering and virtual balance sheets available to senior management in real time (see Section 4).

The IT audit explained to the corporate governance committee of the board (see Chapter 5) that, to reach that goal, the bank had to invest a great deal of thought and research money in the development of a technological infrastructure tailored to support its current and projected business. He also suggested that the bank should develop and support its own architecture (see Section 3), rather than depending on the one-size-fits-all architecture of the computer vendor.

8.2 Opportunities and Problems of Strategic Planning

The good news for the bank's strategic-planning initiative was that both the majority (but not all) of the board's members and the CEO appreciated that their institution had to come up from under in technology, and that future IT expenditures should serve the bank's strategic plan. Correctly, the CEO had decided that this strategic plan should be *lean* and *mean*, integrating into it other, more specific plans that are typically elaborated by different departments:

- Financial planning
- Product planning
- Market planning
- Human resources planning
- Technology planning (see Section 3)

The bank's financial plan was in good order, with the budget roughly divided two-to-one between *interest* and *noninterest*, which is more or less the international norm. In fact, despite the drain because of spending too much money on IT without commensurate results, the audited bank had five successful budgeting years in a row. The asset distribution also looked good. Return on equity was reasonable, although characterized by some volatility. Capital resources were nicely progressing, and (as was seen in Section 1) the same was true of the capital ratio. IT aside, it was essentially the product plan and the market plan that had to be made more focused. The clients' demands for innovation had to be answered, and those "vanilla" products had to be revamped to feature

- Lower unit labor costs through greater productivity, and
- Greater high-tech content to support price competitiveness.

Human capital was one of the basic issues on which the board focused particular attention, recognizing the fact that organizations are made of people and that the whole entity suffers if the human capital is wanting. The challenge was that an expanding financial institution has a great thirst for qualified personnel. Therefore, the auditor made four suggestions on forward management of the bank's human resources, in coordination with strategic planning:

- The building of a management inventory coupled with career development plans
- A schedule for job rotation designed to increase the polyvalence of the bank's professionals
- Intensive computer literacy courses, from board members to clerks and secretaries
- Training in derivatives and risk management to give the bank's professionals a different dimension than that of deposits and loans, which had dominated in the past

In what concerns technology, it was suggested that strategic planning should be given a veto on IT investments, as the only way to bring good sense into IT operations. IT strategy should be decided by the bank's strategic planner, and not in the IT department. Most definitely, this function did not belong where it was at the time of the IT audit, and the incumbent in charge of IT (though a nice fellow) did not have the skill to satisfy further out IT strategy requirements.

The board had correctly decided first to put in place a corporate strategic-planning unit and then to ask for an IT audit. This strategic planning was a sound initiative, provided that the unit was equipped with the means and skills needed to perform its duties in an able manner. At the time of the IT audit, it was composed of:

- A department head with good background and knowledge of the bank, its market, and its operations
- A financial products and markets specialist hired from consultancy because of his brains
- An economist well versed in quantitative methods—not necessarily a rocket scientist, but a valid member of the team

The strategic-planning unit, however, was in need of an IT strategy specialist who had experience in end-user support, software development, and system integration. This position was difficult to fill because the market was aware of the lag in the bank's IT and because this issue was politicized internally within the bank. When such situations exist, the aftereffect is that the best people shun the job for fear of having their skills stagnate. Therefore, even if they qualify for the job, they do not care to apply, with the result that

- This position remained open, and
- The bank lacked a well-versed IT strategist.

The director of marketing, who was very critical of the prevailing IT setting (see Chapter 7), wanted the bank to use computers and communications to (a) cut the timetable for the sale of new services and (b) help his department to fence off competition by raising the cost of entry into the firm's market by challengers—a process known as *entry price*. For the director of finance, the most important issue was the strategic use of technology to bend the curve of steady cost increases and keep the bank competitive.

The CFO made a reference to a study by Arthur Young, the auditors, which demonstrated that there is a dollar payoff that comes about three years after implementation, and he wanted this timescale to be accelerated. While supporting both of his senior executives, the CEO made the point that the salient problem facing the board was to change the firm's IT culture by establishing a work environment and a reward system that would be

- Stimulating to professionals and
- Productive to the organization.

He did mention, albeit in a vague form, that there were some persons with connections to major shareholders who resisted change, adding that he feared they might win at the end. Therefore, he wanted to see constructive plans that could motivate some of the board members and current IT people into abandoning their resistance to change.

8.3 A New Technology Strategy

The constructive part of the report that the external IT auditor prepared for the CEO and the board started with the premise that legacy technological solutions (like the one this bank had been following) featured numerous boundaries between key business functions, between suppliers and departments of the organization, and between customers and the bank. Boundaries are obstacles. In this case, their character was an amalgam of several old-style interfaces. Crossing them was both

- A matter of identifying sometimes hazy boundaries, and
- An issue of defining and managing discontinuities inherent in the transition from old to new technology.

The bank needed to elaborate an architectural solution integrating smoothly into the new system. The principle is that end users of computers and communications applications become more productive through agile, friendly, and fairly uniform interfaces that help them work faster in a comprehensive manner.

Down to its fundamentals, the main goal of a business architecture is to provide a master plan, just like that of a data architecture that is to make data dependable, understandable, shareable, available, and secure. The existence of a valid architectural specification simplifies the development of new applications and also provides the ability to integrate and rationalize existing facilities. In turn, this

- Ensures that technology is able to serve business goals,
- Helps in defining information requirements within a business modeling frame, and
- Makes it easier to develop interactive databases—from data capture (one entry, many uses) to online delivery and use.

The highlights of the business architecture that was proposed paid full attention to the fact that information technology should be employed in promoting and maintaining effective business partner relationships, aptitudes that the audited bank was lacking at that time. The external expert proposed implementing an interactive online delivery mechanism to assist in banking products

- Being customized prior to being sold to the customer,
- Having a higher information content than competitors' products, and
- Moving seamlessly across boundaries, protected by security (see Chapter 11) but unimpeded.

In his oral presentation to the board, the IT auditor pressed the point that architectural solutions must be flexible and capable of addressing ad hoc situations as they develop. Apart from end-to-end integration of interfaces and background resources, they must provide system support for latency control, bandwidth allocation, traffic prioritization, and other issues increasingly needed to deliver a reliable quality of service.

To this, the IT auditor added that flexible solutions require careful planning. A flexible business architecture cannot be assembled atop a system that has resulted from years of haphazard growth. Moreover, a vendor's approach typically lacks the flexibility to support new applications and is unable to cope with unforeseen demands without requiring

- Major system changes and
- Associated tremendous costs.

For cost-optimization reasons, the business architecture must be flexible and adaptable, because information requirements change as fast as business and technology do, and as fast as product innovation and the marketplace require. Adaptation is a never-ending business because, as many firms now appreciate, if they cannot incorporate a new technology within three months they will be left behind in competition.

The external expert also explained to the bank's board members that a more advanced, knowledge-enriched architecture would make timely and accurate information more accessible by modeling information flows by means of

- Job models,
- Organizational models, and
- Design parameter models.

In a rational design approach, prior to effecting changes, these solution models must be simulated dynamically to obtain probabilistic distributions of duration of service and cost, locating clusters of highly interacting information elements and experimenting on ways to address them. The goal is to model all aspects of an information system solution, as well as understand and predict its results. In the IT auditor's opinion, this would help in

- Establishing a work environment in a way that enhances motivation,
- Integrating work across departmental, functional, and geographic boundaries,
- Promoting internal control by bypassing the walls classically separating different areas of authority, and
- Identifying and rewarding gatekeepers who break down internal barriers to enable better collaboration among the bank's professionals.

In this oral presentation of an interim report to the board, the IT auditor underlined that, to his experience, it is not possible to build any long-term structure—whether it be a city, building, business division, sales network, or any other—without some master blueprint. A long-term IT plan needs a blueprint defining infrastructure, platforms, end users, and supported facilities; therefore, he focused the interim report on the needed business architecture.

Moreover, among the services the business architecture will help in establishing is a common approach for the selection of hardware, operating systems, and applications packages, all the way to the definition of technical and enabling functions. Its designers must be careful enough to promote coordinated development of all system parts within different organizational entities, thereby

- Permitting components to be purchased off the shelf and
- Defining common utilities to be shared by all processes.

In an effort to make sure everybody understood that this scenario was *not* some idealized dream world, the IT auditor explained that the first challenge was to hire first-class designers, and that the second was to attend to current real and pressing needs while setting the stage for tomorrow's environment. This, too, is a mission to be addressed by a business architecture characterized by an overall computing and communications framework whose components

- Are designed to execute self-standing while being system bound,
- Can be removed and upgraded independently of one another, and
- Are reusable and can be shared across business products and business functions.

In different terms, while today's goals must be fully met, the external expert did not fail to bring to the board's and CEO's attention the requirements connected to the developing landscape of the banking business—and the audited institution's own strategic plans. This should be achieved by modularizing, integrating, and advancing a policy that promotes the use of the Internet, as far as security considerations allow, and accelerates internal applications delivery, with programs tailored to support the most competitive of the bank's functions.

8.4 Bringing High Tech to the CEO and the Professionals

Most companies initially considered IT to be a support function under the control of the financial officer. However, this limited perspective led to strategic blunders, and some well-publicized failures increased the urgency to rethink the type, depth, and frequency of information support to management. The earlier management information systems (MIS) dating from the mid-1970s were, to a considerable extent, a computer-based form of management accounting. Given the huge advances in technology since that time, those early solutions pale in comparison with what is possible in today's world. The benefits are particularly evident when members of the board, the CEO, and his or her immediate assistants are computer literate. As Louis Pasteur once said, "Chance favors only the prepared mind."

After visiting institutions with advanced technological solutions, the CEO of the audited bank was aware of the level of sophistication in customized support technology and of the services it can provide for senior management. His wish was to have ad hoc information available interactively—not just statistics, but action-oriented information with

- Virtual balance sheets,
- Virtual income statements,
- Patterns of credit exposure,
- Patterns of market exposure, and more.

He wanted to obtain, on request, charts providing a comprehensive view of key corporate variables, along with the ability to call up pages with more detailed documentation, as needed. He also wanted this interactive access to be user friendly, easy to handle, and capable of providing comprehensive information. But he did understand that his bank could not move into this world overnight, which was another one of the reasons he had asked for the IT audit.

The president of one of the banks the CEO had visited told him that, in his experience, technological change pushes a company further into reconsidering how to radically transform the way in which its organization works. Therefore, after the IT auditor's interim report, the CEO envisaged a mission that is best described as an enabling business process, used to both expand and enhance the bank's competitive position by creating new business opportunities. His colleague at a correspondent bank had told him that

- Competitiveness requires finding innovative ways and new ideas to gain market advantages, and
- Technology enables companies to operate on the fly with business units that can be dynamically restructured.

The audited bank's CEO, however, was concerned of a looming failure to grasp this potential because of internal resistances. This, he said to the IT auditor, will be holding his institution at a position behind that of its potential competitors. The challenge was not only to enlighten the IT peoples' views, but also to overcome a wall of resistance.

The external expert advised that, indeed, this was the salient problem, but it was the same challenge the majority of firms are confronted with. Advanced technology provides overwhelming opportunities for information and experimentation on virtually any topic, but resistance to change sees to it that available opportunities are not paid due attention. Even the best technology *cannot* help those companies that

- Are unwilling to change their IT culture,
- Have not sorted out their IT priorities, and
- Have not done the organizational work that is a prerequisite to IT results.

In his efforts to get a first-hand view of advanced IT's potential, the CEO visited the bank of a shipping group. At top management's request, its analysts had written a sophisticated expert system that tracked all transports of oil and minerals. The most interesting aspect of this system was that it could rival the best in business applications. For instance, it could track metal shipments on any boat on the high seas and identify which mine in the world had sold what metal to any wholesaler on any day. At the time this system came alive, its capabilities exceeded those available to most other transport companies, mining entities, and financial institutions.

To make the difference in design better evident to the reader, Figures 8.2 and 8.3 present in a nutshell the audited bank's dilemma. Going from the legacy approach shown in Figure 8.2 to the interactive computational finance solution in

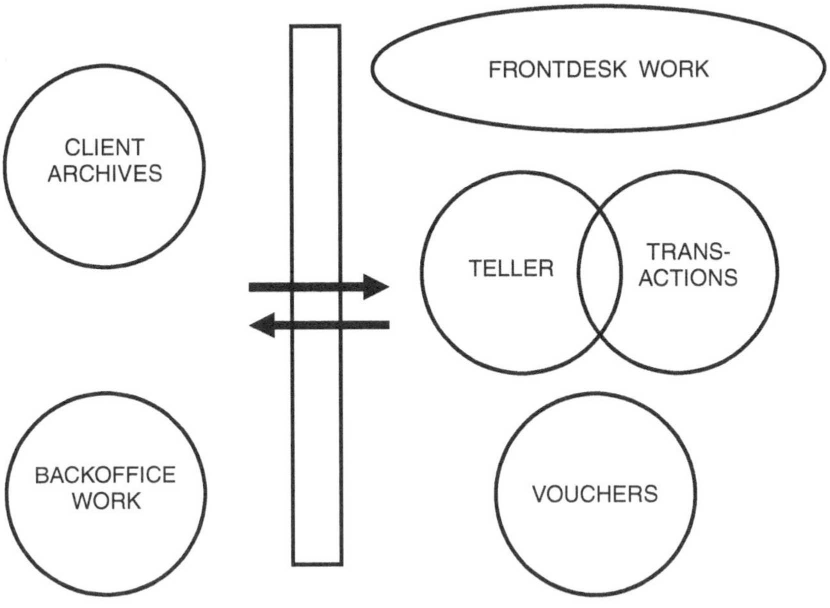

Figure 8.2 The legacy approach to IT services (mainly batch).

Figure 8.3 requires that a giant cultural step be made in a short time. Otherwise, it would never materialize. (The example the IT auditor used was that Mustafa Kemal was able to change the Turkish alphabet from Arabic to Latin in just six months.)

The system in Figure 8.3 brings into perspective the highlights of an interactive computational finance solution that contrasts sharply with the inflexible legacy approach of Figure 8.2. A great deal of competitiveness in banking depends on effectively supporting ad hoc data mining and complex queries, encouraging the use of models as well as of experimentation, and assisting in better understanding the issues associated with the most recent market movements.

- *If* sufficient flexibility is built into the system,
- *Then* responses to ad hoc requests by management can be tailored with modest effort.

Answering a question posed by one of the members of the board on what would be required beyond the business architecture, which had already been explained, the external expert said that a "must" was enhancing the system with algorithms and heuristics designed to serve the end user, thereby enabling every party working for the bank, as well as its business partners, to operate online. This goal also involved the task of elaborating functional approaches that would personalize and customize user-oriented interactivity.

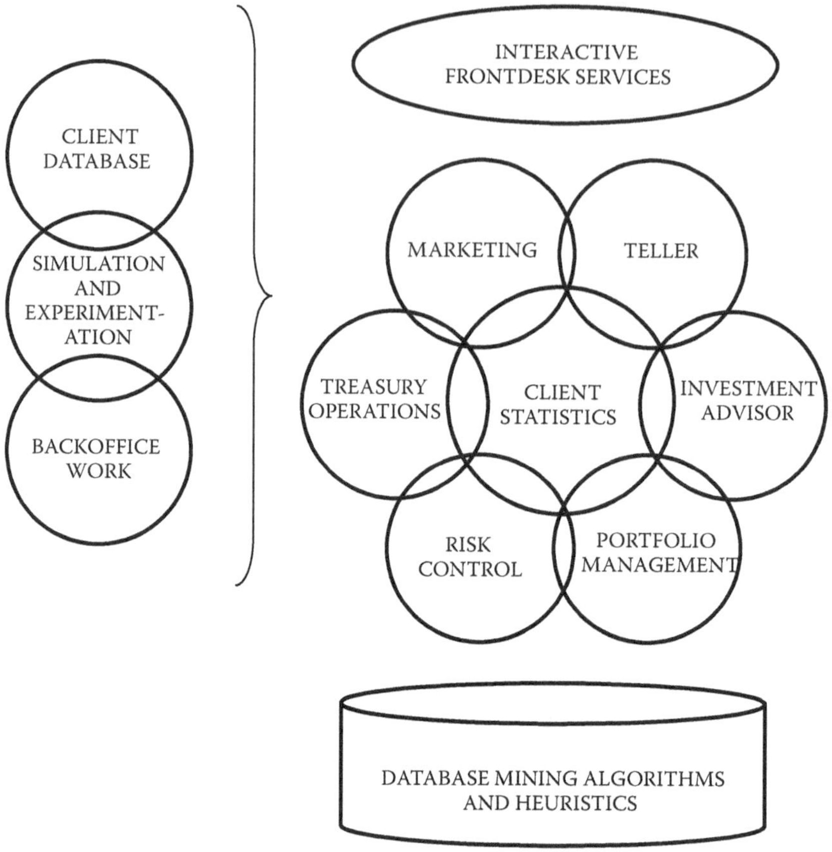

Figure 8.3 The interactive computational finance solution.

During the board meeting, the CEO said that, in the correspondent banks he had visited, interactive knowledge artifacts helped in ensuring that investment advisors, credit officers, and traders attained better domain understanding, used multiple selection criteria, and served client accounts more effectively. In a peer-to-peer discussion, the audited bank's chief executive had heard that interactive computational finance is the mind's eye of the CEO.

8.5 Improving Internal Control over IT

While the information system objectives discussed in Sections 3 and 4 could be the motor enabling the audited financial institution to run in a more efficient manner, effectively facing the growing IT requirements of its clients and of its own management, there were as well other prerequisites to take into account. An integral part of the needed cultural change was the emphasis to be placed on

- Internal control and
- Risk management.

As we have seen since Chapter 1, the responsibility of internal control is to ensure that all of the events that have happened—and those that should have but did not—are brought to the attention of the board's chief executive and senior management. This goes beyond the requirement that annual financial statements be free of material misinterpretation of facts (see Chapters 12 and 13).

If the bank's information technology was to be restructured, then it had to serve both as an engine of greater business opportunity and as a feedback mechanism. A timely and transparent management control was not one of the audited bank's characteristics (see Chapter 7). Mainly because of resistance to change by some of its people, including a few board members, the bank had failed on several occasions to evaluate and revamp internal communications through its organizational levels. This had made it difficult for senior management to identify and correct certain improprieties, or even to be aware of others. In many instances, three reasons were at fault:

- Differences of opinion by major shareholders
- Company politics, which blurred internal control standards
- Information technology that did not serve as an effective feedback mechanism

Because internal control was defective, senior management was slow to react to IT happenings, with the result that this organization had been turned into a parking lot for programmers and analysts. Their productivity was dismal because they had recognized the organization's inability to deal with them. A better internal control system could put an end to such practices by facilitating

- Utilization of internal expertise more effectively and
- Movement of knowledge from one part of the bank to another.

An inherent dilemma in attempting to reward and motivate IT professionals was that incentives that appeal to other people, such as taking on management responsibilities or the prestige of job titles, proved to be less important than working on an interminable application that was (wrongly) considered to guarantee employment.

Other operational-type risks related to the bank's internal control system were loss of data and of customer files (see Chapter 7) due to faulty IT policies, as well as inadequate security and sloppy administrative arrangements. Another problem was the relatively low reliability of its computer systems, leading to unacceptable downtime aggravated by inadequate backup and recovery procedures.

These were no exceptions; they have always been important issues with IT over all businesses and industries. With the audited bank they were even more so, because it had announced to the market that it could support 24-hour retail banking. A combination of poor system design and low reliability saw to it that, while the institution had a network of ATMs, these were not operating in real time in updating customer files. Instead, they were doing data collection and were looking up a black list for purposes of authorization.

The board was promised something that had not been delivered. Internal control should have informed senior management of slow programs well before the IT audit. This issue of questionable dependability was true all the way to erroneous data in management reports because, as always, batch processing was behind the facts.

The external expert brought to the CEO's attention that, during the past couple of years, several credit institutions had experienced severe losses because information in senior management's possession was not updated, reliable, or complete, and because communications within the bank were not timely and effective. An important example of an adverse happening is the use of unreliable information to value financial positions.

Internal controls and the IT supports should be projected to achieve a unified line of assistance to all employees working to meet the bank's objectives—across divisions, departments, and desks. Indeed, the Basel Committee on Banking Supervision advises that controls over information technology should include both general and applications-oriented clauses.

- General controls are those over the computer system aimed at ensuring its continued operation free of trouble.
- Applications-oriented controls focus on software developed in-house or purchased, as well as procedures that command transaction processing, payments, and settlements.

The external expert insisted on the fact that a rigorous approach to internal control over IT should pay attention to these points made by the Basel Committee, and to its statement that banks could experience setbacks without adequate controls over information technology, including systems that are under development. Unreliable or misleading information has been at the origin of many failures whose aftermath ranges

- From serious difficulties for management
- To jeopardizing the bank's ability to conduct its key business activities.

A practical example taken from the audited bank's daily operations documented the existing duality between internal control and IT. This example also demonstrated that while information technology policies, commitments, and operations should be subject to internal control, at the same time technology has a major impact on control operations.

But not all sorts of IT equipment can be of assistance in improving management control. The IT auditor hoped to have convinced the members of the board that the worst thing a bank can do in terms of supporting its internal control through technology is to use centralized mainframes. He gave two reasons for this statement.

The sophisticated software that needs to be used for an effective technological solution in managing risk (see Section 6)—including models, simulators, expert systems, and interactive three-dimensional visualization—will eat up the mainframe's cycle for breakfast. Or, alternatively it will be superficial and incomplete rather than being done in a truly satisfactory way.

The second reason is even more critical. Internal control is by excellence system distributed through the nodes and links of the enterprise. Sometimes it even uses the organizational grapevine to carry information upward. When the channeling of information becomes centralized through a mainframe, selected information becomes subject to editing by the gatekeepers, who have every interest in seeing that "this" or "that" feedback does not reach senior management's ears.

8.6 Instituting a Risk-Management System

Throughout the banking industry, the control of risk has been hampered by problems ranging from lack of appreciation of its vital importance to profitability and survival of the entity, to lack of skills and computer incompatibility. This has left many banks with substandard risk-management solutions or no risk control worth talking about, as was the case of the audited bank.

Because a first-class risk-control organization is key to every financial institution's continuing business success, the IT audit deliberately emphasized this issue. The board and senior management were informed that significant improvements in risk-control tools, methods, and procedures were urgently needed and that they required:

- Far-looking risk-management policies, including supervision of their execution
- Sophisticated models of analytical finance, including risk control
- Doing away with the hodgepodge of inconsistent and aging computer platforms and their archaic routines

In his second interim presentation to the board, the external expert emphasized that risk management does not deal with new product development, but with the fundamental uncertainties that result because of the likely but not the sure market response. Moreover, risk control's main mission is to assess the barriers to unwanted risks, decided by the board, doing so through analytical tools designed to gauge the different kinds of exposure taken by the bank.

The barriers, the members of the board were told, are the limits the board had already established as breaks to exposure, but because of defective internal control it usually had no way to know *if* they were steadily observed. Examples included the barrier of less than 5 percent in loans and investments to the same name. Prerequisites to an effective exposure control were

- Clear risk-management policies,
- Strengthening of the internal control, and an
- Urgently needed higher level of sophistication in IT.

Taking note of the way in which the bank was allocating its IT budget, the external auditor said that, to date, technology has been used mainly as an internal back-office tool. Yet, it is by no means yesterday that IT appeared at the front desk, where it has been playing an ever-increasing role at large and most particularly in information-based financial services,

- Allowing the performance of activities never previously considered and
- Enabling real-time risk control with direct feedback to the CEO and the board's risk committee.

A risk-control culture and skills were evidently a "must," along with the policy to abandon fire-brigade approaches by adopting a strategy assisted through analysis, real-time computation, and immediate corrective action. The good news for the audited bank was that it had in its employment some first-class people who could be effectively trained for enterprise-wide risk control.

For instance, the external auditor had been impressed after meeting with the executives responsible for credit risk. The downside was that their duties were too narrowly defined, strictly focusing on loans. Therefore, the bandwidth of their approach needed to be considerably expanded, and along with this, their authority.

This advice by the external auditor was in line with the opinion of the governor of the central bank who, in a statement a short time before the audit, had said that risk management should be a top objective for the banks under his jurisdiction. Capitalizing on the quality of its personnel—with proper definition of risk-control goals, improvements in internal control, and high tech—the audited bank stood a good chance to become a leader in risk management

- Supported by advanced mathematical models and
- Benefiting from interactive computational finance.

The IT auditor also advised that bankwide risk had to be under the authority of a chief risk management officer (a new position) with ample authority over exposure. Institutions that had maintained parochial controls over credit, market, and operational risk had found that fractured systems were not delivering. An effective risk-control solution had to be well studied and able to work

- At any time,
- In any place,
- Anywhere in the bank, and do so
- In an integrative way.

Informal controls, where they existed, had to be supplemented by formal risk-control measures. The organizational structure itself had to be subject to rigorous auditing, including the omnipresent question of compliance (see Chapter 12). In most countries today, central banks ask the board of directors and senior management of a bank to create a coherent internal control and reporting structure to

- Effectively manage risk,
- Safeguard business assets, and
- Guarantee compliance with rules and regulations.

The IT audit as well suggested that greater management responsibility in terms of risk also requires acknowledgment by the directors that they are responsible for the bank's system of internal control as well as for the certification, through internal and/or external expertise, that the adopted solution can provide assurance against material misstatement or loss.

According to the external expert, sound risk management practice needs risk controllers and analysts who are in a position to investigate the causal relation from symptoms to failures, and vice versa. They must be able to diagnose the nature, location, and intensity of the risks taken by the audited institution to

- Derive patterns of exposure and
- Calculate correlations between different types of exposure.

The development of risk patterns helps in better appreciating the shifts in exposure, and at the same time assists in risk diagnosis. In a pattern defined through the assistance of a statistical quality control chart, the upper bound corresponds to the worst case and least-wanted state among possible states of exposure. Hence there is wisdom in stress testing to examine low-frequency but high-impact events at the long leg of the risk distribution.

Banks are primarily in the risk business and have, over decades, developed processes to monitor and control their risks. However, with the globalization and deregulation of banking, as well as with financial innovations as exemplified by the advent of derivatives, they are finding that their traditional tools no longer suffice. The audited bank was no exception to this most universal finding.

In conclusion, considering the regulatory environment and fiduciary responsibilities confronting the audited credit institution, its management had immediate and deep interest in ensuring a rapid evolution toward bankwide rigorous risk control. This required board decisions, an integrated IT system, and greater sophistication in risk analysis.

8.7 Return on Investment and the Technology Budget

The quality, reliability, and availability of information technology systems are important, but *costs matter*. Sharp businesspeople are keen to ensure that, day in and day out, costs are kept to a low profile. Sam Walton, founder of Wal-Mart, had a principle: "Never buy somebody else's inefficiency" (by buying his high costs). Walton's qualitative benchmarks were that

- *Administrative costs* should never exceed 2 percent of business, and
- *Business trip expenses* should never exceed 1 percent of purchases.

Similar principles that are easy to understand and apply should characterize *return on investment* (ROI) in connection with the technology budget. The information systems departments of the best-managed companies have been moving into the 21st century with a big task: increasing efficiency and cutting costs without losing their edge in

- High tech and
- Competitiveness.

Among the best examples on how to make a technology budget that sustains innovation and promotes ROI comes from the early 1990s from the Mellon Bank, Bankers Trust, and their IT investment guidelines. In both banks, the annual *noninterest* budget invested in technology stood between 20 and 23 percent, up from 10 percent in the late 1970s. An exceptionally good return on investment was instrumental in doubling IT's budgetary figures.

At both Bankers Trust and Mellon, year after year, every effort was made to maintain good ROI figures. Return on IT investments stood at 22 percent, and for every payroll dollar the bank saved through IT, it invested 40 cents in technology. This left 60 cents in profits.

The external expert impressed upon the board members of the audited bank that ROI-conscious institutions were ahead of competition worldwide in information technology; they were not laggards. Their ROI policies looked at costs and benefits in an integrated way, and the CEO asked for documented estimates about costs of present systems and of commitments being made for new installations.

In these firms, the CIOs knew that their cost/benefit estimates must be complete and accurate, including direct labor, overhead, machine depreciation, utilities, supplies, and maintenance. The board paid attention to the CIO's ability to ensure that

- Costs are traceable to accounting records, rather than to vague estimates, and
- Costs included not only those of the IT department, but also equipment installed at the end users.

Regarding in-house projects, IT audit verified that costs are estimated for the complete development cycle and a reasonable operations life after project completion. On the strength of these references, which were among the best that could be found, the external expert asked the management of the audited bank to adopt a similar policy, as well as to authorize verification that its costs estimates reflect

- All commitments in IT and
- Real budgetary figures.

Concomitant with this work has been the need to review estimated operating savings for reasonableness: relating personnel and other savings to present IT costs; examining claims of intangible benefits and similar considerations; and confirming quantification of benefits with user personnel, prior to proceeding with ROI analysis.

The external auditor also advised that IT services should be billed to profit centers (see Section 8) and that the costing policy to be established must look not only at current costs, but also at the longer term because, as a rule of thumb, in information technology,

- For every $1 in the acquisitions budget (capex),
- There will eventually be $5 in support costs.

In his presentation to the audit committee of the board, the external IT auditor documented why a light approach to IT costs does not help technology investments. To the contrary, it confuses the issues and ends up giving the wrong picture, with the result that the IT budget stagnates. A similar statement was made about expected benefits, which need to be examined through both strategic and tactical viewpoints along the line of a business opportunity analysis.

- Large investments in IT cannot be justified without enhancements in business opportunity, productivity, and risk control.
- Not all market benefits are IT bound. Market positioning works in many ways, impacting several critical elements, only one of which is IT.

Figure 8.4 visualizes the market-oriented concept suggested to the board by the bank's strategic planner in the form of a wheel where technology is just one of the nodes, while the pivot point is the *market*. Part of the message was a reminder that strategic considerations precede technological considerations, and in regard to the latter, it is always wise to keep in mind that

- Every IT project should relate to the bank's strategic plan because, if IT is standing all on its own, ROI will be small, and
- If the IT project is too expensive, is late, or has low-quality deliverables, its contribution to business opportunity will be a fraction of the one originally projected, and the same is true of its ROI.

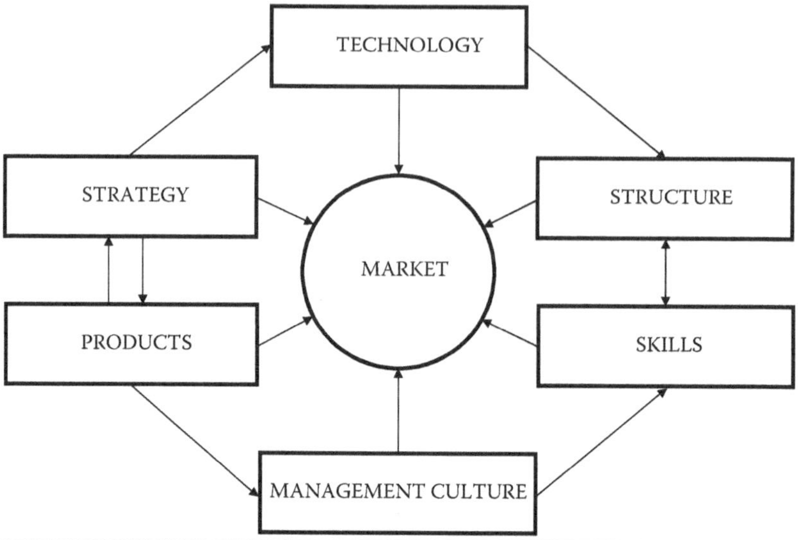

Figure 8.4 Market positioning works both ways, impacting many critical elements

The IT auditor confirmed these statements, pointing out that delays in executing an information technology project cancel out its strategic value. Every IT project has a risk factor associated with it, and this risk factor zooms up with delays. Neither should highly technical details enter the ROI study, because they confuse and deviate the report from its objective.

8.8 Profit Center Organization and Internal Billing

Like so many other companies, the audited bank considered its information technology department as a *cost center*, whose budget is part of general administration expenses and overhead. This is a very bad policy for several reasons, the most important being that:

- Overhead should be cut with a sharp knife; in contrast, the IT budget should grow as long as it provides 22 percent ROI.
- Hiding IT in the jungle of administrative expenses reduces its transparency, most importantly its deliverables.
- A cost center does not bill its services to user departments; a *profit center* does, and this provides a gauge of its acceptability.
- A cost-center approach deprives IT from potential sponsors in the organization, which is counterproductive because new and advanced projects need sponsors.

The last two bulleted items are correlated. When user departments pay for IT services, they are much more careful not only about what they are asking, but also, and most importantly, for the quality, timeliness, and cost effectiveness of what they get. Quite similarly, sponsors of new IT projects are not only cofinancing them, they are also monitoring their progress and exercising pressure so that the deliverables meet expectations.

Because of these reasons, the external auditor advised the board and CEO of the bank that the best way to proceed in terms of visibility, and therefore of personal accountability, is as a *profit center* organization. This should characterize every function and product line in the institution at large, and most particularly its information technology. Clearly, it must include all aspects of IT as billed *services* to operating units.

Performance in information technology and return on investment have very much in common. A profit center must *sell* its services to the bank's departments and branches. If the price is too high, the quality substandard, or the functionality wanting, they would not pay for them. The paying clients are tough critters, and therefore the IT department must be both efficient and effective. Both terms are explained in Table 8.1.

To the question posed by the CEO about which billing method should be used, the IT auditor answered that *activity-based* costing would be the right choice for "profit center IT." The first step is to compute the cost of resources like personnel salaries, computing equipment, databases, communications costs, and other expenses as well as assets such as office space and utilities.

These should be assigned to the *activities* performed by information technology, on the basis of an algorithm to remain stable until proven to be unfair. Cost assignments should be model-based, and they should be simple, because they will be immediately challenged if they are complex.

The second step, as the external expert advised the bank management, is to assign activity costs to *cost objects*. The latter represents an IT service rendered to the end user, for which he or she will be billed. Quite often (as with activities costing) *time* is used as a driver, for instance, the percent of time a certain IT activity, and the resource(s) behind it, is assigned to each end-user service.

The external expert also explained that the IT budget must incorporate all resources employed to deliver IT services to each and every user department, with

Table 8.1 Efficiency and Effectiveness

Efficiency	*Effectiveness*
Doing a given job at least possible: ■ Cost ■ Time	Deliverables meeting goals in a most able manner

expenditures allocated to the corresponding cost object. Care must be exercised to ensure that pricing of services is fair.

- Through accounting, these charges will be billed to the users of IT resources.
- User departments would react negatively if unit costs are too high.

In response to a question by a member of the board on how to handle unfair IT costs, the external expert answered that to make their IT departments sensitive to the need to reduce unit cost, some banks permit user departments to outsource their information technology needs. One of the first banks to do so was Bankers Trust. A better solution than that is to study the cost structure for similar services by

- Insourcers and
- Correspondent banks.

A sample of existing charges for similar services gives the bank a well-documented IT cost distribution. (In similar projects that I have been involved with in my professional work, the policy was to take the mean of the distribution, reduce it by 10 percent, and fix it as an internal cost standard. This made the CIO run fast to meet the challenge, and on many occasions the CIO successfully did so.)

Running fast to meet cost goals is one of the direct benefits of the profit-center solution for IT. It obliges the CIO and his or her immediate assistants to keep the operations under their authority cost effective. Because there may be deviations, it is part of internal audit's mission to

- Control IT's unit costs and
- Compare them with those of the competition and of insourcers.

This was a new concept for the senior management of the audited bank, which saw the annual budget of IT as its undeniable right. The external expert explained that, while this attitude was not unusual, it was wrong. While many people agreed that costs always matter, IT had escaped cost scrutiny for 50 years.

The IT auditor, however, did not fail to bring management's attention to the fact that this flawed policy had changed since the 2000 market downturn. Today, the better-managed companies see to it that, for any IT project and for any information service, there is almost an unprecedented level of scrutiny regarding:

- How it benefits the firm
- What are the deliverables that count most
- How to leave secondary issues out and cut the budget
- How to reduce IT unit costs for the same level of dependability

These questions were simply not asked a few years ago. In contrast, during the last half dozen years, in an increasing number of cases budget approval depends on the answers to these questions and on their documentation. IT expenditures have finally become part of the integrated cost control structure, and this is affecting

- Budgets,
- Timetables, and
- Sophistication of deliverables.

The IT auditor also pointed out that every single dimension of information technology should be subject to cost. For this reason, the obtained results must be compared with the financial plan both systematically and by exception. No department should be permitted to escape managerial control, and this evidently includes IT.

In conclusion, *if* IT has to sell its services at competitive costs, *then* it would care to produce results the operating departments wish to buy. Otherwise, the budget must be cut, because as a profit center IT would receive no income. Accountability is upheld because a profit-center structure promotes visibility. The result of internal billing is much greater care about costs and efficiency, which should always be the two guidelines for all managers and professionals in a firm.

Chapter 9

A Broader Perspective of IT Auditing

9.1 IT Projects That Never Reach Their Goals

Standish is a research firm that produces an influential annual evaluation of IT projects. In September 2006, based on statistics up to the end of 2004, Standish judged that only 29 percent of IT projects succeeded; moreover, in the same reference year of 2004,

- Cost overruns averaged 56 percent of original budget, and
- IT projects took 84 percent more time (on average) than originally scheduled.

These are indeed horrendous statistics, but they are not surprising. From the reported success rate of IT projects, which is slightly over 30 percent, to cost overruns and delays in deliverables, the figures are close to the trend line. Such dismal outcomes persist 50 years after computers first entered commercial, manufacturing, and banking operations.

From this perspective, the banks behind the real-life case studies in Chapters 7 and 8 are not exceptional but, rather, illustrate typical misapplications of intellectual and financial resources. There are several reasons behind the unwanted consequences of information technology investments, which continue to rise while the deliverables shrink:

- Unclear IT goals
- Lack of design reviews (see Chapter 2)
- Lax IT management
- Malfunctioning internal control

This is not only my opinion. According to the research by Standish, the common factors found in failed IT projects have been lack of control and overoptimistic assumptions about costs and revenues. Therefore, the board, the CEO, and senior management of every firm would do well to heed the advice given in Chapter 7's case study that information technology not be considered as just an IT "business." IT is the force driving a company's growth and survival.

CEOs who truly care about the company in their charge should look at IT as an important and integral part of successfully running their enterprise. They should also appreciate that every decade has ushered in a new era of advanced technology:

- 1950s—novelty of the computer
- 1960s—data processing and computation
- 1970s—use of distributed resources
- 1980s—PCs and knowledge engineering
- 1990s—predominance of communications
- 2000+—focus on competitive applications

Companies that have failed to develop and use state-of-the-art computers and communications applications suffer. The same is true of those firms who mismanage their IT projects, who do not push hard for rapid deliverables designed to enhance their competitive position, and who pay lip service to IT costs (see Chapter 8).

In contrast, companies that are ahead of the curve in technology have a management team that recognizes the need to organize greater intellectual effort around the problem to be solved than around such traditional functions as production or marketing. This "problem to be solved" is no legacy-type application. It is a 21st-century novelty that, in the majority of cases, is found in one of the following domains:

- Innovation
- Risk control
- Productivity
- Added value
- Profitability
- Greater competitiveness

The common ground of all six bulleted items is corporate survival. Therefore, tier-1 organizations are undertaking projects in one or more of these domains, and they do not sleepover in their management. They plan the project right, and then they follow up with design reviews (see Chapter 2) and tough evaluations to assess progress and to ensure that it succeeds.

The principle followed by such companies is that the faster technology advances, the more sophisticated *our* information system solutions must be, and the more rapid *our* deliverables. Companies (and persons) who plan and act faster are winners. They are successful not because they know so much more on every subject, but because they have learned how to

- Formulate the problem accurately and
- Channel the needed resources for its solution.

In two sentences, these are the ingredients for success in IT projects. Notice, however, that even a project that succeeds by delivering on time and on budget may subsequently fail in its implementation because its designers did not exercise foresight and its developers did not perform stress tests.* An example is Mizuho's big and costly mistake.

On December 12, 2005, the malfunctioning of the Tokyo Stock Exchange's (TSE) trading system prevented Mizuho Securities, a subsidiary of Mizuho Japan's second biggest bank, from quickly canceling a botched trade. Mizuho Securities faced a stock-trading loss of $333 million because one of its brokers made an error inputting an order for J-COM shares:

- To sell 610,000 shares for 1 yen each, instead of
- Selling 1 share at 610,000 yen (about $5,000).

The error originated at Mizuho Securities, but *if* the Tokyo Stock Exchange's order-canceling system had functioned properly, *then* the amount lost would have been much smaller. In an effort to exercise damage control, Mizuho bought back a majority of the trade, but 96,236 shares (more than six times the number outstanding) had to be repurchased from investors who were owed stock certificates. Two events happened at the same time:

- Mizuho's computer system failed in input control and error detection.
- TSE's computer system proved unreliable. A proper design would have avoided interrupts and downtime during working hours.

This is an example of how low-likelihood events can correlate to produce a high-impact event. It also demonstrates how costly near-sighted information technology solutions can be. In both cases, system designers did not quite understand how a financial transaction must be controlled end-to-end, or they simply cut corners.

---

* D. N. Chorafas, *Stress Testing for Risk Control Under Basel II* (Oxford: Elsevier, 2007).

This horrendous loss because of defective IT is not the only case of its kind. Half a year thereafter, the reliability of computing systems used in Japan's financial markets was further called into question when another technical glitch caused trading in Japanese bonds to be briefly suspended.* This came over and above other problems with computers that disrupted trading on the Tokyo Stock Exchange.

One of the basic reasons for IT failures is that companies, designers, and developers fail to account for the much more stringent requirements posed by *big systems*. For a major organization, the end-to-end IT solution required to manage its business will be a big system, and it is wise to keep in perspective the fact that big systems are not the same as small systems that have grown over time by outpacing their original technical requirements.

- Big systems have their own design characteristics.
- These characteristics must be fulfilled in the most dependable manner if the system is expected to perform its mission without failures.

Design and implementation flaws experienced with complex systems arise primarily from the use of conceptual structures that might have worked well for simpler and static solutions, but that fall too short to answer the requirements posed by dynamic markets. The conceptual structure required by dynamic markets is based on the following pillars:

- A metaphysical view of the nature of complexity and
- *Operational readiness* at 99.9 percent reliability, as a minimum (see Chapter 10).

Designers, implementers, and their managers should keep in mind that, to a considerable extent, complex system structures have nonlinear behavior. Such behavior is generated by the synergy of simpler processes, which individually might be linear but have a nonlinear interaction within the larger system, and this greatly impacts on its output. Stress testing is the answer. Conveniently forgetting the effects of complexity increases the fragility of the information system.

9.2 Why Has the Project Not Been Completed?

This is a real-life case study on a big system. It concerns the audit of an IT project on payments and settlements, which went on for several years and, when the audit finally took place, it was still far from being completed. The code was not quite ready; the tests on ready modules were not finished; some parallel runs were not particularly successful; and the cutoff had been pushed forward four times.

* *The Economist*, July 1, 2006.

A prior IT audit on this same project had suggested that the inputs had to be better defined to avoid duplications. It had also informed senior management that, with a better focused job, over 20 percent of manual input could be eliminated. Moreover, this earlier IT audit had stated that the settlement engine needed revamping from the bottom up and warned that tests of routines providing for online validation were not conclusive. The purpose of the second audit by the same external expert was to

- Evaluate the quality of work done during the elapsed time and
- Make a supertest of completed modules to attest to functionality and dependability.

To protect its flanks, project management rushed to inform that some problems were still present and that "this was unavoidable because of inability of users to quantify their requirements." As the project manager put it: "People don't know how to think in quantitative terms," but he also acknowledged that there had been some delays because of programmer/analyst turnover.

The previous IT audit report had written that, following the external expert's pulling and pushing to get some quantifiable answers, the project manager had suggested that there would be some 85 major modules altogether, and maybe another 20 or a few more that were not yet defined. This was *imprecise*, as well as evidence that both IT management and the project leader had underestimated the job to be done.

By the time of the second IT audit, the number of major modules had grown to 135. To a query by the external expert, who expressed surprise at such an increase, the CIO and his project manager responded that changes in requirements were responsible. In reality, however, the background reasons were not difficult to detect.

- The people working on this project had become too comfortable, with no detectable sense of urgency to complete the project.
- End-user requirements were fixed at the start, so that not all user outfits were committed to them.
- The slow-moving project manager had allowed changes to specifications to occur all the time, which should not have happened.

On the one hand, there were changes between the two audits, with the result that plenty of patching was required, and this alone had taken 20 man-months. On the other hand, the CIO allowed the schedule to be extended, with the result that legacy programs had to continue being maintained at very high cost.

One of the complaints by end users was that the system analysts had not taken full account of their insistence that overnight cash management should be a focal point, because the existing procedure provided a big chunk of the institution's profits. With the new procedure, the standard one-day notice would disappear, the result being that overnight treasury profits would diminish.

The project manager said that this would be counterbalanced by better treasury information, but the head of the treasury department did not buy that argument. The IT auditor requested the project manager to urgently study, through simulation, the impact to be expected on company profits and, also through simulation, to elaborate alternative schemes likely to optimize profit figures in a way satisfactory to the responsible department head.

Of course, this was one of the matters that should have been settled at the earliest phase of the project. But it was not. When the external expert asked for a design review during the first IT audit, in which all responsible department heads were supposed to participate with the aim of reevaluating the system analysis, he was told that the right people were not available—but a design review would be done within a month. It was not; hence the faults persisted.

Instead, what had happened was rescheduling. In the aftermath, the testing timetable became too long, and therefore unsatisfactory to end users. Figure 9.1 gives a snapshot. Another issue that left the external IT auditor puzzled was the bond-redemption lottery. In its background was the practice of partial redemption of non-bullet bonds. However, this seemed to be done sometimes through

- Random numbers (a lottery) and, in other cases, through
- Questionable criteria such as "large size."

The institution's customers had learned of the existence of this second practice (which had also been inserted into the legacy programs), and they complained. Banks and large investors know very well that there is much money to be made or lost with partial redemptions, and they watch carefully the way in which redemptions are decided. Additionally, because this had been an issue with a major impact on the company's business and its reputation, it should have been decided by top management rather than left to the technicians, as proved to be the case. It looked as if senior managers had abdicated their responsibility.

A problem that held back the completion of some modules had to do with the nuts and bolts of IT. Analysts had asked for a change in tools because it takes three to five man days to design a screen under DB2, while it requires only half a day to do so on Oracle. In terms of productivity this meant 600 to 1,000 percent more time and more costs when working with DB2, but IT management was undecided. Some voices spoke of a conflict of interest.

There was, as well, a curious midstream change of platforms that went backward: from client-server to mainframe. Top management should never have approved it, even after the CIO had imprudently bought a couple of mainframes without the authority to do so. Several modules of the new project crashed when converted to the mainframe—a futile exercise that cost over 30 man-years of throwaway investment.

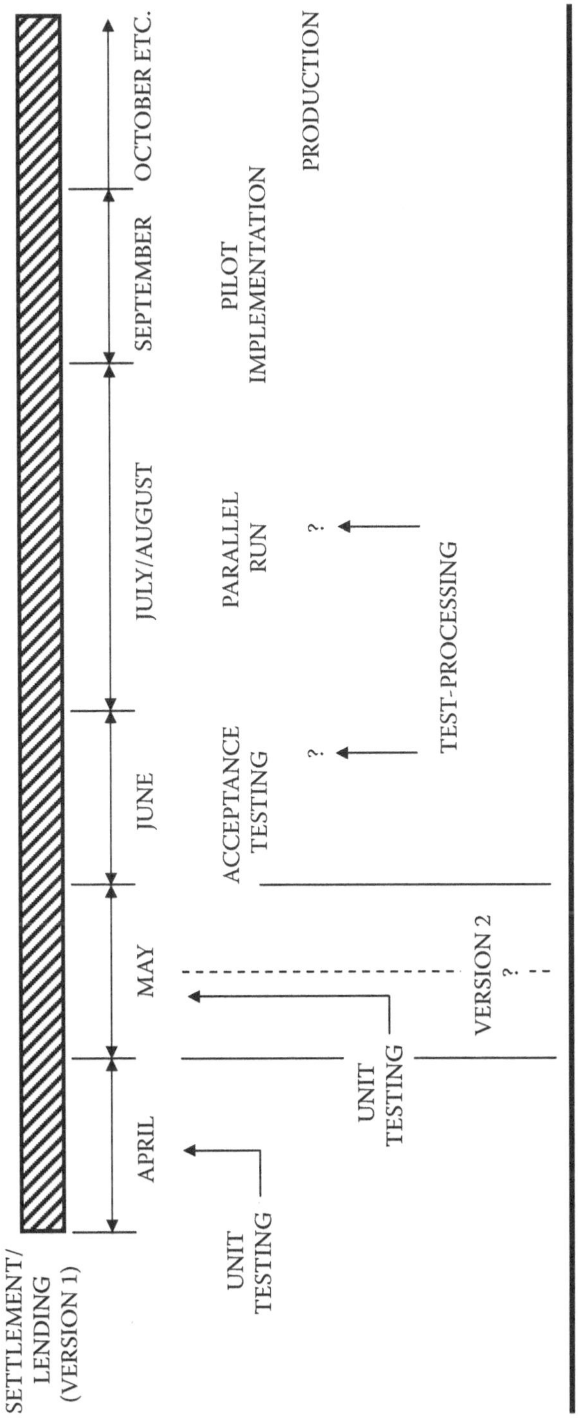

Figure 9.1 Timetable for testing and implementation of the project.

The IT auditor noted in his report that this was not some sort of "once in a lifetime" event that forced top management to accept an irrational solution. Such mishaps occur frequently when the organization's arteries are clogged through the collision of sundry conflicts. In fact, it has happened in the past, and it is safe to bet is that it will happen again for other entities.

Another failure revealed by the IT audit was a design incompatibility. During the parallel run of some of the new modules it was discovered that, while they were supposed to use the same information elements and update the same files, they did so in incompatible ways, thereby creating a de facto file heterogeneity. Nobody seemed to have noticed it until the dry run.

It should be noted that in the background of this fairly serious error was the "common machine" fallacy. System designers failed to appreciate that, in terms of platform compatibility, the software counts more than the hardware. Even on the same type of equipment, *if* two file management/DBMSs are totally different and incompatible, *then* there is heterogeneity, and instead of the supposed integration there is technical disintegration.

9.3 The Fall of a State-of-the-Art Project in Transaction Management

The board of a universal bank decided that, after years of having grown like wild cacti, the presently used business architecture had become inoperative. This made it difficult for traders to access and view customer information across product lines at a moment's notice and, therefore, remain competitive in an increasingly demanding market.

One of the patchworks tried in the past, with no results worth talking about, had been the building of multiple layers of overlapping databases. The process was introduced by one of the main computer vendors, and it aimed to pull data together from lower-standing incompatible platforms. Apart from an inordinately long response time (see Chapter 10), this created

- Redundancies and
- Lots of errors in information elements,

thereby impeding operations.

When the trader/sales support engine on the trader's desk does not help the dealer in getting the appropriate customer data ad hoc, on request, the result is a lack of motivation and poor response to customer requirements coupled with an increase in the risk being assumed. At the insistence of one of its members who was IT-literate, the board asked that this awkward situation be brought to an end through a new procedure.

One of the new procedure's specifications was that not only any-to-any database access should be real-time and seamless, but also knowledge-enriched software should provide the trader with patterns of market prices along with risk profiles for any counterparty, any instrument, and any transaction. Let me highlight this technical requirement. The concept was based in:

- Seamless access
- High functionality
- Pass-through linkages
- Price patterning
- Risk patterning

A preliminary study proposed to deliver enriched functionality at the *metalevel* of commercially available standard supporting software, which was identified. This preliminary system approach was developed by an independent information engineering bureau.

The CIO commented that what the outsourced study proposed was not rational, because the transactions of this universal bank were polyvalent, including credit decisions, market decisions, and execution activities for each specific counterparty. He said that:

- Off-the-shelf software cannot effectively handle such requirements.
- A metalayer would not answer what the board had requested.

The CIO further suggested that the whole new transaction management procedure be done in-house, even if this ended up doubling the time and the budget of that proposed by the independent engineering bureau. His proposal was that the in-house development would retain the handling of credit facilities and trading activities while doing away with knowledge artifacts, since his staff lacked the skills. Instead, the CIO added, COBOL routines would support

- Product pricing,
- Limit setting,
- Risk assessment, and
- Account management.

An independent expert, asked to look into this counterproposal, expressed doubts that it could or would do what it claimed. His pessimism was fed by the fact that the outsourced system design called for transaction management capable of price and control credit exposure for each individual counterparty, after the default probability had been assessed by a loan officer with the help of a scoring system and of database mining. This required a very sophisticated solution, nondeliverable under COBOL.

In fact, part of the metalayer proposed by the independent engineering firm was to implement, at the credit-risk side of transaction management, a contingent claims analysis through knowledge engineering. Also known as *option modeling*,* this assumes the borrower has an option to default that can be modeled as a put option. The CIO considered this facility as being unnecessary, a statement the independent expert rejected.

At the CEO's request, the independent expert explained why this was an interesting concept on which management could capitalize. The underlying basis for the option represents the borrower's assets. Present asset value and the volatility of asset value due to earnings volatility are default parameters. The strike price is represented by the present value of the borrower's liabilities. This type of model assumes that

- The put will be exercised, hence the borrower will opt to default, and
- This will happen when the present value of the borrower's assets falls below the present value of the liabilities.

In fact, to demonstrate to the CEO and the board what can be obtained through high technology, the independent information engineering bureau had designed a prototype of a novel process of estimating expected exposure at time of default, per single transaction. This was structured so as to address the likelihood of both *expected losses* (EL) and *unexpected losses* (UL). In the case of loans, the parameters were loan value plus accrued interest outstanding at time of default. The basic elements in estimating the term structure of default probabilities were

- Transaction structuring and
- The setting of borrower limits.

These short paragraphs help to explain the sophistication of the projected solution which, at the bank side, led to high hopes by traders of having a system able to speak their language. The treasurer to whom the traders reported wanted IT to get busy and develop it as soon as the new business architecture—with trading its first major application—was approved by the board along with authorization to spend money for state-of-the-art models. But the CIO objected and one of the influential members of the board, who was also executive vice president of a computer manufacturer, seconded him. This brought company politics into the picture, and as the argument became amplified, the contrarian board member mastered enough votes to delay the board's approval.

The CIO was particularly concerned that he might lose his status in the company if such an advanced solution saw the light. But what motivated the board member to vote against was a novel database design and associated change in equipment.

* D.N. Chorafas. "Introduction to Derivative Financial Instruments," McGraw-Hill, New York, 2008.

The company database administrator was a young IT graduate whose thinking was ahead of that of his colleagues. He projected a distributed database structure whose files were expressed as a packet with the key being its network address.

- These were to be read and written concurrently so the entire database would become a packet-switching network.
- The network could be used to fetch and store all transferable files in an unblocking way, fully distributed with thousands of accesses happening at once.

The solution was simple and powerful. If applied, it would have eliminated the entire huge and expensive relational database the bank had used for over 20 years with only average results. This was precisely what the dissenting board member and his friends on the board strongly objected to, and with this, strong-arm company politics came into play. The dissent that suddenly showed up was political. It so happened, however, that the universal bank and the computer manufacturer shared some major investors who insisted that the problem had to be solved by means of an exclusive personal discussion between the CEOs of two companies. Guess what happened after that meeting.

9.4 Mismanagement of Client Accounts Revealed by an Audit

If one asks senior bankers to name the top areas of attention that are fueling IT investments, the answers will typically start with special care for institutional investors and corporate customers, followed by regulatory compliance; core value creation; leveraging of existing channels; consolidation, including correspondent banks; security; and disaster recovery.

With regard to IT, some of today's goals among top-tier banks is further cost containment, particularly short-term tangible returns from IT projects; system replacement for treasury management with home-grown software out and a modern package in interactive computational finance; and revamped products, such as electronic letters of credit. (Much depends on standards. The Interstate Commerce Commission (ICC) is setting rules that may open this market.)

Notice, however, that while at the very top of the list is *customer care*, this mainly regards institutional investors and corporate customers, with next in line private wealth management accounts. In contrast, there is a generalized disregard, even mismanagement, of general client accounts as audit after audit reveals.

Several audits demonstrate the existence of different reasons for the mismanagement of clients' accounts, a practice that has also crept into private banking—the theme of this section. These reasons range from outright manipulation with fraud in the background, to ineptitude and plain lack of attention. Whichever the true reason might be, the accountability for what happens lies squarely on the shoulders of senior management whether manipulations are due to

- Lack of training of investment advisors,
- Intermittent or nonexistent supervision, or
- Quotas on sales and profits leading to improper transactions and outright client deception.

This section has been included to document that even small audits, made by the clients themselves to safeguard their wealth entrusted to an institution, can provide a certain sense of security. At least one does not lose one's money without a fight.

The deception of clients can take a number of forms. One of them usually takes place at management's request, and it consists of pushing down the throat of private banking clients unsafe and illiquid instruments, an example being *alternative investments*. These are structured derivative financial instruments of which, by a large majority, individual clients understand nothing and have not even a remote idea of the assumed risk.

Some banks have the bad policy of intensively advertising during a client's advisory meeting that "a modern investor" should have at least 20 percent of his or her fortune in alternative investments (read: a highly unsecured portfolio*). Other institutions have greater pity for their clients and push "only" for a 10 percent share of wealth under their management to be eventually turned into ashes. Needless to say, the bank's internal auditors look the other way.

Some of the manipulations are more classical and more mundane, yet they have the distinction of being brought rather often to court, particularly in the United States. The client signs full powers for management of the account to the bank, and investment advisors as well as traders, generate commissions through frequent selling and buying of securities, with all charges and all risks being passed on to the client.

Scanty or nonexistent supervision leads to still other types of client deception. In late March 1998, for example, the French government made an offer to exchange its 6 percent OAT (Treasury) bonds of 2004 under terms most investors judged as unfavorable to them. The offer said that institutionals (bondholders who are not physical persons or physical persons who tender a total nominal amount greater than a given sum) "will be offered a price for the OAT calculated and published, after the proceeds."

---

* D. N. Chorafas, *Alternative Investments and the Mismanagement of Risk* (London: Macmillan/Palgrave, 2003).

With no covenants attached to these OAT bonds when issued, participation in this offer could only be voluntary. However, some banks and their investment advisors conveniently forgot to inform their private clients about the order's voluntary nature. Instead, the information they provided made it seem as if this was a mandatory change—trapping the client in the process, instead of exercising due diligence, but benefiting the bank, which could have capitalized on the OAT bond's voluntary participation.

Another common trick leading to client deception is a covert play with interest rates by debiting and charging, instead of crediting, a customer account. Here is an example from the French stock market. The market works "à terme," and equities purchased at the beginning of a month are paid at the end of the month. One of my custodian banks sent me the following regarding the results of my audit of its incorrect debits and credits.

> We confirm the purchase of L'Oréal on July 31, XXXX, as well as the complete cancellation of the debit interest rates of 5.626% on your current account, for the third quarter. In the absence of definite instructions, the different (money) transfers *received* during July on your account (for payment of aforementioned securities) were not transferred to a short term deposit.

Behind this message lies the fact that moneys transferred to my account in early July were conveniently parked by the custodian bank to an account from which *it*, not the client, received interest. In contrast, interest was charged to my account for charges that were still not due. If the client does not know the strings this bank and many others are pulling, he is going to lose money.

In fact, what in the aforementioned case came as quite a surprise was that the bank made reference to "absence of definite instructions." Quite to the contrary, there were standing written instructions, specifying that all money must be immediately invested under best conditions on a one-week basis renewed. This had been done by this bank since the beginning of the private account relationship, but then the custodian's policy seems to have changed to the client's disfavor

- Without informing the client and
- Without giving the client a chance to opt out.

This kind of trick with debits and credits is never done to institutional investors because their lawyers are watching out and they are ready to sue. In contrast, several asset managers do not consider the private investors sophisticated enough to appreciate different premeditated manipulations, or to catch up with the fine print of changes in financial statements made without client warning.

Since the financial account submitted by the bank to the client was patently false, I called its director of auditing to discuss the matter and get *his* position in regard to the statement. Subsequently, a fax was sent to him at his request describing step-by-step what the bank had (illegally) done to the account. Among other things, the fax stated that:

> Both debits and credits had nothing to do with reality. The credits were forgotten, the debits were inflated. I did not think there was fraud, but did believe there were unwarranted manipulations of money and of value dates, which should never be repeated, for any client.

"There are some religious rules in accounting," the fax further stated. "One of them is that no debits and no credits can be done without the evidence of vouchers. Where are the vouchers?" The fax also pointed out to the auditor that this was not the first but the third time in that particular year that there was something wrong with this account, evidently asking for needed corrective action.

In the aftermath, senior management and the auditing department covered their people, which raised the likelihood they had not acted without instructions. The whole hierarchy seemed to be rotten, though the bank offered to pay a lump sum and return wrongly debited money—without admitting guilt. The end result was to close the account with this bank and transfer it to a different credit institution, while putting in place a system capable of tracking malfeasance should it occur.

Was this a case of ethics? In his autobiography, Benjamin Franklin writes that at an early age his father convinced him that "that which was not honest could not be truly useful."* Presidents of companies who establish policies, and their underlings who execute them, should read Franklin's book. His advice is the best guide for avoiding reputational risk.

9.5 Wrong Approach to Risk Control: Too Much Manual Work

Describing how members of an investment bank's risk management organization start their day, a financial book gave the following scenario: "The day starts by checking the status of data feeds that come in from the front and back office systems. (The controllers) are members of the risk monitoring team." It sounds reasonable, right? Wrong.

That is exactly what "the controllers" should not do because this is the job of knowledge artifacts—agents and expert systems—and not of highly paid risk managers. Commercial and investment banks who use expensive personnel to do jobs

* Benjamin Franklin, *The Autobiography of Benjamin Franklin* (New York: Barnes & Noble, 1994).

that should have been fully automated long ago find themselves on the wrong track in terms of identification, monitoring, measurement, and control of exposure.

In the bank in reference and many others applying similar approaches, this failure started with system design, filtered through design reviews, and passed the audits of the system. It also violated the principle that experts should be used to handle exceptions and do rigorous analyses, once the knowledge artifacts

- Have detected and possibly corrected errors in data feeds, and
- Have changed each individual transaction against limits, establishing exception reports.

The old-fashioned and ineffectual scenario describing the investment bank's approach to risk management does not end at that point of manual intervention. Once all portfolios are run through a risk model, sometime in the morning, risk controllers review the aggregate risk across the desks. Is that right? Wrong again. The whole culture of such a leisurely approach is for the birds, and for companies who *don't want* to control their risks.

The exposure embedded in derivatives portfolios should be monitored and controlled tick-by-tick intraday, not just when risk controllers wake up and suddenly become busybodies. Exception handling by means of models is doable, executed in real time through knowledge artifacts. If not all banks are doing so, it is because many are mired in ineffectual manual procedures and slow, costly mainframes.

As an IT audit in a different investment bank brought to management's attention, for intraday risk monitoring and exception reporting, a global institution should be using not one but a family of expert systems. These must run in the four corners of its trading empire, working as a network. Other knowledge artifacts must

- Read the journal,
- Examine traders' data inputs and e-mails,
- Flash out extreme events, and
- Focus on inconsistencies and limit breakers.

While the tracking must be done through knowledge engineering, analysis of the findings is the job of human experts, who should concentrate on examination and discovery, rather than sending e-mails to each other as if they are lovers. Moreover, the results of these analyses must be flashed to responsible executives instantaneously and presented in color graphics.

This is just the normal course with current technology, but for many institutions it is mountain climbing, because they have never done it before. As one of my professors at UCLA taught his students, mathematics divides into two parts. One is very easy; the other very difficult. Figure 9.2 tells why. The often-encountered

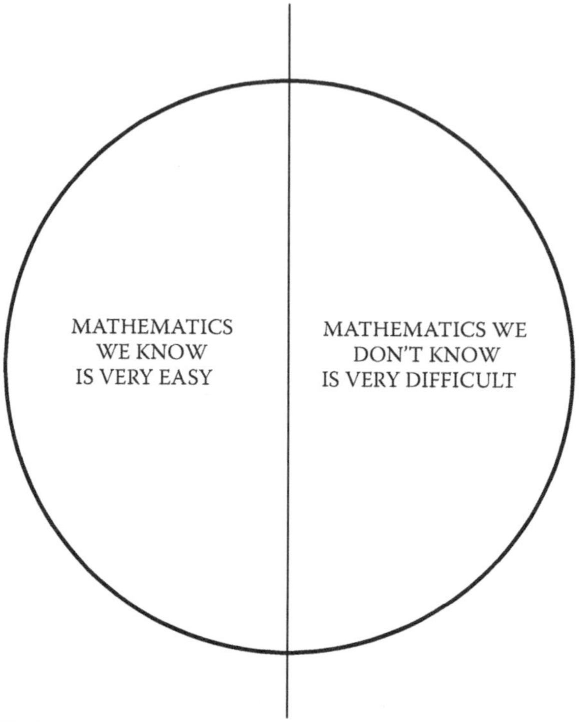

Figure 9.2 Mathematics (noun singular) divides into two parts, and their frontier lies on what we know.

linguistic summaries prepared for senior management have no business in risk control because

- Few people bother reading them, and when they do, chances are that
- Few people would understand, or would want to understand, the message.

Speaking from personal experience, other IT audits have revealed that a mistake often made in connection with risk management—into which both theorists and practitioners fall—is to delay the computation of exposure until the data "is made more reliable." Said a risk manager to my remark about delays in the course of an IT audit: "Because the covariance matrix uses a large amount of historical data, a one-day lag will not have an impact." That is wrong.

- A one-day lag could have a very significant impact, depending on the magnitude and aftereffect of the event.
- The data used by risk-control models should definitely be clean, but this is not the job of risk managers.

Data clearance is the responsibility of information technologists and of knowledge artifacts. The job of risk managers is to make two estimates based on the same data:

1. By the order of magnitude, accepting engineering error (3 to 4 percent). This makes it possible to position the exposure and estimate its size while exercising one's ingenuity in projecting its trend.
2. By the precision of available data, which is, after all, the way economists produce their results.

Let me repeat this message, to be sure that it is understood. The best policy is to proceed with a real-time evaluation of *virtual risk*, as we do with virtual balance sheets, because data inputs must sometimes be corrected. Within certain limits, accuracy is enough. Modern risk-management solutions rely heavily on time-honored engineering principles in computation.

Snap answers on assumed exposure that are accurate but not precise cannot be provided by slow-moving systems based on legacy software and batch work. In modern markets, real-time response is crucial because, as they become more volatile, risk evaluation often calls for management to either stop assuming new exposure or increase risk capital to keep the same overall capital adequacy level. This is written in the understanding that fire sales should be avoided.

- Forced selling tends to drive markets against themselves, ending by selling even more.
- With this, exposure increases because, in turmoil, markets become more interlinked, canceling the effects of previous diversification.

Additionally, the evaluation of exposure should not start with aggregation, but with detail. When risk-management models look at a firm's overall risk, summary hypotheses and interpretations may give misguided signals. That is the herd syndrome. Several banks and other entities started in derivatives trading because the risk-adjusted returns were "thought to be" much better than elsewhere. Now there is evidence that

- The risks are much greater than originally thought,
- While diversification's benefits are much lower.

There is as well a lag in recognition of changes taking place in volatility and liquidity. Most models, including value at risk (VAR), are based on how markets have moved in the past. As such, they assume that extreme movements are rare. In a normal distribution curve, these extreme movements are represented by trivial probabilities. But in real life, the likelihood of extreme events increases, particularly at the long leg of the risk distribution where events have the greatest impact.

9.6 Auditing the Models for Market-Risk Exposure

The development of derivatives markets has given banks the incentive to focus on trading, but it has also underlined the need to control the risk profile of their portfolio more closely and more accurately than ever. Over the last 20 years, the trading of derivatives and securities has seen

- Significant increases in the estimation of market risk, but
- Little effort to audit and stress-test the assumptions underpinning the existing models.

At least in theory, financial risk management has evolved dramatically over the last few years. But in practice, this is not necessarily true if one judges by the models that are being generally used. The prerequisite analytics on which the large majority of current models is based

- Are rather static and
- Do not take into account lagged multiplier effects.

Moreover, model structure is mainly a spreadsheet approach, primarily to the U.S. economy, even if these models are globally used.

With these facts in mind, the executive vice president (EVP) of an international bank asked a consultant to audit the models his bank had been using and come up with an opinion on how well they responded to its need for market risk management. The EVP also offered, and the consultant accepted, to have three correspondent banks participate in the study that his institution had commissioned.

One of the concerns the EVP expressed during the preliminary meetings on this particular project was that derivatives had raised a simultaneous dual challenge of pricing financial instruments and at the same time controlling their exposure (partly due to wrong pricing). Therefore, he wanted to know if it would be possible to develop more sophisticated in-house solutions capable of measuring the range of risk inherent in a given pricing decision.

This theme was discussed in a brainstorming session between specialists of the four banks, a couple of rocket scientists*, and the consultant. The sense of the meeting was that, in terms of algorithms and heuristics, it is not easy to develop a model that accurately represents market movements as a function of small pricing changes, but it is doable. Following this meeting, the sponsoring bank started a project to develop a prototype.

The larger mission of the external expert was that of auditing the quality of models presently used in the control of market exposure. This was a fairly complex task that involved the trading system's three pillars: human capital, information

* D. N. Chorafas, *Rocket Scientists in Banking* (London: Lafferty Publications, 1995).

technology, and the models themselves. Only the latter will interest us in this section. Models connected to trading were mainly designed to elucidate one of two things:

1. Tell something about the future
2. Evaluate an exposure that has already been assumed

Like all forecasting models, those used by the institution tried to accomplish what bankers, traders, investors, and speculators are continually trying to do: Predict the future. While we know that we cannot accurately make such predictions, we do expect that by ingeniously massaging historical data these would reveal a likely future pattern of market movements.

The bank's models were fairly good. Management, however, had incorrectly assumed that future market behavior would follow the same pattern as in the past. That was wrong. Historical data do not remove future uncertainty, which is what risk is all about.

In a seminar held for the bank's senior managers and professionals, the consultant explained that modeling is by definition approximate, and it is not unlikely that its output will leave much to be desired. A great deal depends on the skill with which

- Models are made,
- Models are applied in daily work, and
- Model results are interpreted.

Part of the skill with which a model is developed, and subsequently used, regards an appreciation of its shortcomings. The model, the consultant said, is not a precise predictor. Whenever there is a case of making a choice between precision in modeling and precision in its implementation in risk management:

- The better solution would be an approximate model applied by people with dedication, intuition, and experience.
- The poorer solution would be a "perfect model" in the hands of people who do not quite understand where and how it should be used or who misinterpret its results.

Several of the bank's managers and professionals participating in this seminar took the consultant's remarks badly and went on to complain to the bank's president, who was aware of the shock therapy employed by the consultant and brushed aside the complaints.

The chief risk manager, who participated in the seminar, took to heart the consultant's criticism of the bank's overreliance on the value at risk (VAR) model for sizing up market exposure. To him VAR, and most specifically *expected shortfall*

(ES), its more recent incarnation, were God-given and therefore they could not go wrong. (Yet they do go wrong in an awful way as the 2007/2008 financial disaster has demonstrated.)

The good news about VAR, said the consultant, was that its advent brought a change from past practice, where banks have usually measured the risks in individual parts of their trading book separately, often doing so by rule of thumb. By moving toward a whole trading book approach by using value-at-risk, bankers and treasurers started to calculate on a more consistent basis the *likely loss* they might experience on their trading.

VAR results, however, are very approximate, and they become even more so every day because the model rests on a weak and obsolete basis. Not only have the better-managed banks come up with more-sophisticated VAR versions (like gamma-neutral VAR), but they have also developed alternative market risk-control models. The bank whose IT was audited had not yet done so.

The consultant suggested a dual approach to modeling market risk: instrument-by-instrument and holistic, integrating instrument-level results on exposure through a weighted process by demodulating the notional principal amount (in connection with derivatives). Both should benefit from economic capital (capital at risk, CAR) allocation*, which presents two advantages:

- It obliges management to think in terms of capitalization, as required by the bank's market exposure.
- It leads to an evaluation of whether the accumulation of capital at risk is held at or below a level *our* bank can afford.

Until then, senior management had looked at these issues as being awfully technical. But the shock therapy on model usage had helped in changing this attitude, because many key people appreciated the fact that their bank tended to take rather major market risks. Another contribution of the IT/model audit is that it brought into perspective the need for using experimental tools to evaluate the results of value at risk and other models through simulation of general and specific market factors.

An added value was management's understanding of the importance of stress testing, promoted by the Basel Committee on Banking Supervision. Stress tests and stress scenarios, the consultant said, are eye-openers in connection with the likelihood of catastrophic events in market risk and credit risk. Studying both the body and long queue of the loss distribution helps in distinguishing two different types of exposure; outliers indeed can have plenty of unexpected consequences.

* D. N. Chorafas, *Economic Capital Allocation with Basle II: Cost and Benefit Analysis* (London: Butterworth-Heinemann, 2004).

III
TECHNICAL EXAMPLES IN AUDITING IT FUNCTIONS

Chapter 10

Auditing IT Response Time and Reliability

10.1 Qualifications for Auditing Specific Technical Issues

The four chapters of Part 2 addressed themselves, primarily, to strategic IT audit. But there are as well tactical issues in information technology that have to be audited. This is the theme of Part 3, starting with the present chapter, which addresses two issues: system response time and reliability.

System response time and reliability are often seen as two important but distinct, stand-alone subjects. That is wrong because they are closely related. Improving response time, which is a critical activity with online computers and communications aggregates, makes sense if system reliability is high. If it is low, no matter how well response time has been optimized while the system runs, there will be many cases where it becomes infinite.

Another particularity of the two chapters of Part 3, in contrast to the book's first nine chapters, is that the presentation is different. After the subject of each technical issue has been briefly defined, the reader is presented with a battery of tests or, more precisely, of questions the IT auditor should ask when investigating the subject in discussion.

This is a deliberate choice, intended to guide the reader's hand in auditing each from a tactical viewpoint. Taken together, the batteries of questions addressing the chosen issues provide a body of reference that can also be valuable (as a guide) in auditing other technical subjects.

Of course, as discussed in Chapter 3, the common ground that all IT auditors should share is deep expertise in the practice of auditing. I am proposing this point because many people are termed "IT auditors" when, in effect, they are programmers, analysts, or other IT professionals without the ability or knowledge necessary to tear apart the balance sheet of IT operations or evaluate an ROI (return on investment) proposal. The ability to critically examine technical issues and offer constructive criticism stands on two legs:

- Auditing expertise
- Technical expertise

It has been repeatedly emphasized that the modern IT auditor must be a polyvalent person and, therefore, much more than a mere locator of errors or discoverer of frauds. Here are some leading questions to help managers identify persons qualified as IT auditors in terms of personal and technical attributes.

> Does the candidate IT auditor possess more than IT experience, for instance knowledge of accounting and finance?

It did not used to be that way, but today such knowledge is fundamental, and it will be even more so in the future in IT auditing. Without good training in basic accounting and finance, progress in the field of information system auditing is not possible.

> Does the candidate IT auditor have thorough knowledge of modern IT operations, including knowledge engineering, Web 2.0, and software as a service?

Software as a service has not been included in this text because auditing experience in this field is still very thin—but it is coming. Without knowledge of the next milestone, the technique of the IT auditor will be limited, at best, or it may be counterproductive if there is a delay in his or her contribution to the change in information technology that the company needs to remain competitive.

> Does the candidate IT auditor have a sound knowledge of the business his or her company is in? Of its organization?

As we saw in Chapter 8, a senior IT auditor may be required to give advice in regard to business strategy as well as organizational structure. This goes beyond the firm's IT, such as demands posed by (and satisfaction provided to) end users. Hence the next query.

> How well is the candidate IT auditor aware of the company's strategy and the requirements it poses on IT?

This is a fairly large question because it presupposes knowledge of products, processes, markets, human resources, and finances. It may not look that way, but a good part of the auditor's work deals in terms of money and economics. Therefore, the auditor should never forget that economic principles govern modern industrial life.

> Is the candidate IT auditor well versed in IT issues? How much hands-on experience does he or she have in investigation?

A couple of years ago, the Yankee Group revealed that up to 40 percent of existing access network records incurred some level of inaccuracy. It also found that field visits to determine and fix the cause of different problems were set to increase to five times their current level, with an evident impact on costs.

> Has the candidate IT auditor been involved in this type of study?

This is not an unreasonable request, because the need for such studies is increasing. Many user organizations found out the hard way that they were trapped by their access network, and they had to do something about it. Projects have been set up to that end, but without thoroughly auditing an access network, it is impossible to take corrective measures.

> Does the candidate IT auditor have a good knowledge of cost accounting principles, rules, and procedures?

As Chapter 8 has documented, sound management practice requires that information technology services be billed to the user departments, and before being billed they have to be costed. Costing and billing have to be audited. This is a steady process; it does not happen just once in a lifetime.

> Is the candidate IT auditor characterized by independence of opinion? Does the candidate have the guts to put his/her opinion in writing?

The IT auditor should never be a "yes man." This is the worst choice that management can make. A great many IT audit reports are timid, conservative, and stereotyped, and good managers will have the sense to ignore them. If senior management were truly interested in an audit, this would be the last place to go.

Last but not least:

> Does the candidate IT auditor possess a combination of critical and constructive ability?

Contrary to financial audits (which, as we saw in Part 1, are either unqualified or present different levels of qualifications), after reading an IT audit, management often asks: "If not 'this,' then what else?" The auditor is not expected to present a new system design, but it helps if—through training and experience—he or she can be constructive and advance some suggestions that can be defended.

10.2 System Response Time

One of the topmost characteristics of a system design, the ability of flawless implementation and operation, is largely (though not exclusively) based on system reliability and response time—the way they are perceived by the end user. Both impact on the acceptability of a system solution in terms of its

- Effectiveness,
- Quality of service,
- Cost of operations, and
- Operational performance.

System response time is the time the end user waits. It is measured from the user's signal to the system that there is work to be done, to the point at which the system begins to present the requested information to the user. (It should not be confused with *turnaround time*, which includes the time taken by computational routines.)

Within a given operating environment, the pattern of system response time identifies one of the prevailing operating characteristics of the solution that has been adopted. With the exception of standard tests made to gauge system response, this pattern is always a function of basic technical factors as well as

- System configuration,
- Jobs being treated,
- Type of database access (hierarchical, relational, object), and
- Overhead by physical media and logical supports (operating system [OS], database management system [DBMS], input/output [I/O], transaction handling, and so on)

The message conveyed by these bulleted items is that system response time is more meaningful with centralized operations (of which there are still plenty), where heavy I/O may result in severe time degradation, depending on machine type, OS, and DBMS. For each system configuration, the average operational performance, in terms of response time, means nothing. The only valid approach is response time per

- Individual user and
- His/her job stream

in the realm of a total simultaneously operating user environment.

In principle, higher complexity jobs typically require proportionally more processing power than I/O. In contrast, lower complexity jobs like data processing are characterized by more I/O than processing. These are references pertaining to turnaround time, which is also true of visualization, formatting, and error-assist to individual users.

The transaction profiles, computing functions, data searchers, number of simultaneously online workstations, and overall complexity of the work influence both response time and turnaround time. Since the beginning of online IT operations, complexity has been defined as the ratio of processor use to I/O. Though this definition is only half-valid today, it continues to be used because the majority of installations are still characterized by tonalities of centralization.

What would the IT auditor be expected to do in terms of response time? My advice is that rather than immediately attaching end-user details, a first approach should target representative envelopes of response time connected to fairly homogeneous programs run online.

These envelopes help to identify system capabilities within a given implementation environment. The programs called by users in an envelope will typically represent calls for resource sharing. Questions to be asked by the auditor of system response time include:

> Number, type, and processing characteristics of individual jobs treated within the operating environment under study.

The answer to this query should look not only at stand-alone jobs but also at established priorities, correlations in resource sharing, bottlenecks of that environment as well as response time requirements of each job and other factors influencing and influenced by the creation of envelopes. An example is the type and frequency of file accesses in relation to physical media and logical supports.

> Input/output characteristics and related issues, including visualization, buffering, session and presentation control, front-end solutions (if any), and communications protocols.

Because protocols, basic software, and database architecture greatly impact on system performance, the IT auditor should look at them as design factors with aftereffects on resource sharing and response time. In an interactive application environment, benchmarking of a sample of jobs and simulation based on results of benchmarks can provide useful data on response time evaluation.

Typically, in performing these tests the IT auditors will formulate a number of hypotheses that should be tested against real-life response time results. As an example, Figure 10.1 presents two simulations and subsequent real-life tests.

The way to bet is that, for any given system operating within a defined applications environment, as the number of simultaneous accesses increases, the response

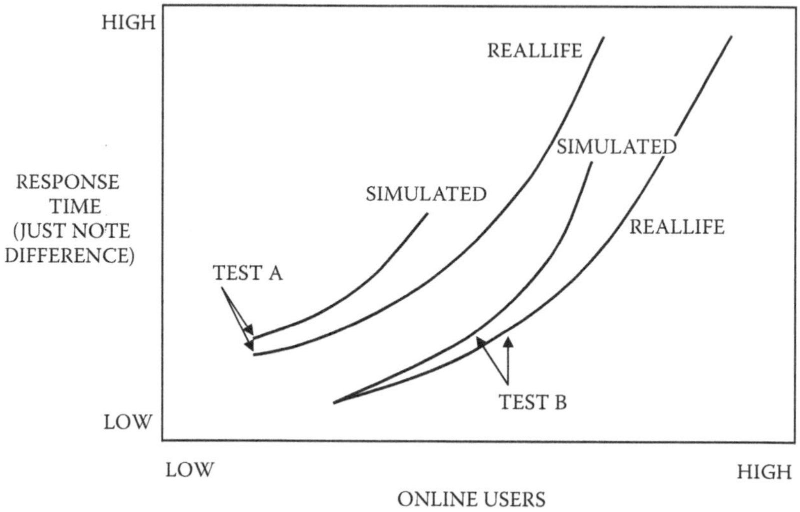

Figure 10.1 Simulated and effective response time.

time degrades. Therefore, other things being equal, if we maximize the number of simultaneous end users, we also increase the number of people confronted by degraded service. But how important is this change?

The easy answer to this query is that accounting routines can be employed to record the number of log-ins by users and corresponding response times. This is not the best approach, because the number of simultaneous system users is a misleading measure of system load. As we will see in Section 3, the system expansion factor (SEF) is a better (albeit imperfect) statistic.

10.3 System Expansion Factor

One of the IT auditor's responsibilities in the study of system response time is to examine the cost effectiveness of resources and their cost versus end-users' productivity and idle time. Up to a point, but only up to a point, we can swamp response time by expanding available resources until reaching the point where this becomes uneconomical.

Within such a briefly described perspective of cost and return, there exists a useful type of measurement known as the system expansion factor (SEF). It can be seen as a way of evaluating IT services relative to the shortest time within which work *could* have been completed with available resources. Therefore, information technology costs serve as a factor in dimensioning the system. SEF is defined as the ratio of

- The *elapsed time* for doing a unit of computer-bound work within a cooperative multiuser environment to
- The *minimum time* to do that same piece of work if the resources were available on a stand-alone basis.

As these two bulleted items suggest, the system expansion factor is broader than a pure response-time estimate in the sense that it includes the execution of a given job. In this sense, it is nearer to turnaround time (see Section 4), although the two terms are not the same. SEF fits well in the coming environment of software as a service and other network-based applications, if the hypothesis is made that a stand-alone engine would practically have near-zero latency.

The term *minimum time* denotes the minimum elapsed time within which a given body of work could be completed without contention. The processor's component of minimum time is the easiest part to estimate accurately. I/O time is more elusive, and it should be calculated using a single job basis as a proxy. On a single job basis, SEF is computed as the aforementioned ratio of elapsed time to minimum time.

$$\text{system expansion factor} = \frac{\text{elapsed time}}{\text{minimum time}} \tag{10.1}$$

For instance, an expansion factor of 2 indicates that the work required twice the elapsed time that would have been needed without contention, which is the minimum time. Expansion factors can be computed by considering only I/O, or only processing component, but it is better to use both because jobs that truly need only one of them are an exception.

A more sophisticated approach is necessary when considering a complex system. In this case, SEF is calculated by dividing the total user-requested action by specific dedicated processor time plus I/O time plus contention. Notice that while this measure is useful, it is imperfect because it was developed for mainframe-based systems and associated number-crunching engines. It also makes certain assumptions:

- There is a fair amount of timesharing performed in the system.
- Computation time and I/O time for any one use are not overlapping.
- At the database-mining level, all paging and mechanical movements are overhead, working by contention.
- Though typically oriented to one industry sector, the work environment does not necessarily imply homogeneous jobs.

Given these assumptions, while not an exact measure, the system expansion factor serves well enough as a first-order approximation of what actually happens. For instance, using SEF statistics, the IT auditor can employ an experimental approach to simulate the degradation in system response.

In many cases, though not always, a first-order approximation suffices because we are often interested in an order-of-magnitude degradation and thresholds having a profound influence on end-user productivity. (Experiments done with online environments document that each second of system-response degradation leads to a similar degradation added to end-user's time for the following request.)

The opening paragraph of this section also suggested that one of the uses to which statistics about system response time can be applied is measuring the cost of available resources. This is the alter ego of estimating delays in system response and the period of time each type of online interactive work might take. To get a better understanding of SEF measurement targets, the IT auditor must appreciate that there are a number of issues associated with expansion factors:

- An expansion factor for a given user can be calculated if one employs all data that apply to that user.
- Changes in expansion factors through time can be shown, if one employs all data collected during successive time periods.
- *If* data apply to all interactive users at one-hour intervals for one day, *then* SEF shows the time-of-day service measure.

These three bulleted items suggest a list of questions the IT auditor should be asking to understand the SEF statistics that he or she is presented with. It is always advisable to keep in mind that information technology is a science whose standardization is often talked about but rarely realized in a consistent sense, and sometimes there are conflicts of interest behind confused statistics.

Expansion-factor reports could address classes of users, time ranges, or specific facilities under investigation. In all these cases, SEF is not only conditioned by the user environment; it is also machine bound. Newer, faster processors in the system turn work to a user faster than older ones. Therefore, expansion factors can also serve in investigating the need for a system upgrade or restructuring.

10.4 User Activity and the Cost of Turnaround Time

While attention to system design, performance factors, machine capacity, functionality, and associated expansion factors is a "must," IT auditors must also pay attention to the individual system users and their work habits or, more precisely, the way each user applies himself or herself to the system (and to his or her work). This has a significant impact on human–machine behavior.

For instance, terminalization in an office work environment allows persons to initiate long-running tasks whose response time impacts upon other end users' productivity. Hence, in order to talk about a user's productivity, it is necessary to estimate the length of time the user is actually working at his or her workstation or waits for a response that comes at slow pace.

As an approximation of the true user-bound time in a man-machine interactive environment, we calculate the *user-active time* (UAT). This is the sum of short elapsed time intervals during which there was system activity by a given end user. By examining UAT, it is possible to classify each user into one of several states that are useful for analysis. For instance:

- *Idle*, keying, "thinking," or absent
- *Runnable*, in relay to use system resources
- *Running*, using system resources
- *Wait*, divided into I/O wait or page-in wait
- *Eligible*, waiting for storage access in data mining

That is a classification from the end-user viewpoint. In contrast, from a system perspective, the total capacity of any IT system, and the cost this represents, will be shared between three main classes: productive time, idle time, and overhead (the system works to keep itself in shape). Figure 10.2 presents two different patterns, each belonging to a different system configuration.

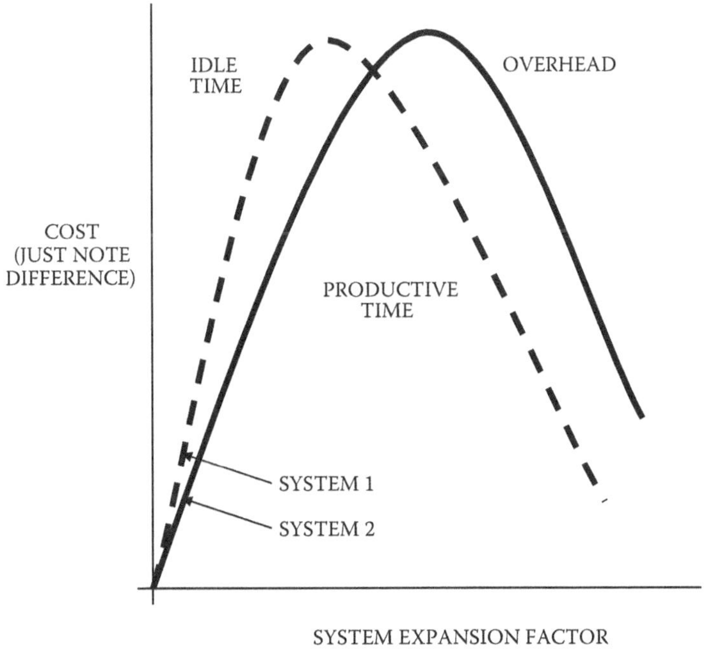

Figure 10.2 Idle time, productive time and overhead of a computers and communications system.

Integrating the elements presented in the preceding paragraphs, we come to the conclusion that—in a system involving local area networks (LAN), wide area networks (WAN), computer resources, databases, and communications switches—the status of idle, runnable, running, wait, and eligible time affect *system turnaround time* (STT). A correct estimate will involve all functions and delays* at client servers, communications nodes, and switches as well as application commands, systems calls, database searches, and more.

While many factors impact system turnaround times, from the end user's viewpoint, STT should be subsecond for about 90 percent of all cases of user access, with 8 percent being less than one second and the balance less than two seconds. This is a good standard, permitting flexibility in system design without undue costs. It can be nicely met at reasonable expense through networked client/servers but not by mainframes.

Analysis of STT state data helps to locate bottlenecks in the system and to measure the effect of bottlenecks on end users. Without time studies at the procedural end, it is not possible to elaborate reasons for idleness. (Even when a terminalized user is working intensely, user-response time, which includes key-in time and output requirements, absorb a large share of the log.)

Another vital measure the IT auditor should include in his or her examination kit is the number of concurrent transactions in wait or, more precisely, the number of commands that have been entered into the system but have not yet been completed. For a given configuration, when the number of concurrent transactions increases, contention increases too. In principle:

- Utilization of available resources goes up until it reaches a saturation level.
- The percentage of time dedicated to end users declines at higher levels of contention because of queuing and because more supervisor time is consumed in managing available resources.

Samples of user activity can give helpful documentation in keeping the system well tuned in order to make more of the current capacity available through better coordination of system components and of work patterns. It is not possible to design, implement, dimension, and maintain interactive systems without proper statistics taken at run time through sampling routines.

This being said, long years of experience with online applications help in documenting that the more centralized is a given system, the greater will be its turnaround time—a fact that mainframers prefer to forget. In the general case, as the number of processors increases, so does the aggregate cost because of underperformance by the user population. The IT auditor should be very sensitive to this fact.

Dr. Michael Stonebraker, of the University of California, at Berkeley, has advanced an important metric of the cost function associated with turnaround

* For instance, *idle time* arising from contention, interlocks, and other mishaps.

time. The principle behind it is that every time the number of *processes* exceeds the number of *processors* in a system, the solution that has been implemented is in trouble.

To account for the expense to the user organization represented by an increase in response time, Dr. Stonebraker and Dr. Wei Hong, also of UC Berkeley, proposed the following algorithm:

$$\text{cost function} = \text{resource consumption} + (W \times \text{response time}) \qquad (10.2)$$

where W is a judgmental factor valuing response time over the cost of resources. Response time is calculated in seconds and fractions thereof, and it is expressed in absolute value.

- If end-user time is expensive, W can equal 5 or more.
- For low-paid clerical work, W may be taken as equal to 1.

The major advantage of the Stonebraker-Hong algorithm lies in the visibility it brings to the *real* costs of computing. The cost function in equation (10.2) does not need to be precise; an order-of-magnitude measurement can ring alarm bells. Every time the response time increases, so does the total system cost.

Experiments done at the University of California help in documenting that this cost function can be instrumental in determining resource allocation, all the way from the purchasing of new equipment (hardware and software) to its online usage. The Stonebraker-Hong algorithm is simple and very effective; therefore, IT auditors can capitalize on this by asking the CIO and his or her people to:

- Present me a documented cost function of the current mainframe-based solution and of a simulated client/server.
- Draw for me isocost curves for system response time, system expansion factor, user-active time, and system turnaround time for the above alternatives.
- Do the same to compare alternative basic software (OS, DBMS, TPR*) for the current hardware platforms.

Armed with answers to these queries the IT auditor should further ask:

- How should the current system be redimensioned to cut response time in half? To observe the 90 percent, 8 percent, 2 percent ratio?
- How much throughput will be required in the next three years? How are you planning to meet the challenge while observing the above ratios?
- What kind of software will be used for cost improvement in the present system's turnaround time?
- Have end-user job streams been thoroughly studied? How much training should take place to reduce delays in user interactivity?

---

* Transaction processing routine.

The IT auditor should only accept answers that are factual, although some will require assumptions. When necessary, such assumptions must be explicitly stated. Otherwise, what the IT auditor gets is seat-of-the-pants answers.

In conclusion, the Stonebraker-Hong algorithm focuses attention where it really belongs, not only at the level of the computer and communications resources, but also at the end-user level. This dual perspective helps the IT auditor in costing resources as well as in performance studies such as the time end users spend on terminals and workstations.

10.5 Auditing Interactive Systems

Sections 2, 3, and 4 have discussed the care that should be paid to the design and audit of interactive systems. Top in the list of objectives is that interactive systems must safeguard the most valuable resources they are set up to serve—the end-user's own time, which is a critical resource for the company.

User-perceived response, functionality, and quality of interactive systems can be defined in terms of dimensioning factors describing essential end-user requirements. Each dimension is defined by a set of system properties that can be quantitatively and qualitatively expressed to reflect values indicating its relevance for

- the type of services offered by IT and
- the aftereffect of system performance on its users.

As the previous sections demonstrated, research projects brought in evidence of the usefulness of a number of criteria for evaluation of an interactive system. These can help in guiding the IT auditor's hand in phrasing the questions he or she should be asking to help in determining the information system's usefulness and its return on investment (see Chapter 8). The following is a list of *show-me* questions:

- Supply examples of help features pertinent to (a sample of) man–machine dialogs.
- Provide comprehensive explanations on a sample of interactive output formats (graphs and tables selected by the auditor).
- Select and present (by the CIO) the best current examples of dialog organization and dialog sequence.
- Demonstrate available user guidance and help-desk support for interactive computer usage.
- Calculate system response time, user activity time, and turnaround time (on a sample of jobs chosen by the IT auditor).
- Test system expansion factor against 10 percent increase/10 percent decrease in configuration cost (and other ratios).
- List the most important and least important system interruptions that took place since the last audit and their background reasons (see Sections 6 and 7).

Other important queries to be asked by the IT auditor concern process canceling without detrimental side effects, the existence of syntactically homogeneous command languages that are easy to remember and apply by end users, the possibility of reducing input/output according to the user's training level, and the flexibility required to allow the user to define his or her set of system functions.

Also subject to audit should be the existence of routines permitting the user to make background processes visible; the availability of a data-management system that obviates, as far as possible, the need for the user to perform clerical and housekeeping activities; simplicity of task handling; and, most importantly, tolerance toward erroneous user input.

In the background of these end-user support characteristics is the need to enable each manager, professional, and clerk to set his or her own pace of interactive work with the information system. This is crucial, inasmuch as many business activities today find themselves in a process of *time deformation*

- From *clock time*
- To activity time, or *intrinsic time.*

This is shown in Figure 10.3. Intrinsic time is one's own pace of work. Aside from the fact that we do not all work at the same pace, there exist significant business time differences between financial centers and industrial areas of activity. Indeed, intrinsic time has been one of the reasons why customization to end-user requirements has become a key competitive advantage. Still other questions to be asked by the IT auditor in terms of system design and an implementation supporting interactivity include:

- Assurance of fault tolerance (see Sections 6 and 7)
- Decision aids (expert systems and models)
- Enrichment of displayed information by means of encoded messages
- Provision of well-rounded safeguards to the user (see Chapter 11)

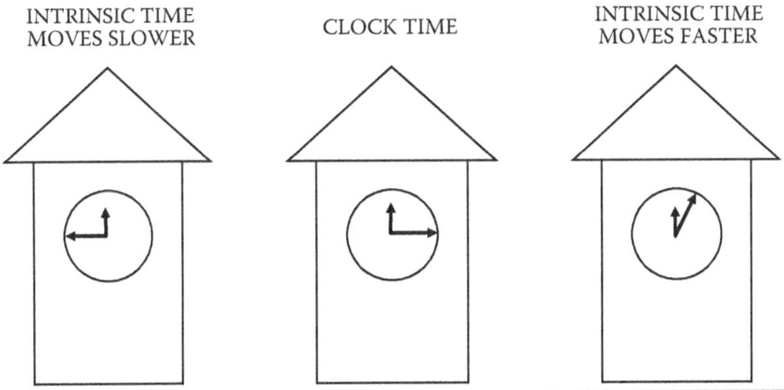

Figure 10.3 Intrinsic time can be shorter or much longer than clock time.

In short, a major preoccupation of the IT auditor should always be whether the system has been projected to enhance the user's ability to do productive work. While some supports represent system overhead, it should not be forgotten that aggregate user time is much more costly than computer time.

A basic consideration in auditing interactive systems is that, while only a portion of the authorized users will be working with the system at the same moment, a small fraction of them will account for the largest share of available resources (Pareto's law). Statistics taken with interactive systems indicate that less than 10 percent of their users consume about 75 percent of available resources. Pareto curves, like the one shown in Figure 10.4, characterize the distribution of interactive computing usage in many installations.

What this application of Pareto's law strongly suggests is that the users should always be a focal point of IT auditing. By focusing on the top 10 percent of an interactive system's users, we frequently find that a fraction of their interactions dominates the overall demand for functionally intensive operations. This leads to specific considerations pertaining to the audit of an interactive system in terms of end-user requirements: an audit to be cast according to user profiles.

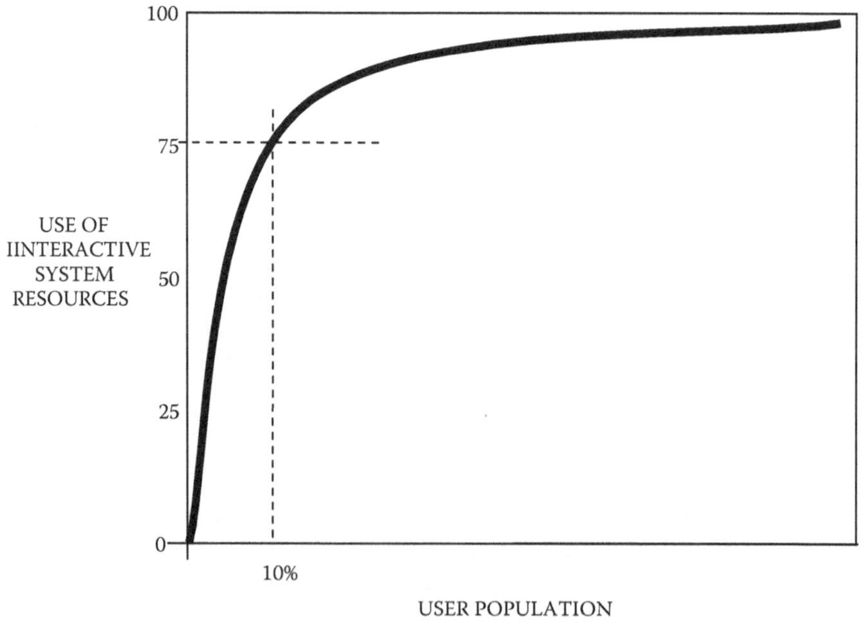

Figure 10.4 Pareto's law applied to the use of system resources.

10.6 Auditing System Reliability

Reliability is not an ability. It is the probability that a machine or a system will work satisfactorily for a preestablished period of time, under operational and environmental conditions defined in advance. For stand-alone systems like a missile, reliability is calculated by the algorithm

$$R = e^{-t/\overline{T}} \tag{10.3}$$

where $\overline{T}$ is the mean time between failures (MTBF, more on this later), t is the time over which a system is expected to operate, and e is the Neperian logarithm radix. Equation (10.3) is not the best for computer centers and networks. Indeed, many IT operations prefer to use a simplified algorithm

$$R = \frac{\text{system usage time}}{\Sigma \text{ interruptions}} \tag{10.4}$$

In this case, *reliability* can be seen as the extent to which a system performs its specified functions (without any failures visible to its users) divided by time lost in interruptions. This is not the same as the first definition of reliability, which is much more rigorous.

The reader should note that redundancy in design may be used to emulate a higher reliability factor. On the other hand, an increase in the number of components also tends to reduce system reliability. As Table 10.1 shows, *if* each component's reliability is 0.999 (which is high), *then* a system of 500 components connected in series will have a reliability of only 0.60 (which is very low). The algorithm is

$$R = R_1 \bullet R_2 \bullet R_3 \bullet \ldots \bullet R_{n-1} \bullet R_n \tag{10.5}$$

Table 10.1 Component Reliability and System Reliability with 500 Components Connected in Series

Reliability of Each Component, Ri	*Resulting System Reliability, R*
0.999	0.60
0.9994	0.70
0.9998	0.80
0.99992	0.90
0.99995	0.95

where

R = system reliability
R_i = reliability of each component (taken as equal to one another)
n = number of components connected in services

With computers and communications, a useful metric is *availability*, defined as the probability that a system is running at any point during scheduled time. An important measurement is percent availability, calculated as

$$\text{percent availability} = 100 \times \frac{\text{system usage time (uptime)}}{\text{scheduled time}} \tag{10.6}$$

Yet another measure of system availability, particularly from an end-user perspective, is *uptime*. A simple equation is

$$\text{uptime} = \text{scheduled time} - \text{system downtime} \tag{10.7}$$

A better and more complex measure of availability distinguishes between machine failures and system failures, then calculates the mean time of successful operation as well as the mean time of interrupts. Both are critical factors in connection with system reliability and availability. For a stand-alone machine, the mean time between failures is computed as

$$\text{MTBF} = \bar{T} = \frac{\Sigma t_1 + t_2 + t_3 + \ldots + t_n}{n} \tag{10.8}$$

where t_i is each problem-free period (uptime) of the stand-alone machine, and n is the between-failures measurements we have in the sample. A similar algorithm is valid for the calculation of mean time between *system* interrupts

$$\text{MTBSI} = \frac{\Sigma t_1 + t_2 + t_3 + \ldots + t_n}{n} \tag{10.9}$$

In this case, t_i is the system uptime and n is the number of measurements in the sample in connection with error-free performance of the whole system. The mean time of system interrupts is

$$\text{MTOSI} = \frac{\Sigma \tau_1 + \tau_2 + \tau_3 + \ldots + \tau_n}{n} \tag{10.10}$$

where τ_i is each time-to-repair period (for the system), and n is the sample size, as in equations (10.7) and (10.8).

The mean time of system interrupts is an important statistic, as demonstrated by the temporary loss of the BlackBerry e-mail service, in the beginning of February 2007. Caused by a system upgrade, this was the second big crash in 10 months; user entities and private individuals had to sweat it out for three whole hours before normal service was resumed.*

As far as the IT auditor is concerned, each of the above algorithms is a useful tool in the IT toolkit. *Availability* and *reliability* apply to the system running at any point during scheduled time, and these must be examined, ensured, and *audited* from a life-cycle perspective because they define the extent to which the system (all components of hardware and software included) can be depended upon to supply its services, including complete and correct results given any combination of inputs.

- "Any combination of inputs" provides the certainty that the system will not fail if some inputs are invalid.
- One of the requirements for complete and correct results is detection, rejection, and error publication, should errors occur.

The IT auditor must be aware that information systems may be designed with a *failsoft* capability. In this case, instead of the whole system shutting down because of a failure, part of it will continue to function, but with reduced characteristics in terms of

- Expansion factor,
- Response time, and
- Turnaround time.

Apart from reliability and availability, the IT auditor must as well examine *maintainability*. Maintainability is the extent to which the system has been designed for easy maintenance and how well preventive maintenance is performed so that availability is not degraded.

Repairability is the speed with which a component failure can be detected and fully corrected without creating system problems. *Recoverability* must be measured following the correction of a component failure. This is the speed with which system failures can be restored, including necessary correction of programs or data damaged as a result of the failure.

10.7 The Investigation of Reasons for Unreliability

One of the obvious places the IT auditor should look for hardware reliability is in the type of components and platforms (including their MTBF, MTBSI, and

* *The Economist*, February 16, 2008.

MTOSI) employed in the system design. Reliability standards must always be requested from the vendor prior to procurement, and they should be reestablished by the user organization itself during operations for

- Each machine and each subsystem, using the expected failure rate of their component parts, and
- Each function being performed based on its criticality to the applications of every defined user environment.

Theoretically, the IT auditor is concerned with the second bulleted item. Practically, he or she must care for both the first and the second items because they are correlated. A factual analysis of problems presented by machines and systems—their hardware and software—leads to a better investigation of reasons behind poor availability, from every end-user's perspective. Crucial questions to be asked by the auditor in a "show-me" manner are

- What has systems analysis and design done defensively?
- Did the designer assume that the worst will happen?
- Did the designer account for invalid data being presented to the system?
- Have unplanned uses occurred in the past? When? How often?
- Have interruptions or failures occurred in the past? How often? Which were hardware- and which software-oriented?
- Were applications programs designed and implemented in a modular fashion? Do they have break points?
- Have operational problems been properly considered at the software design stage?
- What is the setup time required by each major routine? Which ones? Is it always the same?

The reason for these queries is the fact that what lies behind events must always be investigated. For instance, lengthy restart and reboot time, which is part of MTOSI, is certainly inconsistent with the concept of having online systems.

Operational failures may be due to system and component weaknesses, operator training problems, and other reasons. It is part of the IT auditor's job to judge how well the system is scheduled, run, and maintained. Generally, one of the more serious losses of availability is the time required to set up computing facilities after a time-out.

- The nature of the problem is such that this factor can probably never be reduced to zero.
- However, attention should definitely be paid to lowering such loss of availability, and it is one of the auditing responsibilities to establish whether the CIO has done so.

The auditor should also be interested in examining statistics on the difference between consecutive system interruptions and the associated time to repair, as well as the frequency and impact of hardware vs. software system problems. Hardware interruptions tend to be shorter than software interruptions, but the former are often overwhelmed by the impact of other factors affecting time-out.

Software problems, system instability, operator errors, dumps, and recoveries represent a high proportion of hardware downtime. Proportionally speaking, the impact of the aforementioned factors weighs considerably on system interruptions. While less frequent, interruptions due to software have greater impact than those due to hardware. System software and application programs are sensitive to

- Changes such as a new version of a compiler and
- The installation of a new release of an operating system.

It is part of the IT auditor's job to investigate whether the low points in MTOSI are due to new software releases or new hardware features. He or she should also examine what lies behind high points indicating good availability, because these can teach operational lessons. Both positive and negative findings help in

- Improving system availability and
- Designing more reliable computers and communications aggregates.

Section 8 brings to the IT auditor's attention that *operational readiness*, R_o, is much more sensitive to changes in operational maintenance capability, M_o, and along with it the time available for maintenance, than it is to changes in hardware and operational failures. Hence the IT auditor needs to take a closer look at what promotes operational readiness.

10.8 Auditing Operational Readiness

Maintainability has been one of the earliest preoccupations for the purpose of ensuring reliability. With online interactive information systems, this issue has broadened, becoming more complex and demanding a higher degree of expertise as new parameters enter the reliability equation. Here are three interesting questions confronting the IT auditor in this regard:

- Has IT management examined whether the addition of new operational requirements requires new maintainability rules?
- Or, has IT taken for granted that the old rules were sufficient? Was this justified?
- If IT adopted new rules, how effective has their impact been on operational readiness?

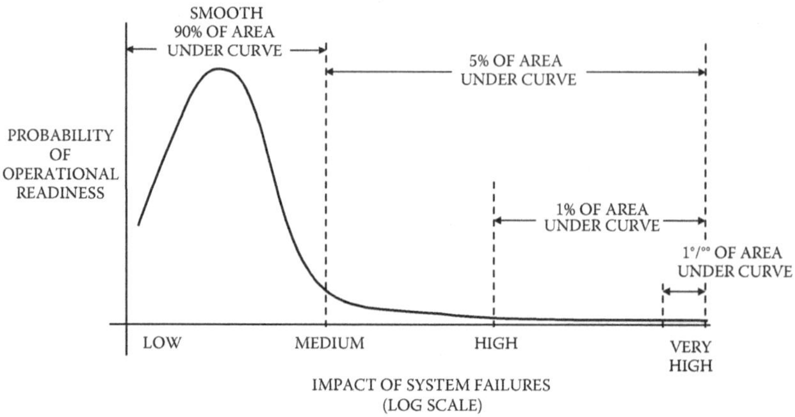

Figure 10.5 Operational readiness and impact of system failures.

Operational readiness expresses the probability of being operational as required by an established time schedule. Its main components are software dependability, equipment reliability, maintenance capability, and operational skill. Adjunct to this definition is the requirement that a malfunction will not occur during a given time period, and if a malfunction does occur (assuming that it is detectable and critical to the operational function), it will be restored within the allowable time limitations. The algorithm is

$$R_o = R + M_o (1 - R) \tag{10.11}$$

where R_o is operational readiness, R is equipment reliability, M_o is operational maintenance capability (probability of restoring in less than an allowable time), and $1 - R$ is equipment unreliability (probability of failures, in any or all combinations). Empirical curves express the impact of operational readiness and system failures. One of them is shown in Figure 10.5. (Financial analysts will appreciate the similarity of this curve to that of expected and unexpected losses, particularly the long leg.)

Operational maintainability can be expressed as a function of four factors having to do with the capability to: (a) restore any single malfunction; (b) restore any combination of two malfunctions; (c) restore any combination of three malfunctions; and (d) restore any combination of N malfunctions, where the N malfunctions (as well the more limited combinations) are defined by the nature, design, and mission of the system, as well as by user expectations.

The IT auditor should appreciate that, to properly define and test operational maintainability, it is necessary to examine not only the system variables, but also the maintenance capability available to take care of *all combinations* of malfunctions within a chosen operational time frame. The probability of successes or failures, in all combinations, is given the Poisson distribution (which itself reflects Pareto's law; see Figure 10.4).

The ability to compute a reliable estimate of operational readiness permits a fairly accurate estimation of the degree of extension of system reliability through corrective maintenance actions. The advantage of a probabilistic approach is that it provides a figure of merit that can be

- First estimated, or simulated,
- Then updated and tested.

Note that equation (10.11) considers both R and M_0, targets the entire support system, is applicable for use within time constraints, can be employed at system and subsystem levels, and it immediately identifies areas of need for further R, M_0, or whole-system improvement.

This is feasible because operational readiness is made up of a combination of probabilities, including what has been mentioned above as well as the highly intangible reduction of human-error probability, which is the domain of human engineering. However, the assurance of successfully completing a real-time system's operational objective within an established time frame further requires the integration of interfacing functions of the user population.

Not all organizations and their auditors have grown accustomed to these various design disciplines and to the need of working separately and independently, comparing their results thereafter. Now, it is necessary to integrate them, as Figure 10.6 suggests. A common bond is needed to provide a unifying effort. This is the job of operational analysis and feedback, and it has become a management prerequisite.

Figure 10.6 lists six components that constitute the core of operational readiness. The first two are R and M_0 descriptors. The third is human engineering, concerned with both reliability and maintainability; the fourth is interfacing; and the fifth's objective is operational analysis and feedback (the latter is provided by internal control, see Chapter 1) the sixth focuses on the improvement of operational readiness by means of simulation and experimentation. All of them must be audited.

The basis of simulation and experimentation in prognostication of future failures ranges from the behavior of each of the aforementioned components to the way they are tied together as an aggregate. Our interest in experimentation is propelled by the study of the interrelationships characterizing crucial factors that make or break a system's deliverables.

During the last 10 years, analytical and experimental techniques have become a "must" for complex systems. They help to provide supportive data used in the estimating, evaluating, optimizing, and controlling processes. The real usefulness of experimentation is that it stresses the need for the management accountability. Decision-making steps are interwoven into the reliability and maintainability program in such a way that R, R_0, and M_0 must be constantly evaluated in terms of meeting the end objective of any system designed and implemented for end-user support.

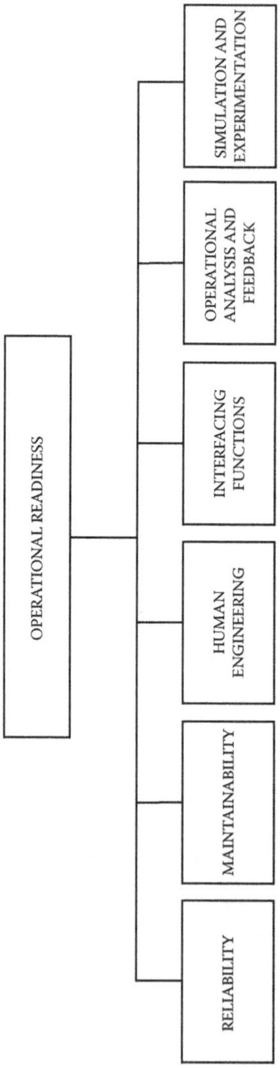

Figure 10.6 Integration of component parts of operational readiness.

Chapter 11

Auditing the Security System

11.1 Information Security and the IT Auditor

Privacy and security are knotty problems, particularly with open systems. When it comes to the Internet, network security is practically a contradiction in terms, because the Web is a medium developed to provide wide access to information, while security focuses on the ability to selectively restrict access.

- In the present business environment, information security is a trade-off between open access and protection.
- This trade-off must be managed through a carefully chosen security policy, a clear selection of security targets, and the availability of effective tools.

The level of detail in integrating security measures is important, but the integration of different security features across enterprise-wide networks can be limited when they bump against constraints imposed by legacy programs and older platforms. Network managers, worried about hackers and internal snoops, often resort to the use of firewalls to seal off access to certain areas of the company (see Section 4). The downside is that the company winds up with

- Spotty security measures and
- A host of incompatible software.

This is making communications more cumbersome than it needs to be because of incompatibilities in protocols, platforms, operating systems (OS), and database management systems (DBMS). The result is that security has become an operation that needs to be qualified and then quantified in terms of risk magnitude. *Security risk* and *information technology risk* are not the same, but one impacts on the other in several ways; therefore, security risk is a legitimate area of interest for the IT auditor.

- The lack of an integrated security solution impacts negatively on the dependability of information services.
- In contrast, information technology, used in an intelligent manner, can significantly improve system security.

Another negative resulting from nearsighted policies (with which the IT auditor will be confronted) is the lack of thoroughly studied security plans, most particularly plans about what to do in emergencies. Study after study on security issues documents that three out of four companies that have suffered a serious security breach had no contingency plan in place to deal with it. Therefore, when examining information security, one of the first queries posed by the IT auditor should relate to the formally defined rules regarding management of information security. Other audit queries should address adjunct implementation system directives as well as the most common company security breaches. In the general case, the latter involve:

- Misused user IDs
- External viruses
- Internal and external theft
- Local-area network failures
- Wide-area network failures
- Power failures facilitating security breaches

The auditing of IT security must follow a broad perspective. In my experience, only 10 percent of security issues result directly from malicious external intrusion, although even that low percentage can lead to uncontrolled security effects. Consequently, several companies dependent on the Internet are using hackers to probe weaknesses in their systems under the euphemism "third-party testing."

A small industry of so-called security companies has emerged to exploit the hackers' expertise. The strategy of these outfits is to buy bugs from hackers, who are now ironically called "security researchers,"* and then they either

- Sell them to software companies affected by security problems (sometimes with a corrective patch), or further
- Exploit them by turning them into more significant (and more lucrative) security instruments.

---

* "Security researchers" and "security companies" might find a rich market in connection with the new menace from cyberspace discussed in Section 7.

To succeed, this new breed of "security companies," which act as a third party, must be trusted by both the hackers and their victims. They must also know the market and properly guess the price that each side will bear in a deal. Their risk is that neither side may trust them well enough to do business with them.

For instance, hackers complain that, when they go to such intermediaries to ascertain what represents a fair price for their (illegal) wares, the value of their proprietary information drops because the act of communicating with the intermediary broadcasts their information to too many people. At the same time, user organizations and software companies often think that they are only being offered uninteresting security information, and they suspect that the more interesting hackers' stuff is going straight to the black market.

Many of the worries at each side of such triangular deals lies in the fact that the sale of hacker-protection devices is a nontransparent business. This statement is neither for nor against using the so-called "security companies" or the direct use of ex-hackers. Its purpose is to alert IT auditors by bringing their attention to the risks involved: Sometimes the medicine may be worse than the illness. The lack of transparency adds one more responsibility to the long list facing the IT auditor on security matters.

A systematic approach to security would trace the problem to its origins and to subsequent developments. Hacking has been followed by organized crime, all the way to identity theft. "There is real financial value here with business models built on this [organized crime]," says Ed Amoroso, chief security officer at AT&T. "Cyber crime is sucking in more and more players as word spreads about how easy it is to make money online," suggests Roei Lichtman, a spokesman of the Internet security company Aladdin Knowledge Systems.*

Cyber crime can be expected to increase in the years to come. Therefore, the IT auditor should pay particular attention to the fact that up to 90 percent of all financial transactions traverse networks. Outright theft is not the only problem; denial of service also means trouble. Service providers should look at the protection of their networks as an essential part of their efforts to upgrade their core infrastructure. Precisely for this reason, user organizations must steadily audit the dependability of their networks.

11.2 Auditing Security Management

Most of the questions the IT auditor should ask with respect to security should go well beyond configuration management, change management, backup/recovery, communications issues, encryption, authentication, and other means of access control for the site and its databases. Apart from the issues raised in Section 1, other examples of queries that go beyond the beaten path are

* *Total Telecom Magazine*, December 2007.

- Weak spots in integration with the corporate infrastructure, including a steady validation of security measures
- The role internal control plays in network and computer security.
- If on the Internet, links to and from Web server security and measures taken to be proactive in a case of external intrusion.
- End-to-end integration with business partner security, including firewalls, access control, and logging.

These are as much technical as organizational aspects of security protection, and the IT auditor should be attentive to existing collaborations with business partners on security planning as well as on maintenance of the security system. The auditor must examine whether IT management has assigned competent staff and provided it with the resources needed to meet security requirements, to identify trends in security breaches, and to conduct risk–benefit analyses of alternative methods of operation.

The counterpart of policy and organizational issues is technical security, including systems architecture, software engineering, information technology tools, and the methods that can automate (or otherwise support) security. It is also important to meet service-level objectives. (For more on physical and logical security, see Section 3.)

Security management and its audit look like complex issues, and they are. Security is probably the biggest single challenge facing network architects, system architects, and senior management. Many parties have good reason to be concerned about privacy and security. Moreover, they know that promises to enhance security, like superfirewalls, come and go; but the security problem remains.

The evidence provided in Section 1 is that (a) the parties posing an external threat are inventive and (b) commercially available security measures do not always provide protection. The lack of security has a high cost. Denial-of-service attacks, for example, are a key consideration for i-commerce, since no connectivity means no sale. Additionally, nobody can guard against attacks it cannot see, like those involving unauthorized dial-up lines.

- A smart crook can find a way to infiltrate online almost any organization, at least for a while.
- If there is a crack in the security defenses, an imaginative intruder will quite possibly discover it. Under this perspective, the responsibility of the CEO, CIO, and IT auditors is to throw as many obstacles in the intruder's way as possible.

Hurdles and deterrents make the life of hackers, intruders, and other parties (whose goal is malfeasance) more difficult. A sense of balance between cost and protection is largely a security-management responsibility.

Quite often, the polyvalence of countermeasures help in obtaining better protection. Therefore, the security arsenal should include a range of tools (intrusion detection systems, gateways, and more) and, above all, vigilant management. The IT auditor must look after both this polyvalence and management skill and include any findings in his or her report.

Some characteristics of a vigilant management program resemble those of the law enforcement industry. While, for moral considerations, some people would not steal even if they could get away with it, others would steal if they thought they would not be caught, but they do not want to risk the possible alternative of facing a severe penalty. There are as well those curious types who set out to

- Intentionally abuse and
- Strip another party of its assets.

Internally, a lack of respect for the organization and its top echelon (or supervisory personnel), frequently results in an "I will get mine" attitude. IT auditors would also be well advised to remember that the internal embezzler is frequently a high-ranking officer. During the past 30 years there has been an increase in the number of people in our society who believe that they are entitled to get their share of good living no matter how this is accomplished.

In the criminal division, said a police officer, we learn of instances where a bank employee is caught directing enormous funds to his own account and is merely dismissed. Not only is there no referral to law enforcement officials, but there is no mention to future employees that a person already in the employment of the firm was caught stealing. When this happens, it should come as no surprise that some employees do not hesitate to try the same scheme. The security problem is merely transferred to the newcomers, thereby identifying very poor security management and an incompetent general management.

Connected to this is the fact that there must also be a *legal system* supportive of security enforcement. The old legal framework should change to account for cyberspace, and the new security rules must become global. The story of a Dutch hacker who broke into Bell Labs' computers system was published some years ago. Although the hacker attempted to destroy the system, he could not be prosecuted because hacking was not illegal under Dutch law.*

Whether we talk of plain fraud or other sophisticated types of database breaches, such as *identity theft*, the fact is that, in a plethora of cases, existing security standards and civil laws are hardly adequate. Yet, like any other type of standards, well-studied security standards are a symbol of professionalism. Board members, the CEO, and IT auditors should heed the advice of an Athenian senator in Shakespeare's *Timon of Athens*: "Nothing emboldens sin so much as mercy."

---

* *ACM Member Net*, 41, no. 3 (1998).

11.3 Physical Security

The reference was made in Section 2 that security standards are in essence an effective management tool, helping to establish a frame of reference and assisting in measuring progress toward stated security goals. A common question hinges on which type of security standards we should mainly depend: physical or logical. And the answer is both, because *both* are important, each in its domain.

Standards for physical security are not part of the present text, but we should at least briefly review some of their highlights, taking a computer center as an example. The typical approach is card-entry areas for building security. For theft prevention, custom-designed approaches are used, including motion detector alarms, fiber-optic loops with transmitters at the nodes, and the like. Additionally, power switch locks, keyboard locks, and portable disc drive locks are employed to control physical access and prevent substitution. Fingerprint-based access and retinal-based access are also employed; their use is not yet widespread, but fingerprint solutions are gaining momentum.

In recent applications for physical security at the PC level, the user has to insert a personalized smartcard and provide the correct password in order to boot the system. Contrary to the approach usually taken for computer centers, with PCs security controls are customized for specific individuals booted from a secure server.

With central installations, communications switches, LANs, and PCs, there should always be audit trails of security so that all violations can be traced to their author and the time of the event. A security audit should do the following:

- First, examine the physical security policy established by the company.
- Evaluate this policy against the best of the line in business partners and competitor firms.
- Examine how well the current physical security policy (even if not highly competitive) has been implemented.

Behind these principles of examination of physical security lies the concept that the organization's computer facility cannot be sealed off from the outside world. For a variety of reasons, even with centralized installations, personnel and materials must regularly move in and out of them. Hence, physical security measures have to be taken, and the auditor should be concerned with

- The adequacy of policies, procedures, and devices used to control such movements, and
- The verification that security policies and procedures are being followed faithfully by all personnel.

The security auditor's ways and means of examination must account for the fact that the movement of personnel includes not only regular employees, but also suppliers, maintenance personnel, temporary employees, visitors, and so on. Furthermore, controlling the movement of materials in and out of the controlled area may at first glance seem straightforward, but in reality there are many subtleties. For instance, waste and spoiled computer outputs hauled away in the trash have often yielded valuable or sensitive information to scavengers. Disks, tapes, or printed reports can easily be concealed in a briefcase or on the person of an individual leaving a computer facility—whether an employee, visitor, supplier, or anybody else.

Ironically, changes in computing technology have added a new dimension to access control rather than easing the constraints. It used to be that data inputs were physically shipped to the computer center. Now much of the input and output process is conducted over communication lines (more on this in Section 5).

Beyond what has been stated so far, an integral part of physical security is effective control of all threats or disruptions such as fire and associated water damage, natural floods, earthquakes, tornadoes, mudslides, and the like. Exposed facilities include central and distributed data processing, databases, data communications switches and networks, PCs, and other interactive terminals.

Every data-processing system and system component is exposed to at least some of the threats that have been listed. Additionally, as we will see in Section 4, data processing facilities are exposed to logical threats. Software is subject to tampering for purposes of embezzlement or simply to inflict malicious damage.

Last but not least, an integral part of a physical security policy is insurance coverage. Most of the risks discussed in the preceding paragraphs can be insured, but insurance policies are not always clear in their clauses. Therefore, they need to be

- Thoroughly audited,
- Carefully negotiated, and
- Carefully examined under a worst-case scenario.

It is unwise to sign any form of an insurance contract under the terms presented by the insurer, and this is not only because chances are it will cost much more money than the one the company can get from an alternative insurer. More important than the premium is the protection an insurance policy provides. Typically, insurance contracts specify: "The following physical risks are covered" and "The following physical risks are not covered." Between these two classes may fall plenty of exceptions. The CIO, and even the legal counsel, might think that the company's coverage is well-rounded when, in fact, it is not. The IT auditor must pay a great deal of attention to what really is and is not insured by reading *between* the lines of a contract, and not only what is written in black and white.

11.4 Logical Security

Much more flexible and adaptable tools are available for logical security than for physical security, and some of the logical security tools are subject to steady development by their vendors. These include firewalls, encryption algorithms, different types of restrictions, sign-ons, session timeout, audit trails, centralized security administration, and much more.

Firewalls are generally considered to provide a critical point of control for allowing authorized traffic "in" and keeping unauthorized traffic "out." They also serve in an effort to mask the overall structure of the company network from prying eyes, denying potential intruders information that could be useful in mounting an attack. Using firewalls, however, is by no means synonymous with a logical guardian. One challenge with firewall management is to tune filter variables in such a way that they can effectively distinguish between authorized and unauthorized traffic. This is particularly important when the controlled parameters change continuously over time as new business relationships and applications are

- Created,
- Changed, or
- Dropped.

Therefore, tuning is one of the key areas to be addressed by the security auditor, after having been satisfied that the firewalls chosen by IT are state of the art. An adjunct problem needing attention is that firewall performance can be affected by the increasing volume and variability of network traffic. This is an often-overlooked issue in security management.

Encryption, too, poses challenges. Theoretically, an encryption provides the people responsible for logical security with the ability to scramble and descramble the binary string of 1's and 0's that make up digital content. This is generally considered to be one of the indispensable capabilities for security, with increasingly complex encryption algorithms being brought to market to counterbalance the decryption techniques used by intruders and eavesdroppers. Practically,

- Encryption keys are often used in a way that lacks a long, hard look in regard to their long-term management, and
- They are steadily the subject of intensive work by code breakers, who often use arrays of PCs and sophisticated intrusion strategies.

In connection with the first bulleted item, the IT auditor should appreciate that encryption is only useful if it is applied consistently and correctly. In contrast, many user organizations have not developed a rigorous key-management methodology that changes keys more frequently to counter the increasing risk of code breaking. Moreover, some companies have found that the 64-bit DES (data encryption standard) is insufficient. Crédit Suisse First Boston, for example, uses a 128-bit key for encryption, much more powerful than the classical DES.

What about other logical security means? Taking a LAN environment as an example of logical security, *user ID* and *password* authentication must have an embedded feature of disable after repeated logon failures as well as register control date and time of access by both legitimate and illegitimate uses. As we have seen on many occasions, security logons are a critical reference for the IT auditor.

Another important issue to examine is access control to serial and parallel ports, and portable disk read and write production. Is the documentation complete and updated? Has the audit of IT operations seriously studied weaknesses in access control? Has the system established password restrictions, such as

- Expiration dates,
- Minimum lengths,
- Inhibition of simplistic passwords,
- Installation of adapter address components, and more.

Other logical security issues to be audited include protection during boot (prevent boot from floppy, lock keyboard during boot); password protection for files and subdirectories; routines to ensure that registers are zeroed after each logoff; implementation of procedures to prevent, detect, and repair virus attacks; and logon/logoff facilities. Have the CIO and his or her people implemented

- Session timeouts after predefined periods of inactivity,
- Background tasks examination, or
- A system preventing the use of unauthorized software.

A crucial question to be addressed by the security auditor is whether IT has in place a single system image of enterprise security. If the answer is yes, is it valid? Is it observed? Has it been able to correlate same-origin security breaches? Can these be effectively be segregated into

- Insider breaches and
- Outsider breaches.

Insider breaches usually include malicious code, infection of company machines through viruses, use of company equipment for illegal communications, abuses of different sorts concerning computer and communications gear, unauthorized access to databases, managing a personal i-commerce site through company Internet resources, gambling, enabling chores for physical theft, disclosure of proprietary data, or plain fraud.

The most worrisome outsider breaches are viruses and Trojan horses, but they are not the only threats. Others include the already mentioned denial of service; acts related to active program scripting; fraud by exploiting insecure passwords, weak firewalls, or encryption codes that are easy to break; attacks exploiting protocol weaknesses; and attacks on buys in Web servers. There are as well other reasons for worry about logical security, such as buffer overflows, that should be regularly audited.

11.5 How Safe Is Network Security?

Some years ago, upon being asked, "What does one do with virtual money?" Walter Wriston, the former CEO of Citibank, responded, "One pays his bills." But then he added: "The problem with this kind of money is the *security* of the networks. There exist too many 16-year-olds with gold chains around the neck, who break into the data system."

Correctly, Wriston pointed out the prevailing lack of security from a network viewpoint. It is possible to work on "more secure" solutions through ingenious use of hardware and software, but this does not mean that one obtains 100 percent assurance about security. There are too many hackers around, and some of them are inventive. Moreover, technology changes so fast that it is impossible to predict what is the life cycle of a secure system solution. The only serious statement that can be made is that the world today has become so transparent, in an information sense, that nothing can be properly secured anymore—let alone secured in a lasting way. Here is an example.

Though widely acknowledged to have one of the best security systems in the world, particularly in New York, Citibank is not immune from security breaches. In mid-1995, a Buenos Aires investment firm (Invest Capital) notified Citicorp, its parent company, about unauthorized transactions. Internal investigators at Citibank immediately sought help from the FBI and, by working in rare collaboration with Russian police, the trail led to two computer hackers in St. Petersburg. The infiltrators moved Invest Capital funds totaling some $24.5 million from different accounts. A company official at Invest Capital was shocked to see unauthorized transfers being made through his workstation, one after another. "He was virtually watching company funds disappear right on the screen," said a report.*

The story of the Citicorp computer crime, which began in 1994, portrays how one of the most tightly guarded computer systems in the world was penetrated 40 times in five months—until a collaboration of the FBI, Russian police, and several other foreign police forces tracked the infiltrators to St. Petersburg. A man nicknamed "Vova," a 28-year-old biochemistry graduate who was working for a trading company AO Saturn, was taken into custody. Among other things, this company wrote and installed computer software. In June 1994, using the Russian and U.S. telephone networks, Vova managed to enter Citicorp's computers. Masquerading as one of its clients, he moved other customers' funds to a bank account in Finland. There, a confederate went to the bank and began making withdrawals.

The irony of this event is that Citicorp's system is so ringed with security that breaking in was considered to be almost impossible by industry experts. The infiltrator allegedly used Citicorp customers' passwords and user identification, going through several additional intricate steps to pluck funds from customer accounts and transfer them.

---

* *Asian Wall Street Journal*, September 13, 1995.

If a break-in takes place in one of the best-secured networks in the world, it is not difficult to guess what can happen with other networks where computer security is low. It is estimated that hackers cost American business $3 billion per year, capitalizing on a number of tools permitting them to break into somebody else's system. They use

- Sophisticated scanners to steal id codes,
- Password guessers, essentially code-breaking expert systems, and
- Programs and keys bought from other members of the hacker community.

The first target is not necessarily money but, rather, poorly protected password files meticulously collected over the years. The threat is particularly important not only because a growing number of vital company resources are now held in databases, but also because the economy of many countries—and the wellbeing of their industries—is conditioned by their ability to filter, store, retrieve, manage, and use the information that is created.

Ironically, in a great number of cases, the whole security system is built in such a way that it is not so difficult to pervert, while current security measures themselves can be turned against network security. Corporate customers must use secret codes to gain direct access to a bank's cash management system to

- Extend credit or pay bills worldwide,
- Make investments in securities and other assets, and
- Transfer hundreds of millions of dollars in corporate funds.

Beyond case-by-case insecurity, the sheer volume and value of online transactions generates system weaknesses. When the aforementioned breach took place, the Citicorp system moved about $500 billion a day, which meant that the St. Petersburg break-in had the potential to become the biggest bank robbery in history. Only because of the timely identification of the intruders did the bank limit its losses.

Security auditors, and Internet or other network users who manage money, should keep in mind that this is no once-in-a-lifetime case. A few years ago, a U.S. study found that half of the surveyed 150 high-technology firms and financial institutions were subject to online fraud, but they chose to keep this fact internal and not to announce it publicly.

It is also interesting to note that banks are not the only target of intruders. Shipping, and the transport industry at large, is another area of vulnerability. The security problems associated with containers are less well known than those of the financial industry, but are arguably far more serious because of the 15 to 20 million containers currently at sea or parked in shipyards.

- The containers' network activity boomed during the 1990s, prompting an increase in capacity that now looks reckless.

- The container industry uses a couple of networks, one for information and the other for physical goods, that exploit open standards to speed the flow of traffic.

With free-flowing traffic comes lack of security. Not only computer criminals but also terrorists and other external hostile activities can prove to be major threats. For instance, if a power really wishes to damage America or any other western country, it would not find it difficult to hit its infrastructure, which is in very large measure controlled by computers. This is true all the way

- From finance,
- To transportation.

Modern terrorism can do more damage operating online through a network than with guns and bombs. This has not yet entered the public's consciousness as a credible threat. Major problems can also happen through accidental failures for which there was no backup. In the mid-1990s, subsequent to a computer failure, the Bank of New York discovered they were $23 billion short in overnight funds and borrowed money from the Federal Reserve to save the day. The glitch cost the bank about $25 million in interest.

In conclusion, with everything taken into account, the main insight regarding network security is that, because the infrastructure is protected in a weak way and the applied security measures are often poorly tested, vulnerabilities are inevitable. Few people truly appreciate that building and maintaining a secure computer and communications infrastructure—essential to provide the technological underpinnings of modern society—is indeed

- A highly complex job,
- Beyond the experience and current competency of many firms, and
- A subject that should be the target of *frequent rigorous audits*.

Moreover, network security constantly evolves in terms of characteristics, requirements, and vulnerabilities. An example is mobile network security, which is becoming month-by-month more imperative as data services increase. The challenge is that by using a fire brigade approach for their growing inventory of applications, many firms take their eye off the threat posed to their infrastructure.

11.6 Information Security in Cyberspace—The Small Fry*

A decade ago, with information insecurity in cyberspace hitting the news at rapidly increasing pace, one could read the following statement in a broker's publication:

* The cyber risks described in this section are not trivial in absolute terms, but in relation to the new menace discussed in Section 7.

"The statelessness of cyberspace is one reason why Schwab insists on keeping the doors of its 254 U.S. domestic and international branches open, and 5,000 human brokers among a total of 11,000 employees."* Schwab management looked at its branches in London, Hong Kong, and the Cayman Islands as a sort of backup, reassuring through their presence and reminding customers that even if the wires are not so secure, or they are not working, they can still walk into a building to get on with their business. Worried about the fact that the underlying environment in cyberspace is stateless, and concerned about how a firm makes sure that he or she connects to the same customer machine every time, other financial companies, too, have strengthened their brick-and-mortar networks.

One of the unknowns in cyberspace is where the thieves are located. Unlike the automated teller machines (ATMs) in a network, whose location is known to the system and whose users are registered through every transaction, the Web sees every turn of the page and every transaction as a new party. This creates fairly complex security problems, complicating

- Security management at large, and more specifically,
- The IT auditor's mission.

What has just been said by no means implies that ATM networks are secure. Not long ago, hackers seized money from Citibank's ATM network by breaking into a retailer's server, stealing customer card data, and duplicating the cards. The bank claims only several hundred U.S. customers were affected, but security experts are not sure about such low numbers.

What is sure is that, other things being equal, cyberspace insecurity is greater; even small payments have come under increasingly more sophisticated cyber attacks. As a way of improving customer protection, banks are looking at a two-factor authentication, such as a key-ring token that generates a password every few seconds. This means:

- When logging into the account, users type a user ID, password, and the additional password generated by the token.
- Access is granted after the token-generated password is synchronized with the bank's server and verified.

Is this secure? Not necessarily. This example suggests two things. First, nobody can certify that token usage will not be implicated. Second, while a two-factor identification may have advantages, this interface code is not the most critical determinant in the security of a financial transaction. Neither is it a generic improvement.

* *Information Strategy*, 2, no. 7 (1997).

- It is, of course, necessary to apply technical solutions at each of the endpoints of the application.
- However, endpoint Internet security is also ineffectual because it remains a relatively technical, local, and distinct issue from the corporate IT design and management.

Additionally, as companies consider and try to exploit the more strategic uses of the Internet, this limited endpoint security becomes even more weak because of the Internet's lack of central control, which is shifting the security responsibility squarely on the user organization—and from there to the shoulders of the auditor.

From a security risk-management viewpoint, using the Internet as a transaction-processing system blurs the information technology boundaries that formerly provided the basis for determining liability in disputes. Stated in different terms, if not designed in conjunction with a comprehensive security management system (see Section 7) the Internet may provide

- A false sense of security, and
- A misleading expectation for the financial benefits of adopting the internet as a transport medium.

To this should be added the fact that hacker activities range from break-in to malicious programs that would wait for people to log into their online payment accounts and then start transferring money automatically to the intruder's account. This tactic is quite different from the more classical Trojan horses, which steal passwords and user names, reporting them back to hackers for illegal employment.

- Known as a piece of *malware*, the *wait-for-a-kill* approach is programmed to be patient until a pigeon logs on to transfer money.
- Wait-for-a-kill is part of a larger class of the "card not present" fraud over the telephone and Internet, where a personal ID number (PIN) is not required.

It is redundant to add that the security auditor must be flexible in adapting his or her work to the developing situation—always remembering that computer crime cuts across lines of government, manufacturing, commerce, finance, insurance, and other sectors of the economy.

While across-the-board statistics on cyber crime are scarce, and the range of losses per incident is wide, in the potential downside it is not only the cash loss that is disturbing, but also the possibility of abstraction of valuable information: scientific, industrial, commercial, or personal, which could be more significant than cash.

Several Web sites, for example, have found out the hard way that the deliberate creation of bogus Web sites that have names very similar to real sites is a growing fraudulent practice. To deceive Internet users who think the Net is safe, intruders create copycat sites that use text and graphics identical to that on legitimate Web pages. In Britain, the Financial Services Authority (FSA) has issued investor alerts about the existence of these sites.

In March 1998, Global Asset Management, a London investment firm, fell victim to the so-called *passing off* racket. It found that its name and a slightly modified Web page was being used by an outfit in Ghana. Because "Ghana" alphabetically preceded "United Kingdom" the pass-off URL was reached first by search engines.* The Ghanian company was using the name of Global Asset Management, hence also its reputation, to gain business. The passing off-scam came to light when the designer of the Web page left a message on the Web: "Don't touch these people; they owe me $6,500."

In conclusion, preventive measures must be built around the necessary conditions of doing business on the Internet and any other network. Because hackers, intruders, and other illegals operating on the Internet are inventive, no security planning can conceive of every possibility that could be germinated by an ingenious and innovative criminal. This should not discourage companies from working to improve *their* security, but it should strengthen the IT auditor's vigilance.

11.7 Information Security in Cyber Warfare—The Big Stuff

The possibility of cyber warfare, as well as of cyber terrorism, being unleashed over the Internet is a real and present danger. The case of Estonia in early 2007 provides a preview of what might happen. Cyber warfare's goal is that of disabling a nation's control and command, emergency services, and economic activities, including banking.

In April and May 2007, Estonia got a taste of what cyber warfare means when its government's Web sites came under sustained distributed denial of service (DDoS) attacks. The immediate aftereffect was that of obliging the Estonian government to close its Web sites to the outside world, though not to domestic access. The April/May 2007 cyber attacks also targeted Estonia's largest banks as well as the Web sites of major national newspapers. According to a report, practically all DDoS events came from highly distributed computers located in several countries. This made it practically impossible to pin the blame on any single source with reasonable certainty.† As Estonia discovered to its expense, cyberspace warriors can unleash distributed denial of service attacks from any region and any place in the world. While the Estonian government has allegedly traced some IP addresses back to Russia, its Web sites also came under fire from PCs in several other countries, while classical countermeasures proved to be difficult to enact and coordinate.

---

* Communications International, London, 1998.

† *Total Telecom Magazine*, July-August 2007.

Several experts are of the opinion that Estonia was nothing more than a test case in DDoS cyber attacks. They are also suggesting that these events were rather simple, and eventually Estonians managed to protect themselves. But until and unless one develops skills in counteraction, protection may be difficult with sophisticated cyber attacks. This is leading a body of experts to request that

- Security measures must be put in place *now*, to defend civil cyber infrastructure, and
- Protection from cyber attacks must cover the whole range of critical communications targets, including social and economic—not only military.

Another conclusion by experts is that the more sophisticated the infrastructure, the greater is the cyber risk. For instance, all-IP next-generation networks that integrate voice transmission put voice communications at risk, not only data and multimedia. This is in contrast to the current system, where if the Internet goes down, the voice network still works.

What this means in technical terms is that we are seeing a shift in the impact of hostile cyber attacks and an opaque identification of originators. Increasingly, cyber exposure originates outside developed countries and tends to be more distributed than ever, leading to network vulnerability.

Some people point to China, saying that the country is developing both offensive and defensive cyber warfare techniques to protect its computer networks and attack those of an eventual adversary. This is interpreted as preparation for the day advanced forms of electronic warfare will be conducted in a virtual battle space, far larger than any WW II theater of operations.

China, of course, is not alone in such exploits. Both the United States and Russia are said to be developing their own cyber offensive and defensive capabilities, integrating them with more traditional military weapons. NATO, too, is stepping up its response to the threat of cyber warfare, which it has allegedly recognized as a major new security challenge.

As to be expected, NATO's first concern is protecting military information systems, with civil information security coming right after. One of NATO's problems seems to be that it needs to rely on communications service providers for some of its defenses, while an attack will most likely be fought also at the level of information service providers (ISPs). This dichotomy raises several unknowns.

NATO's communications experts, and evidently its generals, are further worried by the fact that also in May 2007, though a strange coincidence, Chinese spy software was discovered in computers in the office of Angela Merkel, the German chancellor, and in other ministries. According to one source, the so-called Trojan horse program (attached to a seemingly innocuous electronic file) was siphoning off 160 gigabytes of information when it was stopped. (Germans suspect that China's People's Liberation Army was responsible.)

A few weeks later, in June 2007, it became known that a similar Trojan horse had penetrated computers in the office of Robert Gates, the U.S. secretary of defense. Pentagon officials also think the Chinese were behind the Trojan horse. (The Pentagon says only an unclassified e-mail system was breached.)

According to an article in the *Economist*, U.S. military planners worry that China is using cyberspace for reasons beyond simple espionage.* This is worrisome because currently our society depends too much on computers and communications; therefore a first-strike attack on networks not only can cripple military systems, but also disrupt civilian life. The name of the game is *electromagnetic dominance*, which may be making the nuclear threat obsolete.

In principle, computers and communications systems are only as secure as the weakest link, and a cyber attack might obliterate the weaker ISPs. The Internet is a dynamic market, and new entrants may not be ready to provide countermeasures as part of their critical infrastructure. If so, this will weaken the robustness of the Internet at two levels, that of the

- ISP's subscribers, and
- The services they may provide to other network operators.

For the time being, ideas on how to face the challenge of cyber attacks are rather spotty. One of the better opinions is that—in a way not dissimilar to that used by big private and public buildings, which regularly test fire alarms—networks operators need to reset their ability to deal with cyber attacks. To do so, they not only have to educate individual users of Internet services (including preventive and recovery measures), but also audit these measures and coordinate among themselves drills for worst-case scenarios.

11.8 The Auditor's Target in Network Security

Confronted with the security problems that have been outlined in the preceding section, how should the IT auditor organize his or her approach and execute the mission? This is the object of the present section, while Section 9 presents to the reader an enlarged perspective in regard to the auditor's work in one specific sector: software security.

Many cognizant executives participating in the research that led to this book suggested that the security auditor should start with a corporate perspective, taking note of the fact that, historically, security models have emphasized the role of senior management in setting, maintaining, and implementing security policies

* *The Economist*, September 8, 2007.

and procedures. In contrast, IT management concentrated on solutions and standards, including

- Contingency plans, and
- Disaster recovery procedures.

Starting with the broader horizon, these executives said, allows the auditor to better establish the relative character of security, which greatly depends on policies, assigned missions, acquired skills, purchased tools, and the more general business environment of the company. It also leads to

- Interpreting the board's and CEO's personal judgment regarding the wanted degree of protection,
- Evaluating the means that the company has been willing to put in action to meet its security goals, and
- Ensuring that measures have been taken to protect the network against cyber attacks (see Section 7) and that drills are regularly performed.

After, and only after, these issues have been settled, comes the auditing of the firm's security services—against an established objective whose existence makes it possible to specify sectorial requirements. The security risk assessment that the IT auditor performs must be carried out for each facility and each application, with risk levels scored in terms of fraud potential, privacy, confidentiality, and other chosen factors sorted out by criticality.

In so doing, the IT auditor must keep in mind that the services whose security he or she is examining will provide the company not only a one-point result, but with a framework of systems and procedures that protect not only processing and databasing, but also the dialogue between users, customers, and applications. Hence, there is a need to examine a whole range of services:

- Secure access
- Nonrepudiation
- Data integrity
- User-level security
- Confidentiality and other factors mentioned in preceding sections

Each of these bulleted items poses its own prerequisites in IT auditing terms. Secure access, for example, has two components: *User validation*, that is, verification of the user or application identity; and *access rights*, or determination that the user is permitted to access the requested application, databased information elements, or a specific information service.

Core to the security auditor's work is the way IT is protecting information from unauthorized disclosure, either in storage or during transmission. The security auditor should examine the firm's encryption standards. Have network nodes and links been provided with security solutions commensurate with the most sensitive application that uses them?

Another important element is message authentication, based on a process that implicitly verifies the originator of the message (person or application), and guarantees that the message has not been altered in transmission. Currently, it is achieved either by test words, an aging process, or through cryptographic generation of message-authentication code.

Still another crucial subject in need of security audit is digital signatures, which provide for nonrepudiation. They consist of proof of origin as well as data integrity in a relationship that can be effectively verified. This proof is particularly important if information elements pass across a number of networks. Proof testing applies to both

- Transmitted data and
- Acknowledgments generated by the recipient.

Still another focal point of the audit must be security and privacy of users' services, which generally fall into one of three classes: *individuals*, who may be employees, customers, or correspondents; *business partners* (client companies, suppliers, applications, processors, databases, servers); and *network nodes*, including network management systems, directories, and the security servers themselves.

With *nomadic computing* (as opposed to communications through fixed lines), this classification has taken a higher dimension in complexity. The reason is that as the number of users and locations increases, it becomes more difficult to reach common security definitions and standards or to identify the exact origin of people and programs trying to break into the system.

Security auditors would be well-advised to take note of the following example. An early 2007 survey of 200 mobile network operators worldwide, conducted by McAfee and Informa Telecoms & Media (ITM), found that network security was seen as less important by operators than *applications* and *device level* security when protecting themselves from attacks.

- Over 50 percent of operators surveyed said they had already deployed protection at the network level.
- This share dropped to 33 percent in terms of security for the applications and device-level areas.*

While, according to some estimates, mobile operators can prevent an estimated 95 percent of network security breaches, there is a growing opinion that much of the

* *Total Telecom Magazine*, May 2007.

work has to be done at the applications level and with devices. For instance, phones might restrict applications from accessing functions open to attack by *malware*.

Auditors should be alert to these findings when examining security assurance in nomadic computing. Operators should be aware that mobile malware is becoming a more significant consideration than in the past.

- Malicious software is a bigger issue in data networks because there is more bandwidth and because devices are connected to the Internet.
- Devices are becoming more powerful, given the availability of broadband channels and larger memory capacity, which might host viruses.

Some companies have explored the so-called network security device approach which rests on a single distributed application, with the servers replicated for performance and resilience. This supports network access control, key management (for symmetric key services), and key certification (for asymmetric key services) with both public and private keys. To my knowledge, however, the jury is still out regarding this method's dependability.

11.9 Auditing Software Security

The last two words in this section's title may have several meanings. One that will not interest us in this section is software piracy—a business that is huge, amounting to well over $70 billion worldwide, with over 75 percent of this amount in Asia (having grown from under $10 billion a decade earlier). Worse yet, networks running on pirated software are prone to viruses, which is not to say that other networks are free from them.

Piracy left aside, a crucial mission in software security is of evaluating, testing, and auditing mission-critical software and other routing. This sort of software security should be near the top of the list IT auditor's tasks.

Starting with software dependability, as a rule, proprietary applications' programs and packages do not work well until they have been used and have failed repeatedly in real-life applications. While testing is a long-established discipline, the way to bet is that many uses and several failures have to take place before a software product is considered reliable (see also Chapter 10). In principle,

- Software products behave like other products of evolution-like processes, and
- When operating conditions change, they may fail even years after they were built.

What is a *software test*? A software test can be defined as the method of ensuring that written code is functioning correctly. How and why can it fail? In the general case, the code might have been written incorrectly, or it might fail after use due to a number of other reasons, such as a change in operating system or configuration or the effects of a virus or malware.

While all newly designed products have "this" or "that" oversight or functional error that must be identified and corrected, errors (bugs) are more common, more pervasive, and more troublesome in software. This reference must be understood in light of the fact that it is a standard practice among software professionals to have their products go through an extensive series of carefully planned tests before use.

Often, programming products fail in their first real-life employment because of situations not anticipated by programmers and also overlooked by the tests. With this reference in mind, the software auditor should familiarize himself or herself with software test practices and procedures before making an examination. This familiarization will also assist the auditor in

- Targeting viruses,
- Searching for weak points to be used by intruders, and
- Examining whether, in all likelihood, a piece of downloaded code is malicious software.

The reader can better appreciate the functions an IT auditor should perform in this connection by keeping in mind that security testing of any piece of nontrivial software is a difficult task. While software engineering has been evolving from an ad hoc craft into a discipline, this is not true of all its aspects, and most particularly of testing functions.

In regard to software security, the testing problem is not over whether a good test can be bought off the shelf (it cannot), but what kind of test methodology we develop to serve our needs. One way is the so-called *functional test* (input/output or black-box test), which applies test vectors to inputs and monitors outputs. This is, however, impractical for software programs of reasonable complexity. In black-box testing,

- Tests are chosen without knowledge of the internal workings of the program, and
- Tests are constructed from the functional properties of the program given in the specification and may account for operational effects.

Dynamic testing is functional and structural. Structural, or white-box tests, are chosen by knowing the internal structure of the program. Commonly used criteria for selection of such cases are execution of every statement and execution of every branch in the program.

An alternative to this method, borrowed from circuit testing, isolates each critical program component and tests it separately. Libraries of tests for commonly used components can be assembled, thus reducing time and cost.

Still another approach is *statistical testing*. Based on the requirements specification, the IT auditor employs statistical techniques and watches carefully to see whether program performance is shown to be sufficient to certify product reliability. The specification is analyzed to identify the set of inputs needed to exercise all product functions, under different error probability distributions.

It should be noted, as a general principle in the aftermath of the IT auditor's work, that a software test does not determine whether the modules and their code have been *designed* correctly. Such tests are not a design verification, although many professionals (incorrectly) believe that software tests are nothing else other than that. In reality, what counts is the results obtained from code testing through processing or, more precisely, the consistency of these results from one run to the next.

Can such tests tell whether code errors have been weeded out? Down to basics, despite postdevelopment tests, program errors are elusive, and they could be more or less fully detected only by running, over time, real-life input data and comparing program output to expected output.

A frequently heard argument supporting the thesis that software testing is design testing runs this way: Coded modules are checked against module design, and any errors are readily corrected. This is not so; what is tested is not the program's architectural design (right or wrong), but coding proper. Errors found usually require a change in code by

- Reworking the module, or, more frequently, by
- Developing patches.

Errors in output are elusive. They may lie anywhere in tested code. Therefore, to avoid long reruns, programmers are advised to institute breakpoints between phases, but for reasons of expedience, they rarely do so. Yet, everybody knows that it is rare to find a substantial piece of software that is error-free, one of the reasons being that there are as yet no established engineering methods for the production of software.

The IT auditor should as well appreciate that program testing can be used to show the presence of programming bugs, but never their absence. It follows that nearly fully guaranteeing correctness in a piece of software implies exercising the program with all possible combinations of input data, with each information element varying over its entire possible input range. This is clearly impractical.

The only exception to the foregoing statement is that program testing can be facilitated with prototyping; visual programming methods also permit design testing. Many companies, however, steer away from prototyping because their analysts and programmers are not trained in it and lack its culture. This is a pity, because prototypes present tremendous advantages:

- Hugely improved programmer productivity
- Feasibility for the user to see and evaluate what he or she will get
- Tests that are much easier than with compiled programs
- A reference frame for efficient program update and for recovery in the case of viruses and malware

Additionally, prototype solutions are the best for *safety-critical* processes—those in which system failure could lead directly to a major upset in computers and communications operations. This is not written only with respect to reliability (see Chapter 10). Functions such as data filtering, early-warning diagnostics, analysis of sequences, and more, are software based, and the consequences of errors may well be safety critical.

IV

CAN IT HELP IN COMPLIANCE? THE CASE OF SOX

Chapter 12

Sarbanes-Oxley Compliance and IT's Contribution

12.1 Compliance Defined

This chapter pursues two purposes. The first is to define compliance while positioning it in the context of the much-criticized, but still enduring, Sarbanes-Oxley Act (see Chapter 3). The second aim is to bring into perspective the better side of information technology's contribution to compliance.

- Section 6 explains the reasons why the corporate memory facility (CMF) is so important, and
- Sections 7 and 8 document how and why knowledge artifacts contribute to the compliance effort by automating the more mundane chores needed to achieve compliance.

"There will not be a different ethical standard for corporate America than the standard that applies to everyone else. The honesty you expect in your small businesses, or in your workplaces, in your community or in your home, will be expected and enforced in every corporate suite in this country." So said George W. Bush in July 2002 as he signed into law the Sarbanes-Oxley Act (SOX).

Observance of rules and regulations is a matter of corporate ethics, and when ethical values are not present (see Chapter 13), no matter who is the external auditor or what sort of technology is used, *corporate cleptocracy** will be king. Precisely because of its zeal in applying Sarbanes-Oxley, the Bush administration may be remembered as America's most active in pursuing errant bosses. On July 13, 2007, it added to its list of successful convictions when Conrad Black, a Canadian-born newspaper "magnate," was found guilty on

- Three counts of mail fraud and
- One count of obstruction of justice.

What is meant by *compliance*? Indeed, there are several definitions of the term. The best definition reflects its holistic nature and was given in the late 1990s by the Bank of England (BOE), in connection with the Year 2000 (Y2K) problem. Addressing itself to British banks, BOE stated: "To be Y2K compliant you must be able to work any date in the 21st century." In terms of Y2K solutions, this definition blew out half-measures, such as windowing and other incomplete approaches. As banking companies confronted the regulators' pressure that their applications programs might confuse 20th and 21st century dates (because of a punch-card legacy), nearly everyone claimed in the abstract to be Y2K compliant. The question is,

- Was this a factual long-lasting statement, or
- Was it temporarily valid today but untrue in the longer run?

The fact that compliance is not a notion that one can interpret in this guise did not escape the attention of well-governed financial institutions that have used the term *compliance* in a more extensive way than others. But the Sarbanes-Oxley Act further tightened the degrees of freedom in its interpretation: The company's CEO and CFO must sign the financial statements, and external auditors must answer questions like:

- What control does management have over compliance?
- What, precisely, is covered by management control?
- How often has management exercised direct control?
- Who is responsible for ensuring that every rule and regulation is generally observed?

At Zurich-based Bank Leu, for example, one of the deliverables for which the internal compliance operation is responsible is to produce the documentation of management control action. This is considered important for effective exercise

* A term used by an internal corporate inquiry at Hollinger International, Conrad Black's outfit.

of compliance measures, because internal control (see Chapter 1) cannot be exercised without senior management knowing what the different professionals do, by means of feedback that is

- Frequent,
- Uninhibited,
- Complete,
- Correct, and
- Accurate.

Precisely on this issue, the use of information technology can make a contribution. Companies that are fully terminalized—with financial and accounting operations executed by computers, management decisions registered in the corporate memory facility, and knowledge artifacts used to test for compliance—are better positioned than their competitors because the system will work as a watchdog,

- Testing virtual balance sheets and virtual income statements and
- Immediately informing the board's audit committee (see Chapter 5) that rot has been found or that creative accounting practices have been detected.

There is also another, more critical contribution to compliance by information technology: ensuring that the back office works like a clock, which is far from being the general case. No better example can be found on this issue than what became known as the *Wall Street back-office crisis* of the late 1960s, which nearly brought down investment banks and brokerages.

The back-office crisis started in 1967, when equity trading volumes in the major stock exchanges zoomed. In both the United States and Europe, many banks were ill-equipped to handle the resulting mass of paperwork in spite of big money they had spent on electrical accounting machines (EAM) and on computers, the latter for about a decade.

Matters came to a crash in New York City, where many brokerages were slow and ineffective in putting their back offices in order. The fire-brigade approach they eventually adopted was to hire more personnel, but talent suffered, resulting in a sea of

- Unprocessed and
- Inaccurate transactions.

This lasted several years, and it has been one of the reasons why a *crisis committee* was established by the New York Stock Exchange (NYSE), which confronted several disasters. One of them came in July 1970, when one of the Street's largest brokerages, F.I. DuPont Glore Forgan, started to fail six months after a shotgun merger that had brought three brokerages together: F.I. DuPont, Glore Forgan

Staats, and Hirsch. According to a published news item, the merged firm found itself in deep distress:

- Its account ledges were mired in red ink.
- Its back office had become an insoluble snarl of paperwork.

"Figures from firms with huge back office problems are meaningless, because you can't really know their position," commented Felix Rohatyn, the investment banker chairing the crisis committee, in an interview with *Fortune* magazine.* He was right. When the CEO and CFO are not *personally accountable* for the mess in the front desk and in the back office, anything can happen—any malfeasance—and they will walk out like gentlemen. This is what SOX aims to correct.

12.2 Beyond Compliance with the Sarbanes-Oxley Act

One of several critiques heard from Wall Street about Sarbanes-Oxley is that the act could lead to a number of European companies severing their ties with the U.S. stock markets by delisting. Or that it might prevent others from listing there in the first place. As an example, critics sometimes point to the delisting of Telekom Austria, which was listed on both the Vienna exchange and the NYSE in 2000, when it was common for European telecoms to list in the United States in order to gain access to a large pool of capital.

This argument is utterly misplaced. To start with, former national telecom monopolies of European countries, with their bureaucratic thinking, have no business listing on the NYSE. Second, the changing behavior of U.S. investors, rather than SOX, has made a U.S. listing unnecessary. These days, the knowledge of how to tap the global capital market is no secret for

- American institutional investors and
- High-net-worth individuals who want to diversify their portfolios.

Neither of these parties needs to look at U.S. stock exchanges to find foreign companies. Additionally, while the Sarbanes-Oxley Act indeed increased the regulatory burden, Telekom Austria's deregistering was primarily motivated by capital considerations. After all:

- This company is a big cap (albeit one that is sleepy).
- If big caps are unable to comply with SOX, including Section 404 that covers management accountability for financial reports, who would?

* William D. Cohan, *The Last Tycoons* (New York: Doubleday, 2007).

While Telekom Austria, Cable & Wireless (C&W), and O2 (three telecoms) have delisted from the United States since 2002, other telecoms have chosen to stick with their U.S. listing and indeed have found *benefits* with SOX. Christine Maxwell, director of IT advisory services at KPMG who oversaw the SOX compliance project for a U.K. mobile operator, says there were a lot of inefficiencies in telecoms in general but "SOX has flushed a lot of this out thanks to general improvements in internal processes. Section 404 caused all the work."*

True enough, compliance deadlines were delayed a number of times for European companies. This was, however, the result of confronting change to International Financial Reporting Standards (IFRS)†, rather than of SOX. It is to the credit of Christopher Cox, the SEC chairman, that he sized up the pluses and minuses of doing away with SOX compliance, and in mid-2007 he eased only internal control's audit for *smaller* registered firms because of compliance costs.

To put it bluntly, the bigger United States or foreign companies who complain about compliance with the Sarbanes-Oxley Act either have something to hide or they are unable to manage their financials. As Sections 7 and 8 will bring to the reader's attention, advanced technology offers tools that not only ease compliance burdens, and associated costs, but also make management control more effective.

On the other hand, it is understandable that companies whose IT is still in the Paleolithic age, have to pay a SOX penalty for being in the rear guard. Let me add, as a general statement, that the goal of new legislation has been to protect investors and close the loopholes opening up. Correctly, the act's authors were worried about

- Creative accounting,
- Massaged financial statements, and
- Their hugely negative impact on the market.

This is true of all companies, and most particularly of those with light supervision or none at all. The reason why William Donaldson, former chairman of the Securities and Exchange Commission, and Harvey Goldschmid, former member of SEC's five-person board, wanted to bring hedge funds under regulatory control is that they were highly concerned about companies prone to taking investors for a ride.

In March 2005, in an article in the Notre Dame Law Review, Goldschmid called America's financial scandals a "systemic failure" requiring serious correction. On the SEC, he pushed not only for stiffer penalties and more explicit rules, but also for more regulation of both hedge funds and stock exchanges as well as the possible regulation of rating agencies.‡ What has happened subsequently with AAA-rated tranches of subprimes is testimony to Goldschmid's foresight.

* *Total Telecom Magazine*, July/August 2007.

† D. N. Chorafas, *IFRS, Fair Value and Corporate Governance: Its Impact on Budgets, Balance Sheets and Management Accounts* (London: Butterworth-Heinemann, 2005).

‡ *The Economist*, June 11, 2005.

Part of the problem lies in the fact that SEC's authority over fund management is not clear-cut. Broadly it covers mutual funds, very slightly hedge funds, but not at all pension funds—a huge money machine of great importance to both companies and individuals, particularly retirees. It is the duty of regulators to let it be well known that conflicts of interest are not tolerable.

Neither are other jurisdictions soft on malfeasance. Take conflict of interest in insider trading as an example. On July 2, 2007, Britain's Financial Services Authority (FSA) let it be known that investment banks that do not put in place proper controls to stop price-sensitive information leaking into the market could, in future, face hefty fines. Circulated in newsletters, this caution underlined FSA's determination to crack down on insider trading ahead of mergers and acquisitions (M&A).

According to published information, FSA's research is suggesting that about a quarter of all price-sensitive announcements by companies listed in London are preceded by share price movements. In turn, this is an indication of possible insider trading, and it has prompted criticism that the regulator has not brought more high-profile insider trading cases to court.

"Recognizing the evidential challenges in bringing successful enforcement cases, we will take a robust line where we identify leaks that may have been caused either deliberately or due to serious weaknesses in controls or behavior," the FSA wrote in a newsletter.* This provided evidence of the British regulator's determination to be in charge of cases where

- People may think FSA is not willing to use broad principles to bring about changes in behavior, and
- Investment banks may make some money on the side while involved in organizing and financing M&A deals.

Those who complain that London has recently become the global financial hub instead of New York should also remember the existence of other, more potent reasons than changes in financial regulation. While the United States has a 100 percent right to protect itself against terrorist attacks from hoodlums coming from abroad, outsourcing of the U.S. consulate's duties to private companies, as it now happens in Western Europe, has deprived the American security system of

- The experience of State Department professionals and
- Long years of databased information on visa applications and temporary residence permits, which can be instrumental in screening.

In my view, the difficulty of obtaining U.S. visas by foreign businessmen should be rated at par (if not higher) with that of SOX compliance in terms of promoting

* *Financial Times*, July 3, 2007.

London (within easy reach) over New York as the global center for financial and business activities. There is always the law of unexpected consequences, to which there does not seem to have been given enough thought when the new U.S. entry regulations were drawn.

12.3 Both Regulation and Management Watch Should Be Proactive

The use of technology for improved governance, such as compliance with Sarbanes-Oxley, can be described as "back to basics." What could be more fundamental than asking for, and obtaining, a confirmation signed by the chief executive and chief financial officer, that rules and regulations are observed by everybody working for the company, including the top brass?

Simply stated, in a globalized market characterized by deregulation and a golden horde of innovation opportunities, the tendency to run wild of the rules may be difficult to resist. While technology is a key ingredient in new products and services, it also serves

- In compliance and
- In the management of risk.

In both cases, technology has to be audited. The need for IT auditing was shown in Section 1 with the example on the snarl in back-office work. Merely paying for technology is no evidence of using it the right way.

On the other hand, as we will see in this section, there are issues against which even the best technology is powerless, because they do not fall in its domain. These are *political* issues that have to be resolved, and decided upon, before we can talk of applying high tech to help in compliance with rules and regulations.

Options trading provides an example. In the United States, options were traded in the grain markets back in the late 1800s, and this continued into the Great Depression throughout the early 1930s. However, unlike other assets traded at the Chicago Board of Trade (CBOT) and other exchanges, options trading was generally considered as being *privileged trading*—a question that was also addressed by the Illinois Supreme Court.

During that period, in the absence of clear definitions and regulations, the overall image of the options business was less than respectable, and in 1910, to protect the public, the federal government became involved in prudential supervision. Slowly, the rules were modified by the exchanges to

- Develop a plan of accountability and
- Guarantee a form of cash settlement.

Books on the history of finance say that the U.S. government attempted to cure certain flaws that were subject to public objections by imposing a heavy tax on all exchange-traded commodity options. The *transaction tax* quite literally killed options trading for a time, but it rebounded in 1926 when the tax was declared unconstitutional by U.S. courts.

From 1926 until 1933, the trading in exchange-style options flourished and came to represent 10 percent of futures trading volume, a significant share. Then came a price spike. On July 19, 1933, the July CBOT wheat contract went from around 44.5 cents per bushel at the start of the year to $1.17. The following day, a dramatic drop brought the market back down to 90 cents and wiped out fortunes.

Trading was suspended for two days following this event, officially because of a backlog in accounting work, just like it happened in 1967 to 1970 with the Wall Street investment banks' back offices. But the way market rumor had it, the price swing was caused by a single private speculator who cornered the wheat market through the cunning use of call privileges.

A short time after this incident, a Chicago crop authority made the statement that the drop in price was "fully justified by legitimate conditions of supply and demand" that stemmed from a severe drought and crop failures. No matter the reason, however, the turbulent advance and subsequent caving-in of the wheat market had two unwanted consequences:

- A public fear that food shortages could occur
- A general negative reaction against economic forces

In the aftermath of these events, in a move to improve the way options were handled in a free market, on July 24, 1933, the Chicago Board of Trade moved to prevent huge volatility swings in the future by imposing daily trading limits on grains. For their part, federal legislators correctly considered the wild market gyrations to be the result of excessive speculation, and this led to serious controls that were legislated into the Commodity Exchange Act of 1936.

- The new laws placed restrictions on commodity options trading.
- Despite government action, scandals continued and options trading was eventually banned.

Some years later, the U.S. Commodity Futures Trading Commission (CFTC) approved a pilot program to trade commodity options in a handful of commodities, including gold, sugar, heating oil, and Treasury bonds. Only designated contracts were initially approved, but many more markets were later authorized as additions to the scope of this initiative—but really as a way of lowering initial restrictions. There are lessons to be learned from the ups and downs of options trading in the United States:

- Regulations are largely of a political nature.
- Rules, regulations, and controls that are imposed in response to past excesses are eventually bypassed.
- Bypassing previously imposed regulations twists the broader sense of compliance, leading to starting all over again with tougher rules that will eventually be watered down.

The Sarbanes-Oxley Act of 2002 was passed in an attempt to stem the reaction against economic forces by all types of investors who got burned by Enron, WorldCom, Adelphia Communications, Global Crossing, and many other companies who, in the go-go late 1990s, thrived by taking to the cleaners legitimate and hardworking investors.

- What preceded SOX was not a once-in-a-lifetime happening.
- What preceded SOX was a series of events with a certain similitude to other events, some of which, in 1929, led to the Great Depression.

Regulators have the duty of being proactive. If they fail to do so, they forgo their responsibilities. The shocks from the financial scandals of the late 1990s/early 21st century changed the political climate in the United States by reducing political opposition to increased regulatory burdens on business. This would not have happened if management had been in charge and if its decisions and actions had been ethical. Corporate wrongdoing and noncompliance with laws and rules flourished because the proper control system for self-regulation was not in place. (It very rarely is.) And it is just as true that the absence of regulations creates more opportunities for legal risk.

12.4 SOX Is a Friend of Business, Not a Foe

Many questions have been raised by the rather frequent inaccuracy of financial statements as well as of both internal and external auditing reports. Such events involve the entire concept of regulation. If our accounting and auditing practices are inadequate, who will find the wrongdoers? Who will do the policing?

If there were no management risk* and no misuses of financial information followed by abuses of corporate money and outright fraud (Adelphia Communications being an example), there might have been no urgency for a law that significantly increased the regulators' watch. However, the massive disregard for ethical values made it imperative to reestablish public confidence.

---

* D. N. Chorafas, *Management Risk: The Bottleneck Is at the Top of the Bottle* (London: Macmillan/Palgrave, 2004).

- If senior managers are to handle compliance risk in an able manner, they must be much more proactive than in the past.
- The corporate-responsibility law foresees a maximum penalty of 20 years, which is a huge incentive for not cooking the books.

In this sense, SOX protects rather than inhibits or damages business because the new economy depends on intangible assets, with business confidence at the top of the list. If the CEO and CFO cannot or would not be able to value the assets and liabilities, then nobody else, including investors and regulators, can say what a company is worth.

An example of how difficult this becomes is provided by the mid- to late-1990s go-go market. To keep at high gear their company's equity, some CEOs deliberately steered their financial records toward creative accounting practices. They began to fake financial reports, and they tried to corrupt the markets. Professional managers, financial analysts, certified public accountants, lawyers, and others became greedy, with the result that

- Financial information turned out to be very unreliable, and
- In the aftermath, investors first became concerned, then scared, and the bubble burst.

Deceived by corrupt and unethical behavior on a grand scale, Western European markets used the Sarbanes-Oxley Act to recalibrate their rules and regulations,* requiring transparent easy-to-understand financial statements. In America alone, in 2002, nearly 1,000 companies restated their previous earnings, thereby

- Establishing more credible financial statements while
- Trying to escape from the stigma and consequences of corporate malfeasance.

People still wanting to escape their responsibilities rose against the SOX reform bill on the basis that it is hard to value *intangible assets*. Others said that there is a general disagreement on how to value them, or that the government just tries to read *management intent*. These are lightweight arguments.

Regarding *intangible assets*, companies have been valuing and misvaluing them for a long time. An evidence is goodwill and the huge 2001 and 2002 write-downs at the level of $50 billion by JDSU, AOL Time Warner, and others (though the "other" write-downs were at lesser level). Let us also not forget that cases similar to those that shook America have happened elsewhere in the western world. German

* For instance, in February 2003, the German government introduced a law similar to SOX, holding top executives personally liable for misleading investors.

examples are Balsam AG, Flowtex, and Philipp Holzmann; in Austria the name of the wrongdoer is BAWAG (see Section 5); and an Italian example is Parmalat.

An irony with the argument against the corporate responsibility law about valuing intangibles is that companies have been steadily feeding the market with *their* financial estimates, which are heavily based on intangibles. So are pro forma reporting and EBITDA (earnings before interest, taxes, depreciation, and amortization)—statements that are so much loved by financial analysts.

With Enron, WorldCom, and many other problem cases, pro forma reporting and EBITDA were financial statements that misled investors, while their CEOs and CFOs played both ways: benefiting from pro formas but renouncing any responsibility for these statements. Transparency was at a bare minimum when SOX saw to it that accountability should be increased across the board.

In connection with the second argument, in America, the need for explicitly stating *management intent* entered the letter of the law in June 1998 with the Statement of Financial Accounting Standards 133 (SFAS 133) by the Financial Accounting Standards Board (FASB). It is nothing new. While SFAS 133 has been updated twice since then, the requirement of explicitly stating management intent is always supreme.

Clear-eyed CEOs appreciate that the so-called "voluntary corporate governance codes for companies" have neither a soul to blame nor a body to kick. This is another reason why legislation bringing personal accountability to the foreground is a step in the right direction. At the same time, one thing shown by the controversy surrounding SOX that there is still no consensus about the right levels of

- Corporate transparency and
- Personal accountability.

Along with the able use of technology, these notions are pillars of the book of management; indeed, they are at the heart of it. What several texts on management do not state so clearly (though they should) is that the use of information technology to help management perform its duties did not start with the need to confront SOX challenges; rather, it is more than 30 years old.

In the mid-1960s, Citibank developed the Internal Accounting Management Information System (IAMIS), enriching it in the 1980s with knowledge artifacts (see Sections 7 and 8). And in the late 1980s, Bankers Trust designed and implemented Magellan, a corporate memory facility (CMF, more on this issue in Section 6). The fact that several financial institutions and other companies remained behind and did not benefit from such development is clearly their fault, and not the fault of the regulator.

Markets and supervisors rely on dependable financial reporting for their decisions, and high technology can be of help. Additionally, all stakeholders have to gain from financial transparency. The first golden rule of governance is that there should be penalties for misdeeds. In the Enron case, rating agencies came under fire for having given the enterprise an investment-grade rating just before its collapse. (This repeated itself in 2007 with high credit ratings of top tranches of securitized subprimes.)

The second golden rule of governance is that accounting standards are sacrosanct, but at the same time accounting rules that produce reliable financial statements are, by themselves, insufficient if there is no credible institutional procedure for enforcing them. In the United States, this is the role of the Securities and Exchange Commission, which does not make the laws; it enforces them.

In conclusion, one way to look at SOX aftereffects is through the fact that the SEC has ordered the CEOs and CFOs of the 1,000 largest U.S. companies to attest personally to the accuracy of financial statements, starting with their most recent annual report. The New York Stock Exchange has also proposed new rules on corporate governance. But the question remains: For how long is this going to right the balances of financial reporting?

12.5 The Fear of the Policeman Is Greater than the Fear of IT

From the examples we have seen since Section 1, it is not difficult to conclude that IT has a role to play in compliance, since in several cases this statement could be documented. For instance, the able use of information technology might have broken the back-office bottleneck that shook Wall Street in 1967 to 1970. Still,

- In all likelihood, the legacy solution used at that time (and even today) would not have lasted for long.
- The back-office applications had to be regularly revamped and restructured to continue providing a valid solution.

On the other hand, while it is undeniable that IT has a role to play in assisting management's compliance with the letter of the law, in the longer run—human nature being what it is—a more significant role in compliance is played by the fear of the policeman. Moving from the executive suite to a prison cell has been a traumatic experience to many executives.

Intelligent people appreciate that compliance with laws and regulations is not just the best policy; it is the only sound one. For instance, in the decades prior to the passage of the Sarbanes-Oxley Act, board seats, particularly those of big companies, were much sought after by bankers. This was a prestigious job that also enabled the banker to get the most insight into his client firm's strategic thinking, ensuring that his institution walked away with the lion's share of the business the company did with financial entities.

- SOX made it untenable for an investment banker to sit on his client's board.
- SOX put new restrictions on insider information that bankers and other professionals might obtain.

A Sarbanes-Oxley Act in the Austrian Republic might have saved the country from the serial BAWAG scandals of the 1990s and early years of this century. Owned by the federation of Austrian labor unions, this bank nearly collapsed in 2006, and the case is currently at the court of justice. According to published accounts, Helmut Elsner, BAWAG's former CEO, lived in a penthouse flat with a swimming pool built for him at the bank's expense on top of the bank's office in central Vienna. From there, he allegedly supervised:

- The financial speculation that began in the early 1990s
- The bank's bloodletting of $600 million in October 1998, after a gamble by his own son, a freelance banker* (To plug that hole, money was taken from the strike fund of ÖGB, the labor union federation that owned BAWAG.)
- The April 2006 torrent of financial losses, which prompted a run on the bank
- The subsequent aversion of panic by throwing good money after bad money—fresh funds from two insurance companies and an Austrian government guarantee

Overall, BAWAG losses rose to an estimated Euro 1.4 billion—just short of $2 billion—seriously wounding the institution and the labor unions' treasury. It remains to be seen what sort of sentence will befall the bad management, as in 2007 the Austrian prosecutor finally brought Elsner and his pals to court. (In 2006, following huge losses, BAWAG was bought at a bargain basement price by Cerberus, the U.S. private equity firm.)

In America, the impact of the Sarbanes-Oxley Act has been, by all evidence, on accounting fraud. In March 2004, Jamie Olis, a former tax planning executive at Dynegy, the Texas energy company, was sentenced to 24 years in jail with no prospect of parole. The reason was his role in *Project Alpha*, an accounting fraud that inflated the energy company's cash flow by $300 million. This was an interesting case of jurisprudence because:

- On October 31, 2005, though upholding the conviction, an appeals court threw out the sentence.
- The appeals court concluded that Sim Lake, a Houston judge, had greatly overstated the losses caused by Olis, who had no criminal record.

---

* *The Economist*, July 21, 2007.

In the case of Jamie Olis, Judge Lake had probably based the sentence on the $105-million loss to the University of California Retirement System (UCRS) that, he said, was due to Dynegy restating its results to correct its dodgy accounting. The appeals court found that the lower court's loss calculation had ignored some facts:

- UCRS bought its Dynegy shares at top of the market, and both the overall market and shares of similar firms had since fallen.
- Dynegy's share price may have been hit by its failure to acquire its faltering and fraudulent rival Enron.
- Over two-thirds of the loss occurred either before the accounting restatement or more than a week after it.

Based on these premises, the appeals court said that at least $100 million of UCRS's loss cannot be attributed to Mr. Olis,* making this decision an excellent example of a sophisticated approach to the attribution of financial responsibilities, probably elaborated by Olis's lawyers in their conclusions to the court. But the conviction was upheld.

Some people argue that when the law enforcement industry and the courts function properly, existing laws are plenty. In July 2007, Yoshiaki Murakami, Japan's best-known shareholder activist and former trade-ministry official, was found guilty of insider trading and sentenced to two years in prison. His Murakami Fund was charged with receiving inside information from an entity presided by Takafumi Horie, who is appealing against a separate sentence.† Prison convictions in white-collar cases are rare in Japan, but the wind is changing.

Four years earlier, on June 13, 2003, two of South Korea's high-profile businesspeople were handed prison sentences for their part in a $1.2-billion accounting fraud at SK Group, the country's third-largest conglomerate. Both were at the company's vertex: Chey Tae-won, chairman of SK Corporation, South Korea's biggest oil refiner, was jailed for three years; and Son Kil-seung, chairman of the parent group, got a three-year-term suspended sentence. Chey, who received the firm prison sentence, was the grandson of former South Korean president Roh Tae-woo and nephew of SK Group's founder. Son was chairman of the Federation of Korean Industries, the country's most powerful business lobby group. Allegedly, he was more responsible for the accounting manipulation than Chey (but probably he knew somebody).

As it happened in the United States with Enron and WorldCom, the SK Group scandal revived concerns about standards of corporate governance in South Korea, years after the country's financial sector was thrown into a major crisis and its economy was at the edge of going bankrupt. The cases of other formerly mighty South Korean companies, like Daewoo and Hanbo Steel, were even greater scandals.

---

* *The Economist*, November 5, 2005.

† *The Economist*, July 21, 2007.

After the fraud, Kim Woo-Choong, Daewoo's founder and president, ran for years from country to country until he was finally caught.

Technology might have played a role in early discovery and prosecution of the aforementioned cases if all internal control information was by law databased; and if regulators were given the right to examine online, ad hoc, the companies' databases and corporate-memory facilities to unearth cases of fraud. Powerful expert systems, too, would have helped. The knowledge artifacts, developed by the SEC in the early 1990s for mining its own huge database for a web of insider trading, provide a good example of what can be done.

12.6 Contribution to Compliance of the Corporate Memory Facility

The *corporate memory facility* (CMF) is one of the most significant developments in financial and industrial databases. Unlike other database structures, which basically store transactional and accounting information, CMF registers decisions, the reason for decisions being taken, and their aftermath. This process became increasingly important during the 1990s, first with contractors to Pentagon projects and then with corporate walkthroughs and postmortem analyses. Implementation examples abound, ranging

- From board decisions
- To risk management, design reviews, and more.

Starting with the fundamentals, a *database* is an organized collection of information elements stored on magnetic, optical, or other media that is accessed ad hoc, online, by data-processing programs and end users. (Batch databases are of no interest to this text.) These information elements can be seen as a model of the real world

- Made available to diverse applications and
- Calibrated, updated, and supported by housekeeping services.

Modern databases contain qualitative information, not only quantitative data, as used to be the case in the 1950s and 1960s. Therefore, the databased information elements may be *hard numbers*, subject to objective verification, and softer, *future-oriented* numbers, the results of simulations plus comments and other text.

The corporate memory facility may also include ideas, concepts, and graphical information stored and retrieved online. For instance, there may be pages of specific customer commitments as well as customer wishes, whose nonobservance—let alone violation—would alienate the customer from his or her bank.

Softer information elements are increasingly popular because companies are interested in storing and retrieving hypotheses, assumptions, and results of decision processes, where the main source of data has so far existed in the minds of managers and professionals. These are *knowledge assets*, widely considered as the most overlooked corporate resources over the past decades.

The best-governed organizations appreciate that they have a need for technology that can capture, monitor, and manage knowledge assets, and that this must be done in an organized and cost-effective manner. Not surprisingly, compliance is a good field to apply CMF solutions.

The contents of CMF may consist of the reasons and justifications for why a loan was given, balance sheet analyses, evaluation of collateral, dissenting voices, and qualifiers of the loans. An integral part of the CMF will be the client's quality record built over the years by distilling experience from lending, investment, trading, and other operations. Two uses can be made of such records:

- A regular review, leading to a pattern of behavior for each counterparty
- In-depth studies to unearth who has made what violation of compliance, how often, of which kind, and when they were found out

Figure 12.1 provides a snapshot of a web of database accesses plus compliance knowledge stored in the corporate memory facility. The careful reader may wish to compare this reference to what has happened with valuable database records of the bank that provided the background for the case study on IT audit in Chapter 7.

A different example with additional information elements that also find their way into the CMF is the outcome of design reviews. As we saw in Chapter 2, in many companies, projects are subject to weekly management control, usually done through physical personal presence. An alternative is by means of video-conferencing events, often held in a war-room setting, with all the division's main operating data projected on screens and databased. Management control at large may follow a similar approach, as several chief executives do,

- Painstakingly taking the people reporting to them through every line of figures and
- Maintaining this ritual throughout their tenure, so that they always know exactly what is going on.

This policy of direct control—with storage of decisions (and of the reasons behind them) to enable future walkthroughs—allows the person in charge to make up his or her mind based on documented evidence rather than vague hunches. Therefore, CMF solutions and postmortem analyses are practiced by companies who realize that their business success, productivity, and profitability depends on *shared knowledge*, not just on exchanged information.

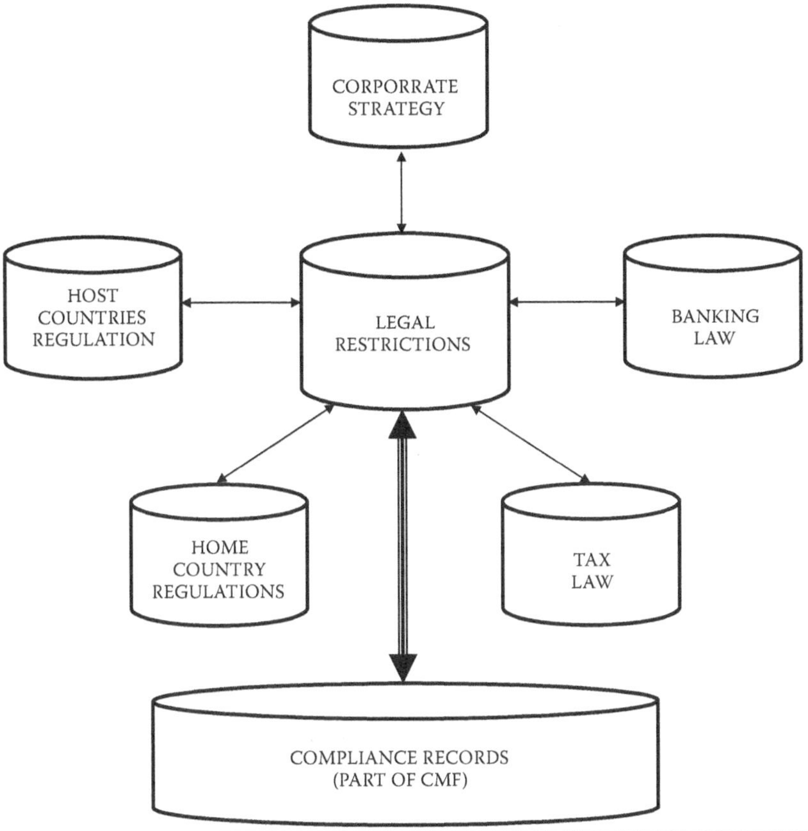

Figure 12.1 Compliance is a polyvalent issue which requires both hard data and soft data.

What has surprised me in my research is that, despite the advantages a CMF provides, relatively few organizations have done fundamental studies on how to capitalize on a store of knowledge. Xerox is one of them, and it has found that

> 46 percent of corporate knowledge is captured by documents in paper form.

The problem is that this knowledge is scattered all over the firm. Therefore, it is often difficult to locate it, and it is even more difficult, if not outright impossible, to exploit it in an effective manner. CMF does away with these constraints.

> 42 percent of corporate knowledge resides in the heads of individual employees.

This knowledge is inaccessible to their colleagues, and it will ultimately be lost for the organization as some of the firm's more knowledgeable people change employment or simply retire. Even if these employees continue working for the firm, such knowledge cannot be easily extracted under current conditions, while CMF makes possible both effective access and immediate usage.

> Only 12 percent of a company's knowledge is captured in a shareable electronic knowledge base.

The majority of this 12 percent is handled through expert systems (see Section 7). Tier-1 companies believe that this is the part destined to grow over the coming years, at least among firms who take seriously the issue of safekeeping precious corporate assets. Furthermore, while the knowledge base of an organization has so far been mainly used to represent scientific, engineering, financial, and trading experience, it now starts to involve

- Compliance results and
- Internal control findings.

Some companies shy away from their responsibility to safeguard knowledge resources because they are afraid of the unknown. In contrast, the best-managed entities have implemented (or are implementing) a corporate memory facility. Eventually CMF may become as common as the telephone. "Wherever there is a telephone, there is Chase" was the message in a long-running Chase Manhattan advertisement that aired many years ago.

12.7 The Contribution of Knowledge Engineering

The contribution of knowledge artifacts to compliance has been referenced throughout this chapter. To provide the reader with a broader perspective on what modern technology can deliver by way of sophisticated software, this and the next section are dedicated to definitions of and documentation on what expert systems and agents can achieve.

Back in the 1960s and 1970s, the domain we presently call *knowledge engineering* was known as *artificial intelligence* (AI), and to a large extent it was a field of interest for university professors. But it should as well be noted that "thinking" and "intelligence" constituted a more general way in which some people looked at computers. Published in the 1950s, one of the earliest books on computers and computation was entitled *Machines that Think*.

Because the search for more sophisticated solutions by the leaders of industry is never ending, artificial intelligence did not remain for long the toy of university professors. As their students graduated and went to work in business companies, they were eager to apply in their profession what they had learned in the lab.

- AI processes and tools migrated to the data-processing departments of several companies, and they started to produce some very interesting results.*
- By the mid-1980s, the artifacts these young scientists had built were rechristened as *expert systems*, and top-tier firms were proud to show what they could do with them.

Today, more than two decades down the line, knowledge artifacts can be found in the IT departments of companies that are operating with state-of-the-art high tech. The ample use of knowledge engineering provides the leaders with a significant competitive advantage; it also helps to distinguish between those firms that are well managed and those that are not.

Clearly, expert systems cannot change a company's ethics (or those of its CEO), but in entities where the CEO, CFO, and all other executives abide by ethical standards, they can be of invaluable assistance. Similarly, auditors can put the information provided by expert systems to great use in their work. For instance, on the basis of information revealed by expert systems, the board, CEO, and senior management must decide on

- Which control process best fits the bank's profile or
- How often and which type of spot audits need to be made.

Expert systems, however, are not all-weather artifacts. For instance, those designed for compliance will not be effective in auditing, and vice versa, because each field demands a different type of functionality from the knowledge artifact. Day-to-day compliance is a steady process, while auditing should be independent from day-to-day business activities and dig deeply into one chosen subject.

Audit's mission, said a senior executive at Bank Leu, in Zurich, is to inspect; it is not supposed to operate in the sense of controlling ongoing business events or enforcing the observance of rules and regulations, which is the business of compliance. On the other hand, at the end of the day, internal auditors and compliance officers are asking fairly similar questions:

- What has gone wrong?
- What can go wrong again?
- What is the likelihood of each type of incident occurring under a different form?

---

* D. N. Chorafas and Heinrich Steinmann *Expert Systems in Banking* (London: Macmillan, 1991); and D. N. Chorafas, *Rocket Scientists in Banking* (London: Lafferty Publications, 1995).

- What will be the impact of each failure in terms of damage to assets?
- How can this failure be avoided or its aftereffect minimized?

One of the ways expert systems map these questions for computer handling is through rules (see Section 8). The same is true of *agents*, which are mobile knowledge artifacts residing in network nodes, testing for vulnerabilities and serving as "assistants" to their masters.

The programming of expert systems and agents has little to do with classical programming approaches. For instance, in programming an artifact for surveillance, the regulations to be observed will be painted through visual programming, which significantly facilitates this task; then, they will be compiled in rule form and the rules compiled in C++, an object-oriented language.

There are, of course, prerequisites. The technical infrastructure must consist of a platform capable of handling a number of compliance artifacts in real time. Flexibility is at a premium because this application will continue to evolve in response to changes in compliance requirements. The focal point of each expert system must be the area from which violations of compliance may come. Examples include

- Lending,
- Investments,
- Private banking,
- Trading, and
- Risk management.

Trading is an activity that banks carry out primarily on their own behalf and only secondarily sell to their clients as a service. The client sees trading functions primarily in the form of an execution of a financial order, but this execution might violate supervisory, fiduciary, or other standards. Hence there is a need to monitor and control for compliance purposes.

To explore what a knowledge artifact can do in this connection, one should place oneself in the shoes of a financial trader who operates in several markets and a variety of financial instruments, constantly looking for opportunities. Because each trader works in the context of a portfolio according to his or her behavioral pattern, the knowledge artifact for compliance watch must be

- Tailored to each trader and
- Designed to explore his or her unique profile and strategy.

This can be achieved by segregating functions, analyzing them into discrete components, and testing them. Subsequently, during operation, the knowledge artifact must have in its knowledge bank (or be able to data mine) not only behavioral aspects, but also portfolio analytics; an algorithm to monitor risk and return; and, most importantly, compliance parameters to be observed at all times. Section 8 provides more insight on this issue.

12.8 Why Knowledge Artifacts Are a Major Advance in IT

Applications aimed at compliance control provide plenty of opportunities for imaginative approaches. Their common ground is that a certain level of sophistication is needed in tracking violations of compliance, because many of the financial instruments, such as exotic derivatives, are complex. The essential nature of this type of usage of advanced IT is that of using intelligence, not force, in order to ensure observance of laws and of regulations.

This has not been at all surprising because, as Dr. Robert Oppenheimer of Manhattan Project fame predicted in the late 1950s, computers can be used for much more than just numeric processing. Indeed, during that same period while languages like Fortran and COBOL were being defined, people at Carnegie Tech and MIT were investigating the simulation of human problem solving on a computer (see Section 7 on AI's origin).

Typically, these job-oriented artifacts will be agents, the smaller, mobile artifacts that serve a master (or a small part of a bigger process). They will operate in a distributed computer and communications environment working in an autonomous manner and communicating with the

- System resources and
- End users for whom they execute a self-contained mission.

Agents may also communicate with each other, cooperating to carry out jobs beyond the capability of a single artifact. Increasingly, they also feature the capacity to acquire knowledge through learning; therefore, they are an interesting product (which finds its origin in von Neumann's automata theory).

The careful reader will recall from Section 7 that there exist different ways of acquiring, mapping, and exploiting domain knowledge obtained from experts, which is distilled and compiled for further, wider use. One of the more successful structures of knowledge artifacts has been rule based. Here is a brief example:

IF <Clause 1>
THEN <Clause 2>
ELSE <Clause 3>

For instance, in an ultrasimplified form:

IF <Sarbanes-Oxley is the law>
THEN <CEO and CFO must sign financial statements>
ELSE <Annual accounts are suspect and CEO/CFO may be subject to prosecution>

Section 7 also made the reference that expert system rules are compiled into a self-contained software program responsible for executing part of a process for which they have been designed, in this case, SOX observance. In a way fairly similar to that of human experts, the knowledge artifacts use information

- Coming onstream through the network,
- Obtained from information providers, or
- Contained in corporate databases and in public databases.

Some 30 rules can make a simple but fairly good expert system. Although complex structures like DEC's *XCON* or Mitsubishi Bank's Underwriter had thousands of rules, neither was a monolithic system. Both were aggregations of smaller artifacts that made the knowledge-enriched solution

- Flexible and
- Easy to update.

Updating the rules is vital, because the knowledge of an artifact is never cast in stone. Contrary to legacy data processing, a basic characteristic of expert systems is that they are very sensitive to changes in the environment they are designed to operate or control. Olivetti, the computer and office equipment company, had built in its Palo Alto Labs an expert system for production planning that was used in its factory in Ivrea, Italy:

- The artifact identified many things that were wrong with production planning.
- After these were corrected, it became useless because its rules reflected the company's previous organization of manufacturing operations.

This is a different way of saying that knowledge artifacts are both focused and dynamic. While they perform very well for the specific domain or fraction thereof (and its parameters) for which they were written, when conditions change, or when they are carried to a different domain, they would not work. The reason is that the knowledge reflected in their rules no longer applies.

- An expert system written for compliance with Sarbanes-Oxley is not going to work in the French jurisdiction because the law of the land is different.
- More than that, an expert system written for the original SOX will work poorly for smaller companies because of the recent changes in SOX rules (see Chapter 3).

For a better appreciation of the situation, the reader should note that compliance is far from being the only domain effectively assisted by expert systems and agents. From the mid-1980s to today, applications domains for knowledge engineering have substantially widened. Here are, in a nutshell, some interesting areas:

- Financial applications in budgeting, loans, and investments
- "Assistant to" implementation (perhaps the most widespread case)
- Data analysis and presentation, substituting middle management levels (becoming increasingly popular)
- Tracking a professional's work productivity and performance (IBM example)
- Embedded fuzzy chips in autos, appliances, photo machines, and other engines
- Restructuring and making more efficient legacy computer programs (easily the least successful of all these examples)
- New developments in computer applications, with a target of fast delivery and low cost (often in conjunction with an operating unit acting as sponsor)

Training is another implementation domain in full expansion. Using the knowledge of their experts, companies create a help-desk expert system to assist junior-level persons in responding to the customer in an able manner. As added value, this help-desk expert system teaches the junior-level person on how to become a better professional.

Similar applications examples exist in trading and in investments, where knowledge-based artifacts help companies leverage the skills of their employees. At Harvard Law School, researchers developed the Diplomat expert system to train professional negotiators and diplomats. The interaction with the knowledge artifact is on a case-by-case basis. Rules used as a metaphor to make the exchanges between human and computer more realistic.

A program similar to Harvard's can be written to *train* IT auditors and Sarbanes-Oxley compliance personnel, prompting its users to clearly define issues under investigation, including the way violators would look at and react to opportunities for fraud or for escaping compliance. As an example, Harvard's Diplomat prompts the user to

- Rank his or her own goals and requirements,
- Rank the goals and needs of the opposite side,
- Identify and outline disputed items,
- Try out different negotiating strategies, and
- Assist in elaborating ways and means to find common ground.

If finding a common ground is not feasible, then the Diplomat system assists its user in selecting an adversarial strategy or, alternatively, a conciliatory course. With a knowledge artifact containing a senior negotiator's knowledge and judgment, junior members of the team can obtain focused answers to their queries quickly. Though the knowledge bank will necessarily contain different domain rules, the training of IT auditors and of compliance officers will basically be no different than Harvard's approach.

Good corporate governance has much to gain by blending high technology and SOX. The Sarbanes-Oxley Act has an interesting clause, No. 304, which so far has been only partially applied. It states that companies can recover money taken by managers and other beneficiaries of options and bonuses whether these unwarranted rewards were due to fraudulent reasons or accounting errors.

A 2008 study by The Corporate Library (TCL) suggests that till mid-2007, five years after SOX, only 14 cases were found in American industry where clause 304 was put into effect. But with the subprimes and credit crisis of 2007, just a year later the number grew to 297 companies. Knowledge artifacts can be effectively used to:

- Track all options and bonuses to their receivers
- Follow-up on their recovery, and
- Document whether SOX Clause 304 has been applied fully or only partially

It is an interesting statistic that, according to the TCL study, in the US industry: 44 percent of unwarranted bonuses and benefits from options are due to outright fraud; 39 percent are linked to performance which has been badly presented, due to accounting error rather than plain fraud; and the 17 percent have a variety of causes in the background - but still have caused significant loss to the shareholders of companies which paid out money in an unwarranted way.

Chapter 13

What If: Backtesting Sarbanes-Oxley

13.1 The Concept Underpinning Case Studies and What-If Scenarios

This book has presented a number of case studies: Those in Chapter 2 focused on internal control's contribution to better management; in Chapter 3, the theme was auditing practices; in Chapter 6, the case studies concentrated on the audit of information technology; Chapters 7 and 8 presented the condensed version of a strategic IT audit requested by the board of directors; and Chapter 9 presented more case studies on IT audit.

This approach of alternating between the definition of key corporate functions such as internal control, audit, and technology—and how they are put in practice (expressed through case studies)—was continued in Part 3, with two chapters on technical audit: Chapter 10 on response time and system reliability, and Chapter 11 on the many aspects of system security. The first of the two chapters in Part 4 has concentrated on the aftereffects of the Sarbanes-Oxley Act (SOX) and the contribution of IT to SOX compliance as well as its limits. For this purpose, the necessary IT tools and methods have been examined, with each case presenting an actual event at the time it happened.

The large majority of the previously cited cases are unlike the case studies of Harvard Business School, which present situations where something is yet to be decided, or redecided. In those instances, the reader is expected to make his or her examination, interpret the data into a diagnosis, and prescribe a treatment. Instead, the case studies in this book report facts, and from time to time they also

- Report opinions of people within the companies or
- Provide the reader with a battery of audit queries to be used in professional practice.

Moreover, it has been a deliberate choice to evaluate the facts and opinions included in each case study, as well as presenting a follow-up on problems being discussed and sometimes suggesting solutions. Such an approach helps the reader to discover and analyze challenges associated with an IT audit. Another deliberate choice has been that several parts of the text include suggestions to help the IT auditor in similar situations, in his or her professional work.

Typically, the problems the case studies bring to the reader's attention may be desperate emergencies in the use of information technology, or in compliance, calling for drastic action. Or they require basic policy changes of longer range significance, though not emergencies. Along this line of reference, an important addition to this text is a chapter on *what if* scenarios connected to the Sarbanes-Oxley Act. Ideally, these should have been cases looking at:

- How companies organized themselves to confront SOX challenges
- How they used their IT to be truly in charge of financial statements (in cases where they did so)

But it did not happen that way. While research usually provides a rich amount of information, getting material for a couple of chapters on companies' experience in implementing Sarbanes-Oxley, including IT chores, proved to be quite different than it was for other research issues.

Perhaps the subject is too esoteric and controversial and, therefore, CEOs and CFOs keep such information close to their chest. As a result, the alternative has been to use an emulation

- Capitalizing on the fact there is plenty of information about what has happened pre-SOX, and
- Writing scenarios about what might have been the case *if* the Sarbanes-Oxley Act had been enacted in 2000 after the burst of the Internet companies' bubbles, or even earlier.

This is, of course, a big *what if*, but as long as we appreciate that emulation is not an exact science, it can make an interesting case study and present the reader with a pattern. Is it possible that Enron, Enron's banks, and WorldCom—the three case studies in this chapter—would have benefited from a tightly audited internal control and the CEO/CFO's legal accountability for financial statements? Could high tech have made a difference? These are the key queries.

For starters, *what if* scenarios are based partly on facts and very much on judgment. This policy has been followed in backtesting the likely effect of Sarbanes-Oxley. Because the hypotheses made are a *what if*, the publisher was concerned that it might be "that readers won't get past it ... [they] will get all the way through the book, be hit with this big *what if* scenario, and not value all the material they had read previously."

In my opinion, this need not be the case. First, because the reader is informed in advance that, unlike the previous case studies that have been based on fact, the present scenario is only a way of thinking and feeling based on assumptions about doing something that complies with the letter of the law. The scenario that follows is looking at compliance as a matter of

- Intellectual power,
- Judgment, and
- Practical common sense.

But it also accounts for the fact that it is very difficult, if not impossible, to change human nature— hence, the second point. As Demosthenes, the great orator and philosopher of ancient Athens, once said: "Business is built on confidence and we all know from our professional life that confidence is promoted by

- Stricter corporate governance,
- Accurate financial reporting, and
- More oversight by regulators."

Within this broader concept of business confidence and lack of it, the pre-SOX events back played in the following sections should not be seen as concerning only "this" or "that" company but all of corporate America, of corporate Europe, and of corporate Japan. All companies have plenty to lose from accounting improprieties committed in public markets, while they can make good profits from strong business management and transparent balance sheets.

13.2 Replaying the Enron Scandal under SOX

Enron started life as a sleepy gas pipeline company, but under chairman Ken Lay it transformed itself into what was basically a "hedge fund with a gas pipeline on the side." In its Lay-time incarnation, Enron was a holding specializing in the energy industry and in derivative financial instruments.

In its filings with the Securities and Exchange Commission, the new Enron identified itself as a securities broker and dealer. This is precisely the classification followed by investment banks and used by companies like Morgan Stanley, Goldman Sachs, and other Wall Street firms.

With a regulatory blind eye from the Commodity Futures Trading Commission (CFTC), which had wanted to regulate derivatives but whose top was decapitated by political action, Enron created an over-the-counter derivatives market in energy contracts, becoming over the years a major derivatives dealer and player. (In May 1998, under Brooksley Born, CFTC issued a concept release regarding new derivatives regulation. This caused anxiety among banks and brokers, bringing into action some heavyweights like Alan Greenspan, Robert Rubin, and Phil Gram. The rest is history, but it is also a lesson.)

Until Enron's energy derivatives put their weight on the market, most energy companies backed trading operations with hard assets such as power plants. These allowed them to guarantee energy supply to the instrument's buyer. To the contrary, Enron worked furiously to shed power plants and oil- and gas-generating fields. Its management believed it could earn higher returns by

- Using its trading and technology expertise, and
- Tapping assets owned by others in widespread markets, including steel, pulp, paper, and broadband communications—not just energy.

Critics, however, say that more than anything else, Enron suffered from a crisis of confidence, not a meltdown of its core business, because financial assets are more easily manipulated than physical assets, and Enron leveraged itself at unreasonably high levels, which proved to be unsustainable.

Looking back in corporate history, had the Sarbanes-Oxley Act passed in 2000, it would have changed absolutely Enron's rise to power as well as the behavior of its top brass. Its board, CEO, president, and CFO were not part of the solution in following Demosthenes' advice on building business confidence; they were part of the problem. Sarbanes-Oxley

- Punishes corporate malfeasance,
- But it does not change human nature.

According to *Swaps Monitor*, at the end of 2000 Enron had $201 billion in derivatives exposure. While this may seem peanuts in comparison to JP Morgan Chase's (then) $24.5 trillion and Deutsche Bank's $9.1 trillion for the same period, it did make Enron one of the top derivatives players—which was also its downfall. The beginning of the end for Enron came on October 16, 2001, when the company stated that:

- It had lost $618 million in the third quarter of 2001, due to write-offs of just over $1 billion.
- It was proceeding with early termination of certain structured financial arrangements, a sign that something big had gone wrong.

In a conference call that day announcing this news, Enron's Ken Lay made a quick reference to a $1.2-billion write-down in the company's equity capital. More announcements like that were to follow. In mid-October 2001, the *Wall Street Journal* and other papers began questioning Enron's bookkeeping, charging that the company's actions raised vexing conflict-of-interest questions in its relationship to some of the partnerships it had created.

Sarbanes-Oxley would not have made much of a difference in this case, except for the fact that Kenneth Lay and Enron's CFO would have had to sign financial statements about derivatives exposure, which should not have posed them any problem. To the contrary, what might have saved Enron was Brooksley Born's proposed derivatives legislation. Had it been enacted it would have

- Brought Enron and other derivatives players under CFTC's watch, for their own good, and
- Informed the market about derivatives volcanoes, so that Enron's huge exposure (and that of other overleveraged firms) would have been unwelcome and counterproductive.

Not only are derivatives leveraged instruments, but Enron also had other means to load itself with debt. It issued large amounts of debentures based on practically nothing. Money-market funds and other investors who bought them now say they trusted Arthur Andersen, the now-defunct auditors. According to some reports in Japan, Citibank, through its partner Nikko Securities, had sold many Enron debentures to Japanese investors.*

(As a hindsight on how investors are taken for being stupid, with 2001 coming to a close, Tokyo money-market funds, which held most of the Enron and Argentina paper in Japan, reportedly lost an estimated $25 to $35 billion. This situation had become so dangerous that the Bank of Japan had to conduct direct money-market operations, purchasing large amounts of commercial paper from money-market funds and banks to avoid a deflationary crash.)

13.3 The Worst Continued to Worsen

Ernest Renan, a 19th-century French philosopher, once observed that national identity requires a collective work of amnesia. The same is true of business strategies

* *EIR*, January 18, 2002.

that bet on leverage and promise an uninterrupted stream of returns without concern for major risks being assumed.

- Those establishing them have more reasons than most other executives to want to forget the lessons of the past, which is a mistake.
- While the strategic thinker at the top has to look years ahead, he or she must also be very sensitive to what business history teaches as the sure road to oblivion.

At the end, except the "selected few," practically all of Enron's stakeholders were duped. Its shareholders lost their shirts; the regulators looked stupid; and, most importantly, Enron's employees lost their jobs, their pension fund money, and the equity investments they had made in the company for which they were working.

Dramatic as it may be, this example also shows the limitations of the Sarbanes-Oxley Act. If SOX had been enacted in 2000, or even 1998, it probably would not have inhibited Ken Lay who, a short time prior to Enron's bankruptcy, flooded the e-mail circuits with assurances to his employees that the company was in good financial health. Subsequently, it was revealed that:

- The accounting had been awfully manipulated.
- Debts of about $23 billion were hidden.
- The company's decision makers knew very well its disastrous financial condition.

In fact, after the bankruptcy, 29 people from Enron's senior management were indicted because they sold a huge amount of their Enron stock just prior to the crash.* Profiting from insider trading, they collected hundreds of millions of dollars, while the company's employees and small investors lost everything. (In the United States, laws against insider trading were enacted in the early 1960s, nearly four decades before Enron, but the practice is alive and well, and it is prospering as well all over Europe and Japan.)

After years of rapid growth in both revenue and earnings, with profits surging up to 24 percent per year (at least on paper)—which made it the stock market's darling—in mid-November 2001 the energy company acknowledged that results for the previous three years were overstated by more than a half-billion dollars. Investors might have been spared that kind of bad surprise

- If Sarbanes-Oxley had been enacted a few years prior to 2001; but the result might still have been the same because
- This was not a problem of management's ignorance but of management's complicity in cooking the books.

---

* *Libération, Paris*, June 27, 2002.

The bad news for Enron stakeholders was carefully hidden for several years. Only in late October 2001, a mere five weeks prior to its bankruptcy, did Enron announce a big drop in shareholders' equity, igniting fears that its most complex financial statements were distorting its true financial picture. Additionally, to cover itself, its management pointed to a number of factors supposedly responsible for the entity's distorted financial reports. One, but only one, of them was both

- A questionable decision to exclude the results of three partnerships from its financial statements, and
- A billion-dollar "error" several years earlier that had inflated the company's net worth.

Yet, there existed a long list of reasons for worry, as Enron's performance fell far short of the cozy picture painted by top management in its earlier earnings releases. This would have changed little with SOX compliance. Given the pattern of faking financial statements, its CEO and CFO would not have had much difficulty in signing them. (Neither was Enron alone in reporting bad news. In 2001, corporate America charged off a record $125 billion, much of it for assets, investments, and inventory that were not worth as much as management had previously reported.)

For the same reasons that downplay the results of SOX compliance, even if the now-defunct company had had the most advanced information technology, this would have made little difference. Enron would not have been using its IT to enhance SOX compliance (see Chapter 12), because SOX provisions would have been violated as a matter of policy, which is practically the fate of other existing laws.

Even the now-compulsory auditing of internal control would not have made much change, because Arthur Andersen was part of the deception. But if the external auditor was honest, then, and only then, it would have provided interesting evidence to the court following Enron's collapse (see Section 4). Theoretically, at least, one of the escape valves that top management has often used—that of "being busy with other things, we knew nothing about financial malfeasance"—would have been closed.

13.4 Ignorance as a Way of Running a Big Firm

It is not known whether Enron ever audited its IT, but it should not have done any audit of its internal control system because, otherwise, it would have found that it was in shambles, and maybe purposely so. In June 2002, half a year after the firm's bankruptcy, many members of senior management and of the board, most particularly its chairman Kenneth Lay and its president Jeffrey Skilling, pretended plain ignorance of what was happening with their company's financials as an excuse.

Chief executive officer and president said they knew nothing about a long-term policy of fake financial statements, justifying their ignorance about wrongdoings because of being busy in other matters. This earned Lay the epithet of "the most out-to-lunch CEO in America" ("out of touch" would have been a better fit). It needs no explaining that being busy is no excuse for

- Being inattentive to one's duties and
- Failing to oversee the transactions that eventually ruined the company.

Investors, investigators, the U.S. Congress, and Enron employees angrily dismissed such disclaimers, though this did not discourage the claims of amnesia. In testimony to the U.S. Senate committee investigating the Enron scandal, Jeffrey Skilling used the incompetence line of defense as he continued pleading ignorance.

Nobody seems to have asked the questions: "What about your system of internal control?" "Was it nonexistent or was it turned off?" Michael Kopper, a former executive of Enron, had a better memory than his bosses. He was the first among the company's senior people to face the consequences, and he became a government witness helping the Department of Justice (DOJ) in the continuing investigation of his former chief financial officer, Andrew Fastow—who was the next in line to "remember" Enron's events. (Kopper pleaded guilty to conspiracy and wire fraud, agreeing to pay back $12 million.)

Even if the memory of Enron's chairman and president was so weak, each of them had a chance to refresh it by reading the press. In mid-October of 2001, the *Wall Street Journal* published a seminal article whose coverage focused on a handful of the 3,000 or so partnerships, affiliates, and off-balance-sheet operations of the firm. Additionally, as Enron plunged, a special three-man committee of its board was formed to investigate the allegations of illegal activities. Is it possible that this internal committee would have had an easier time in hunting down illegalities if the Sarbanes-Oxley Act had taken force in, say, 1998? The answer has to be "not necessarily," because the auditors were part of the deception (as explained in Section 3).

The findings of the internal Enron committee were, however, interesting, as it concluded that Skilling bore substantial responsibility. Comments made by the committee in reference documented that Enron's president was responsible for ensuring that

- Those reporting to him performed their oversight duties and
- Internal controls put in place by the board (surprise, surprise) functioned properly.

An article in the *Financial Times* expressed the following opinion about Enron's former president: "He has described the detail of his expressly assigned oversight role as minimal. That answer, however, misses the point [because] the committee said, 'Skilling certainly knew, or should have known, of the magnitude and the risks associated with these transactions.'"*

Beyond this, the investigators pointed to the pattern of deals Enron entered with off-balance-sheet partnerships, some of which involved Enron employees, adding that "Skilling, who prides himself on the controls he put in place in many areas at Enron, bears substantial responsibility for the failure of the system of internal controls to mitigate the risk inherent in the relationship between Enron and the LJM partnerships."

This is most likely because, in February 2001, just 10 months before the bankruptcy of Enron, Jeffrey Skilling, then Enron's president, had suggested that the most logical owners of the power plants and transmission grids were the big financial institutions because of their access to cheap capital. Skilling added that energy companies like Enron would be the

- Derivatives traders and
- Intermediaries,

using a complex and dangerous mix of futures, swaps, and other instruments. But the derivatives trades and the sophisticated intermediaries ran into a sea of red ink, and so did the company that had initiated the deals, whose equity went up and then swiftly down to zero, as Figure 13.1 documents.

Would a strategic IT audit have been material in Enron's case? If a company decides to play fireworks with its equity, collect fast money and glory, and then fall to oblivion, high technology might be useful in the rapid upside, but it would be totally irrelevant in the downside. And an IT audit would have been unimportant in both ways.

On the way up, for example, models and simulations surely helped Lay and his people in creating and manipulating the California power crisis of 2000 and 2001. By upsetting and squeezing the electricity market, Enron was able to boost prices and profits artificially while its chairman was blaming regulators for that crisis. The way a *Business Week* article had it,

- Enron's executives manipulated markets,†
- Misled the public and their own employees, and
- Created an environment of mistrust that struck credit like a hammer.

Augmented by fake financial analyses that some brokers were happy to provide, the crash of the big company led to investor unwillingness to take risks, as they felt they had been lied to and deprived of dependable financial information. After

* *Financial Times*, February 7, 2002.

† *BusinessWeek*, May 20, 2002.

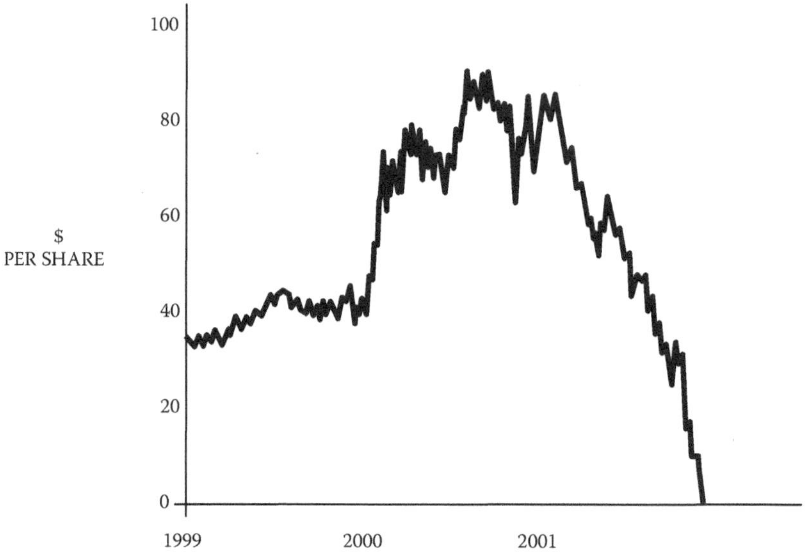

Figure 13.1 Three years of an equity swindle lifecycle: take off, year of glory, and year of demise – the Enron story.

the stock market crash of 2000, December 2001 was an unmitigated disaster for Greenspan's New Economy, which depended on innovation and markets rather than the status quo, but also needed a dependable environment in which the players are not cheating.

13.5 Modern Financial Alchemy: Prepays

Banks that lent to Enron lost a small fortune, and this weighted on their financial statements. Table 13.1 provides a snapshot of the bleeding of credit institutions. While the game was going, however, some of these same banks made a hefty profit, particularly those who were inventive enough and brought to life new instruments in the twilight of what is right and what is wrong.

An example is *prepays*. In its time, this was a fairly new sort of transaction, coming onstream silently but in big sums. The label does not quite explain what the term means. In a nutshell: for a commission, banks put money up-front roughly equal (after a haircut) to what specific trades, like the sale of energy, *might* realize sometime in the future.

Unlike discounted commercial paper, which (also after a haircut) represents what is due by the issuer in the aftermath of a commercial transaction, prepays are based on a hinge about future income. The banks take a risk and buy credit insurance to cover this risk (see Section 6). By all evidence, this was first tried with Enron—and at big scale.

Table 13.1 The Biggest Creditors Who Lost a Fortune with the Bankruptcy of Enron

Institution	*Country*	*Estimated Exposure*
$1 Billion or More in Losses		
JP Morgan Chase	United States	$3.3 billion
Citigroup	United States	$3.0 billion*
Bank of New York	United States	$2.4 billion
Bank of America	United States	$1.0 billion
Below $1 Billion but above $200 Million in Losses		
FleetBoston	United States	...
John Hancock	United States	...
SunTrust	United States	...
Wachovia	United States	...
Aegon	Netherlands	...
Canadian Imperial Bank	Canada	...
Crédit Lyonnais	France	...
ING	Netherlands	...
Sumitomo-Mitsui	Japan	...
Tokyo-Mitsubishi	Japan	...

* This is, of course, a drop in the bucket compared to the tens of billions of dollars Citigroup lost with subprimes in 2007/2008.

Prepays permitted Enron management to beef up quite substantially reported earnings, and thereby impress the market. At least on the surface, the banks that helped Enron in this scheme did not necessarily do something illegal (more on this later). JP Morgan Chase structured 12 prepays, providing among themselves an awesome $3.7 billion. Citigroup structured 14 prepays, providing $4.8 billion.

- The two added up to $8.5 billion in Enron's hands.
- This money was pouring in through shell companies registered offshore, particularly in the Jersey Islands.

As far as the backtesting of the Sarbanes-Oxley Act is concerned, the same thinking is valid with the then-existing financial reporting laws. The big accounting question with prepays is whether such money should have been counted as a loan, or they should have been seen as something close to a loan using as collateral future business by Enron. If they were loans, their impact on Enron's balance sheet would have been profound in a negative sense:

- Enron's debt would have risen by 40 percent.
- Its cash flow would have fallen by 50 percent.

Significant balance-sheet changes such as these would have had a harsh impact on Enron's creditworthiness. The true risk to investors resulting from that kind of huge debt obligation would have been quite different from what was portrayed in Enron's incomplete and misleading financial disclosures. Enron incorrectly

- Had registered the prepays money as profits, and
- Turned a bleak financial condition into a major business success.

Such glaring manipulation of financial statements would have come squarely under Sarbanes-Oxley if it had been effective at that time. But then what? Despite declaring ignorance and amnesia, Lay and Skilling were not the sort of chairman and president living on cloud nine, unaware of what was going on in their company. As Skilling's trial proceeded, it became evident that the bosses were the ones giving orders.

The reader should note that prepays were assorted over a horde of shell companies, the whole plot being designed to bring goods to every one of its members. The banks themselves profited by using the money from the first prepays to fund the next prepaid transactions, thereby creating what became a vicious circle—but they took pride in it. "Citi promised investors that the credit-linked notes would perform similarly to straight Enron bonds—and they have," said Rick Caplan, a Citigroup executive.* JP Morgan, the other bank in the prepays business, probably felt the same.

At the end of July 2002, in their defense before a U.S. Senate committee, executives from Citigroup and JP Morgan argued that their banks were little more than Enron's victims. If blame were in order, they suggested that it should be directed at Arthur Andersen, Enron's auditor, which signed off on all transactions. But the Senate committee had evidence, including e-mails, proving that bank executives were aware of what was going on.

On July 25, 2002, dissatisfied by some of the answers the Senate committee received from representatives of JP Morgan Chase and Citigroup, Senator Carl Levin demanded that the banks' CEOs tell him whether they owned some of the special-purpose entities used to disguise loans to Enron. Two days earlier, at a Sen-

* *The Economist*, July 27, 2002.

ate hearing, representatives of the two banks could not describe the exact nature of the relationship between

- The two big banks and
- The smaller offshore entities that funneled money to Enron.*

Levin wanted precise answers from JP Morgan Chase's CEO Richard Harrison and Citigroup's Sanford Weill. Some lawmakers alleged that both the banks had helped the fallen energy giant to hide debt. Both credit institutions denied the allegations, yet their stocks plunged more than 15 percent. Congress aside, the Securities and Exchange Commission had also been examining the banks' relationship to Enron.

"The financial institutions (JP Morgan Chase and Citigroup) were aware that Enron was using questionable accounting," said Robert Roach, chief investigator for the Senate Permanent Subcommittee on Investigations, which scrutinized the role of Wall Street firms in the Enron scandal. "They actively aided Enron in other business dealings."†

In a jammed hearing room, lawmakers blasted JP Morgan Chase and Citigroup, calling their behavior "a charade" and "a cancer" on the financial markets. During the 10-hour hearing, the Senate committee revealed document after document appearing to show the banks and their overseas law firms had set up and run secretive, offshore shell companies that funneled billions of dollars in financing to Enron over the past years.

- The 26 transactions, designed to look like legitimate energy-contract trades, were accounting trickery that served no good business purpose, the senators said.
- Heavier debt on Enron's balance sheet would have seriously hurt its credit ratings and hastened its meltdown, executives from Standard & Poor's and Moody's Investors Service testified.

Through the investigation, prepays were looked at as the new alchemy of turning liabilities into assets that find their way into financial reporting. This was not lost on the credit-rating agencies in terms of creditworthiness of the two banks. On July 25, 2002, Moody's changed its outlook on JP Morgan Chase from positive to negative because of three reasons:

- Deteriorating asset quality in the portfolio
- Concentration in telecoms, media, and technology lending
- Damage to the bank's image and reputational risk

---

* *USA Today*, July 26, 2002.

† *USA Today*, July 24, 2002.

The Senate Permanent Subcommittee on Investigations believed that hundreds of pages of documents indicated the banks knowingly used secretive, overseas shell companies, with names such as Mahonia and Yosemite, to engage in the deals with Enron. The subcommittee's seven-month investigation found e-mails showing that, while prepays appeared to be energy commodities futures trades, in reality they were loans.

Could a Sarbanes-Oxley Act, if it were enacted in 1998, have made a difference? The answer is *yes*, but not directly on Enron. The difference is that neither Richard Harrison nor Sandy Weill (I suppose) would have signed false financial statements as CEOs, and Enron would have found it tough to get reputable banks as partners in its prepays.

13.6 Credit Insurance, Surety Bonds, and Out-of-Court Settlement

Citing evidence that the company possibly engaged in sham contracts with Enron, on March 5, 2002, a federal judge in New York denied JP Morgan Chase's efforts to immediately collect $1 billion in insurance coverage on trading losses with the bankrupt energy company. This was a legal setback for one of Enron's leading creditors. The judge's decision:

- Threw cold water on a novel legal argument JP Morgan Chase had mounted, arguing that the insurance firms were on the hook whether or not fraud was present
- Was on its way to create jurisprudence, with the result that Enron's and similar financial debacles spread to Wall Street's commercial and investment banks

The reason for this fairly curious argument by JP Morgan had been that, in the contract, the insurers' obligation was described as "absolute and unconditional." That does not mean that fraud is a protected business practice, wrote U.S. District Judge Jed Rakoff, who called JP Morgan Chase's thesis an "extraordinary proposition."*

The insurers listed as defendants in this case were a "Who's Who," including Fireman's Fund, Hartford, Liberty Mutual, St. Paul, Safeco, and Travelers. The coverage they had provided to the Morgan Bank was through a financial instrument known as *surety bonds* supposed, or at least intended, to cover JP Morgan Chase's potential losses on energy trading with Enron. It may not be amiss to give some account of the court case.

Morgan Chase sued to collect $1 billion from insurers to cover losses related to Enron, but it suffered a setback when the judge said a bank e-mail referring to

* *USA Today*, March 6, 2002.

"disguised loans" could be read to a jury. "If the jury accepts defendants' view of what the e-mails are referring to (as the jury reasonably might), the term 'disguised loan' is highly relevant and precisely descriptive of what is involved," Judge Rakoff wrote in a 10-page ruling.*

JP Morgan vice chairman Donald Layton had described the transactions as disguised loans in one of the e-mails, and in another he had discussed the consequences should the bank's internal records about the loans be subpoenaed. That is a very interesting reference in connection with the Sarbanes-Oxley Act back play, because the records would have provided indisputable evidence that

- Chief executives signing the financial reports would have misstated such a transaction, and its balance-sheet impact, and
- Knowing in advance the personal accountability involved in such an act, I do not think they would have signed the financial statements in the first place.

"We are making disguised loans, usually buried in commodities or equities derivatives (and I'm sure in other areas)," Layton wrote in one e-mail. "With a few exceptions, they are understood to be disguised loans and approved as such. But I am queasy about the process." Subsequently, however, Layton told the court, outside of the jury's presence, that none of the 1999 e-mails referred to transactions involving Enron.

JP Morgan Chase Mahonia transactions with Enron were being also investigated by the U.S. DOJ, the Securities and Exchange Commission, the Federal Reserve Bank of New York, and Manhattan District Attorney Robert Morgenthau. Morgenthau began a grand jury investigation of JP Morgan's relationship with Mahonia, which handled billions of dollars of gas and oil trades with Enron (more on this later).

During court hearings, JP Morgan stated the insurers knew the true nature of the transactions and went ahead with the surety bonds anyway. The insurers had refused to pay after Enron defaulted on the trades after it collapsed. "The bank has classified the contracts as nonperforming assets, and won't write off the money unless it loses in court," Vice Chairman Marc Shapiro said.†

JP Morgan Chase claimed that Travelers Indemnity must pay $240 million and Travelers Casualty & Surety $25 million; Federal Insurance, $184 million; Lumbermens Mutual Casualty, $156 million; Fireman's Fund, $154 million; and St. Paul Fire and Marine Insurance, $135 million. Other claims were Continental Casualty and National Fire Insurance of Hartford, $77 million; Safeco Insurance of America, $55 million; Hartford Fire Insurance, $41 million, and Liberty Mutual Insurance, $25 million—altogether a rich windfall at its time.

---

* *Bloomberg Professional*, December 23, 2002.
† *Bloomberg Professional*, December 23, 2002.

The foregoing list adds up to a whole bunch of CEO and CFOs who might well have been prosecuted under "Sarbanes-Oxley 1998," even if they claimed that they had signed their insurance companies' financial statements in good faith. No wonder that so many senior executives are openly against SOX.

The violation of regulations might have been even more flagrant given that one of the picturesque aspects of these surety bonds, and the trades of natural gas and oil that they covered, were conducted through Mahonia Natural Gas—a curious nontransparent organization based in the tax haven of English channel islands.

The fact Mahonia was based in the Jersey Islands came to the public eye with unusual detail. The plan was for Enron to sell the commodities to Mahonia. Chase Manhattan Bank, the predecessor to JP Morgan Chase, had drawn up the transactions between June 1998 and December 2000, and it financed them. In this way, the money for the commodities

- Came from Chase,
- Moved to Mahonia, and
- From the shell company it was transferred to Enron.

The insurers answered the bank's request for coverage by saying that they did not know Enron was contracting to repurchase the exact same amount of natural gas and oil from a third entity called Stoneville Aegean, being allowed to pay for its purchases in the future. They argued in court that the fact that Enron was simply

- Keeping Chase's money while
- Getting its commodities back

made this a disguised loan.

This case became even more colorful when it was revealed that the "trading" organizations of Mahonia and Stoneville Aegean were both set up by the same person. They also had the same director and the same shareholders. One of the names was a red herring, but being based in the Jersey Islands, both of them would have been beyond the reach of "SOX 1998"; however, this would not have been true for Enron and Chase Manhattan.

In his opinion, Judge Rakoff wrote: "Taken together, these arrangements now appear to be nothing but a disguised loan." At the very least, he said, the case merited further investigation, particularly because the insurers uncovered a striking series of rather curious coincidences; and insurance companies could then obtain evidence from Enron and JP Morgan Chase.

The die seemed to be cast in favor of the insurance companies, but there was a final twist that changed the casting. In Houston, Texas, an insurance agent who allegedly acted as a go-between for Chase and the insurers said the latter knew very well that these were disguised loans.

This led to an out-of-court settlement. In the aftermath of this revelation, the probability that each party believed to have in winning the case can be judged by the way the money was split: 60 percent in favor of the bank and 40 percent for the insurers. The likelihood that what had happened behind the scenes at the negotiating table would have fallen like a hammer on all parties concerned, if Sarbanes-Oxley were enacted in 1998, is in my judgment better than 90 percent.

13.7 Sarbanes-Oxley and the WorldCom Scandal

According to some estimates, in 2002, as money went down the drain through bankruptcies and near-bankruptcies of telecommunications companies and their suppliers, the telecoms' bust became an order of magnitude bigger than the better-known dotcom crash. All counted,

- Telecommunications firms had run up total debts of $1 trillion, and
- This industry disgraced itself by using fraudulent accounting tricks in an attempt to conceal the scale of the disaster.

In retrospect, what the Sarbanes-Oxley Act might have had as an effect, had it been enacted four years earlier than 2002, would have been to trigger, at an earlier date, WorldCom's and other telecom companies' crisis and collapse. They would have been under intense scrutiny for plenty of issues associated with their financial reporting, extravagant bonuses paid out to their executives, and unaffordable amount of debt.

There were plenty of dirty tricks. For instance, to hide its huge losses, WorldCom had classified $3.8 billion in network-maintenance costs as capital spending. This chapter alone represented about one-third of an $11-billion scam that, so far, was the biggest in American industrial history. (Not long thereafter, it was eclipsed by the Parmalat scandal in Italy, which has contributed some of the better known names in U.S. and European banking, with court cases against several banks still pending).*

Bernard Ebbers, the CEO and guiding light of WorldCom, spent almost two decades building up his company into one of the biggest worldwide long-distance carriers and Internet pillars. In so doing, he exploited the freedoms made available by U.S. deregulation of the telecommunications industry, specializing in acquisitions, building capacity, but also paying attention to costs.

- Through deal-making, Ebbers showed that it was possible to undercut AT&T in the long-distance market and still make profits.
- But in doing so he got WorldCom overleveraged, entered into murky accounting practices, and brought himself down by wounds that, to large measure, were self-inflicted.

---

* If the subprimes are seen as scams, which they are, these numbers are eclipsed by the $165 billion so far lost by big banks, while the International Monetary Fund (IMF) estimates that the total bill will be nearly $1 trillion.

While watching other costs, the company was very liberal in showering its founder with money. When he resigned as CEO of MCI WorldCom, Ebbers personally owed the company more than $366 million for loans and loan guarantees to cover potential losses on his stock speculation, as the company's share price plummeted. Also, WorldCom became the subject of a continuing investigation by the Securities and Exchange Commission, which scrutinized

- Its accounting practices and
- Its financial relationship with its CEO and animator.

In a way fairly similar to the case of Enron, had the Sarbanes-Oxley Act been in force at the time of WorldCom's wheeling and dealing—say, since 1998—its effect (in my judgment) would not have been substantial. As subsequent events demonstrated, the CEO and CFO, who would have been required to sign the untruthful financial statements, would have found no difficulty in doing so.

Much more difficult to state is how wide the scam spread within the company. Just two months prior to its collapse, WorldCom's senior executives from around the globe gathered at its headquarters in Clinton, Mississippi. There, they heard CEO Bernard J. Ebbers reveal his grand vision for rescuing a company mired in

- Huge liabilities,
- Sluggish growth, and
- Rising controversy about its accounting practices.

In that meeting, Ebbers said that from then on his executives would follow a checklist of priorities referred to as "Bernie's seven points of light." One of them was to count coffee bags, another to make sure no lights were left on at the end of the day, and the like.* In short, WorldCom's grand strategy was reduced to saving pennies at a time when its problem was not pennies but billions of dollars. By 2002, in the telecommunications industry:

- Fast growth was gone.
- Competition was driving down data service fees, dropping WorldCom group's revenue growth from 19 percent in 2000 to practically zero in 2002.

While revenue was flat, debt skyrocketed. With its huge leverage, WorldCom featured $30 billion in debt, and it had to pay $172 million in interest and maturities in 2002 alone. This was expected to rise to $1.7 billion in 2003 and $2.6 billion in 2004, well beyond the company's ability to face its financial obligations.

---

* *BusinessWeek*, May 6, 2002.

The glut of network capacity, which was built by start-up companies fueled by easy financing during the stock market boom of late 1990s, further depressed pricing of telecommunications services. Additionally, the bursting of the stock market bubble in 2000

- Made it more difficult to raise money, and
- Put a temporary stop to deals such as WorldCom's acquisition of MCI for $30 billion in 1998.

After years of euphoric pronouncements that had found their way into its financial statements, the company had to admit that revenues in its WorldCom Group unit, which served business customers, would be flat in 2002 at $21 to $21.5 billion, down from previous expectations. Also, with the consumer long-distance business shrinking, overall revenues were expected to slip 5 percent in 2002 to $33 billion, while net income was projected to drop 40 percent, to $1.6 billion.

In parallel to this, the SEC was probing WorldCom's *take or pay* contracts, whereby customers got a discount if they agreed to use a certain volume of service over a specific period of time. If not, then they had to pay a penalty, and this was interpreted as a hard sale.

WorldCom's pessimistic projections prompted Merrill Lynch, Crédit Suisse First Boston, and A.G. Edwards to downgrade WorldCom to *sell*. For their part, Standard & Poor's and Moody's Investors Service cut the company's debt to two notches above junk status. With that, its stock plunged 43 percent in two days, to $3.41 a share from a high of $64 in June 1999; and it fell to around $1.20 after Moody's downgraded WorldCom's debt to junk status.

By the end of April 2002, the company's debt indeed traded as junk. The price dropped from 85 cents on the dollar in March 2002 to 67 cents following WorldCom's latest profit warning. The SEC inquiry also gave investors more reasons for concern, because it revealed that, in all likelihood, Ebbers beautified financial results through aggressive bookkeeping. A short time thereafter, on July 21, 2002, WorldCom filed for Chapter 11 protection. This was (at its time) the largest bankruptcy in U.S. history, promoting congressional action that led to the Sarbanes-Oxley Act.

13.8 The Contribution of the Sarbanes-Oxley Act to the American Economy

On August 1, 2002, 10 days after Enron's collapse, Scott Sullivan, WorldCom's former CFO (he was sacked by the firm after the $3.8-billion accounting fraud had come to light), and David Myers, the firm's chief controller, were the first to be arrested among the company's top brass, on criminal charges. In Manhattan,

Sullivan and Myers surrendered to agents from the Federal Bureau of Investigation and were charged with

- Conspiracy to commit securities fraud and
- Five additional counts of false filings with the SEC.

It is not far-fetched to guess that, if the Sarbanes-Oxley Act had been enacted in 1998 (rather than 2002), it would not have changed these charges. However, as in the case discussed in conjunction with Enron, it might have acted as a deterrent or, alternatively, as an early trigger of WorldCom's debacle.

As it was, the arrests of Myers and Sullivan came amid a controversy over the billions of dollars in salary and share sales pocketed by executives of U.S. companies before they collapsed into bankruptcy. For his part, at the beginning, Ebbers feigned ignorance, even though he was a micromanager who endorsed the idea of saving money by scrapping free coffee for staff. But he was not featured in the first lot of arrests.

John Ashcroft, then the U.S. attorney general, said that the arrests were part of a stepped-up effort by the Department of Justice (DOJ) to move decisively against corporate wrongdoers. In essence, SOX enabled the hand of the DOJ in pursuing this course.

As the investigation proceeded, it was revealed that Scott Sullivan was among the 25 most highly paid executives of companies involved in the largest U.S. bankruptcies, between January 2001 and mid-2002. He had received a total of $49.4 million in salary, options, and other rich favors.

There was a similitude between Enron's and WorldCom's accounting scandals, and their synergy was an arrow at the heart of a standard bull-market assumption. This states that the United States has the most well-regulated financial reporting system of all of the world's free markets, and it is also characterized by the highest accounting standards. A tandem of scams put that assumption in question.

Has Sarbanes-Oxley changed anything, steering senior management toward a more ethical behavior? *If* one believes the argument that SOX is the reason why global companies desert New York in favor of other more go-go financial centers, like London, *then* there may be truth in it. But as we saw in Chapter 12, that argument is nuts. There are other major reasons about why companies delist.

The WorldCom disintegration was instrumental in convincing the American public that this plethora of bankruptcies was not one of independent events. It also played a role in convincing Congress that, with midterm elections looming, they would pay a political price if they did nothing. "Sarbanes-Oxley wouldn't have passed without WorldCom coming along," claimed Mark Roe of Harvard Law School.*

In mid-March 2005, two years and nine months after the bankruptcy of WorldCom, Bernie Ebbers, its former chief executive, was convicted for his part in the

---

* *The Economist*, March 15, 2005.

$11-billion fraud, while Scott Sullivan, the company's former chief financial officer, who had already pleaded guilty,

- Appeared as a government witness and
- Testified that Ebbers had told him to fiddle the accounts to prop up the firm's share price.

Eleven former board members of the once powerful carrier agreed to pay $20.2 million out of their own pockets to settle a lawsuit related to the accounting fraud. JP Morgan Chase also agreed to pay some $2 billion to settle a class-action lawsuit from investors suing the bank because it sold some $5.1 billion worth of WorldCom bonds just months before it went Chapter 11. (Indeed, the amount paid out by investment banks settling WorldCom cases eventually rose to some $6 billion.) After Ebbers's conviction was made public, some people asked:

- Should he and other executives at former WorldCom have been the only ones on trial?
- Where were the financial analysts, other industrialists, and pundits, as well as the regulators who had oversight of the deals that brought down the firm?

When Ebbers was building WorldCom in the 1990s, investors were thrilled at the prospect that he was producing a telecom challenger to AT&T and incumbents worldwide. But why did the markets never question what was going on behind the scene? Postmortem, it became known that some parties had their suspicions about an overachieving startup. It was telling that British Telecom insisted on taking cash, instead of WorldCom stock, in exchange for surrendering its 20 percent stake in MCI.

An interesting hindsight in this case has been that Bernie Ebbers did not use e-mail, and few documents linked him decisively to the fraud. But other companies with which he dealt had kept incriminating records. Beside this lies the fact that, with the Sarbanes-Oxley Act and the precedents of convictions, company CEOs and CFOs should assume that they could be sent to jail for destroying their firm's assets, even if there is no smoking-gun memo linking them directly to wrongdoing.

All things considered, instilling the fear of the policeman is one of the most significant contributions of the Sarbanes-Oxley Act, because it contributed to the good of the American economy. Plenty of evidence suggests that white-collar crime of the worst variety found its origins at the very top echelons of financial organizations.

While signing unfaithful financial statements by CEOs and CFOs poses no problem to a small number of criminals, SOX is a shot in the arm for those executives who care to be in charge of their companies and want to know exactly what is happening with the company's books. Uncovering of big scams in regulatory financial statements is not done outright by Sarbanes-Oxley, but such scams can be found by reading between the lines of that act. Hopefully, said one of the participants in the research for this book, SOX will animate interest in

- Having a first-class internal control system,
- Implementing real-time technology for financial statements and risk management, and
- Establishing rigorous audit procedures that unturn every stone to uncover and report on malpractice.

There is, as well, another class of CEOs and CFOs that stands to benefit from the Sarbanes-Oxley Act. These are the people who find themselves at the junction of right and wrong, being uncertain in their mind about which way to go. The reality of statutory signing of their companies' financial statements and of having their internal control inspected by external auditors may help to guide them to the right path.

In conclusion, SOX is a reminder that vicious actions are not harmful because they are forbidden; they are forbidden because they are harmful to everybody—the state, the economy, the company, the stakeholders, and the person who initiates such actions. Take a look at Lay, Skilling, and Ebbers. They would have been much better off by always rendering accounts and making remittances with greater clarity and punctuality.

"History is full of the errors of states and princes," wrote Benjamin Franklin in his autobiography. "Look round the habitable world; how few know their own good, or knowing it pursue."*

* Benjamin Franklin, *The Autobiography of Benjamin Franklin* (New York: Barnes & Noble, 1994).

Index

F

G

H

I